Economy of Words

Economy of Words

Communicative Imperatives in Central Banks

DOUGLAS R. HOLMES

THE UNIVERSITY OF CHICAGO PRESS   CHICAGO AND LONDON

DOUGLAS R. HOLMES is professor of anthropology at Binghamton University, SUNY. He is the author of *Cultural Disenchantments: Worker Peasantries in Northeast Italy* and *Integral Europe: Fast-Capitalism, Multiculturalism, Neofascism*.

The University of Chicago Press, Chicago 60637
The University of Chicago Press, Ltd., London
© 2014 by The University of Chicago
All rights reserved. Published 2014.
Printed in the United States of America

23 22 21 20 19 18 17 16 15 14   1 2 3 4 5

ISBN-13: 978-0-226-08759-7(cloth)
ISBN-13: 978-0-226-08762-7(paper)
ISBN-13: 978-0-226-08776-4(e-book)
DOI: 10.7208/chicago/9780226087764.001.0001

Library of Congress Cataloging-in-Publication Data

Holmes, Douglas R., 1949–author.
  Economy of words : communicative imperatives in central banks / Douglas R. Holmes.
    pages cm
  Includes bibliographical references and index.
  ISBN 978-0-226-08759-7 (cloth : alkaline paper)—ISBN 978-0-226-08762-7 (paperback : alkaline paper)—ISBN 978-0-226-08776-4 (e-book) 1. Banks and banking, Central.
2. Monetary policy. I. Title.
  HG1811.H55 2014
  332.1'1014—dc23
                          2013016606

FOR ELI AND PAM

Contents

Preface: Backstories

For the first time [August 12, 2003], the [Federal Open Market] Committee was using communication—mere words—as its primary monetary policy tool. Until then, it was probably common to think of communication about future policy as something that supplemented the setting of the federal funds rate. In this case, communication was an independent and effective tool for influencing the economy. The FOMC had journeyed from "never explain" to a point where sometimes the explanation *is* the policy. — Janet Yellen, Vice Chair, Board of Governors, Federal Reserve System, April 4, 2013

This is the third volume of an ethnographic trilogy that began with the publication of *Cultural Disenchantments* in 1989 and was followed by *Integral Europe*, which appeared in 2000. *Economy of Words* continues to explore themes introduced in these earlier volumes, but of all these texts it has taken the most unusual and unexpected turns. Collectively, these books cover an extended journey, spanning three decades, that ultimately brought me to the kind of experiments with language that Janet Yellen and her colleagues are pursuing in central banks. The three volumes are linked by, among other things, a full appreciation of what "mere words" can accomplish. In the chapters that follow, I tell the story of how words have come to underwrite a monetary regime (Austin 1961; Burke 1974; Searle 1969).

In the early 1980s, while working with Paolo Rondo Brovetto in the rural districts of northeast Italy, we discussed the role of monetary policy in promoting the *idea* of economic growth in the minds and in the conversations of the people we were studying. During our walks in the foothills of the Julian Alps we also wondered about the consequence of a common currency for Europe and how it might impact the lives and livelihoods of the Italian people. Also in the early 1980s, I began a long conversation with Robert Reichlin, exploring, among many other things, how we might

extricate ourselves from notions of culture rooted in convention, tradition, and the past, and re-engage our thinking to address cultural practices
that are emphatically future-oriented.

George Marcus and I began talking regularly while we were both living in Houston. The Late Editions Project, which George orchestrated,
served as the initial setting for our conversations, but in the ensuing years
these discussions expanded and, as the reader will see, they are manifest
in all the approaches to ethnography that animate this book. Most notably, Marcus and I have grappled with the analytical possibilities posed
when our subjects, in this case, central bankers, are pursuing sophisticated anthropological experiments (Fischer 2007; Marcus 2012). David
"Bert" Westbrook joined this conversation about a decade ago, and with
great energy and wit he has written a compelling articulation of what is
at stake in this kind of endeavor (see Westbrook 2008). Over and above
Bert's technical insights on the issues I examine here, I have benefited
from his ability to destabilize my disciplinary conceits with a humane and
rigorous reading of my work. At the University of Chicago Press, David
Brent grasped the intellectual possibilities of the conversation among
George, Bert, and myself. Early on, he expressed interest in this book, and
he has energetically supported it throughout the review and production
processes.

When I returned to New York from New Zealand in 2002, I met two
colleagues, Annelise Riles and Hirokazu Miyazaki, who had also recently
arrived in upstate New York. They too were beginning to investigate
issues of finance drawing on a similar set of intellectual commitments and
a complementary set of ethnographic sensibilities to my own. Over the
last decade, we have begun, I think, to develop a shared view of the implications of this kind of work, not merely or necessarily for our discipline,
but for other audiences. It was Annelise's comment on an earlier draft of
this manuscript, that "markets are a function of language," that proved
decisive in the final revisions of this text.

I also met Peter Katzenstein shortly after I returned to New York,
when he invited me to participate in a project on "European identities."
He graciously agreed to read earlier drafts of this text, and I have benefited from his provocative questions and insightful comments. The discussions that follow, on performativity and on the analysis of the current financial circumstances in Europe, were written with him very much
in mind.

On many occasions I have drawn on the work of Ann Stoler, and in a conversation at the New School she contributed a crucial insight for this book. She provided a means to conceptualize the intellectual dilemmas of technocrats—whether colonial officials or central bankers—and thus a means to investigate the production and/or mis-production of knowledge that is key to their expertise and the institutions they manage.

Michael Herzfeld and I share many interests, notably in how bureaucratic discontents shape the predicaments and the intimate struggles pervading the lives of Europeans. Though not directly addressed here, these struggles nonetheless serve as the backstory to this volume. By that I mean they predisposed me to pay close attention to how, during a period of great difficulty, the efficacy of monetary policy increasingly depended on its ability to address, so to speak, the sentiments and expectations of the public. Not insignificantly, these preoccupations with the circumstances of the public also became an overriding concern of central bankers. Though my account lacks the richness and exuberance of Michael's narratives, I think the ends of the ethnography are similar.

I was very fortunate to have had an extended conversation with Julio Rotemberg at an early stage of this project. He listened to my account of what was, at the time, a still very much ill-defined research plan, providing very generous advice on how anthropologists might, or could, address issues of interest and relevance to monetary economists, and perhaps even central bankers. I have tried my best to follow his guidance, most importantly by acknowledging, as noted above, that central bankers are confronting challenges that are in many respects anthropological in nature.

Christopher Hanes kindly listened to some of the key ideas that have guided this project. He helped further refine my views concerning those issues of central banking that an anthropologist might illuminate.

I am very fortunate to be a member of the Meridian 180 and Tobin projects, and I have had the privilege to participate in their ongoing conversations—conversations orchestrated with great care and foresight by Annelise Riles and John Cisternino, respectively. I find it hard to put into words precisely what I have gleaned from my participation in the discussions with the students, scholars, and government officials who Annelise and John bring together. That said, it is clear to me that as I wrote this book, my thinking about the operation of central banks increasingly became aligned with the aims and agendas of these two remarkable projects. I hope I have done them justice.

Although the research for this volume spans a decade or so, the most important insights coalesced rather quickly, between September 2008 and

August 2010, in a sequence of conversations with a relatively small group
of people. What I gleaned during this time was that the monetary regime I
was studying was about language, about communication, and that the ultimate aim of these communications was to recruit the public, broadly conceived, to collaborate with central bankers in achieving the ends of monetary policy. I also learned that this monetary system is aligned with an
unusual intellectual apparatus that generates knowledge and intelligence
that is resolutely ethnographic. Furthermore, I determined that the current monetary regime is the outcome of a distinctive institutional history,
a history that anticipated what would be the financial and monetary exigencies that commenced with the collapse of Lehman Brothers in 2008.
These are the people who informed my conversations: in Wellington, Arthur Grimes, Mike Hannah, and Tim Ng; in Frankfurt, Jens Ulbrich and
Regina Karoline Schuller; in Stockholm, Stefan Ingves, Lars E. O. Svensson, and Anders Vredin; and in London, Neil Ashbridge, Chris Piper, John
Young, Peter Andrews, Rosie Smith, and Gareth Ramsay. Finally, it was
during conversations initially undertaken with by Arthur Grimes, Mike
Hannah, and Jens Ulbrich, and later given clarity by Anders Vredin and
the people working for him at the Riksbank, that I was able to recognize
that the contemporary task of central bankers encompasses the humane
articulation of a public interest.

This book relies on documents, all of which were originally drafted in
English or are English translations produced by the central banks, notably the Riksbank, the Bundesbank, and the European Central Bank.
The dominant role of English is interesting for many reasons—most obviously insofar as it is an acknowledgment that every central bank speaks,
as it were, to a global audience—but also because it points up that research reports and policy statements currently draw on academic traditions in economics and finance that are by and large Anglo-American. I
have been continually struck by the careful and, at times, highly nuanced
use of spoken and written English in all of the institutions I studied. At
one central bank, I actually sought out these translators, so I could begin
to understand their role in the creation of a technical argot. Ultimately, I
did not pursue this line of inquiry, but I am indebted to them, and to the
technical writers and editors who manage the rhetorical expertise of these
institutions (see Smart 2006).

The members of the Chicago Center for Contemporary Theory
(3CT)—Andreas Glaeser, Gary Herrigel, William Sewell, Lisa Weeden,
and Anwen Tormey—provided an invaluable critical reading at a key mo-

ment in the development of this manuscript. The concept of a "public currency" advanced herein is in many respects a response to their insightful commentaries.

A number of people read earlier drafts of this manuscript in whole or in part. I am enormously grateful for the comments and suggestions provided by Julia Elyachar, Neil Fligstein, Vinny Ialenti, Daromir Rudnyckyj, Evan Schnidman, Josh Reno, David England, and Peter Andrews.

I have also benefited from the remarks of colleagues and friends at presentations, guest lectures, and workshops on various aspects of the material that forms the basis of this book. They include Paul Rabinow, Bill Maurer, Genevieve Bell, and Don Brenneis, at a workshop sponsored by the Center for Ethnography at the University of California, Irvine; Susan Gal, Kaushik Sunder Rajan, Joseph Masco, and John Kelly at the University of Chicago; Christina Garsten, Anette Nyqvist, Ulf Hannerz, and Helena Wulff at the University of Stockholm; Michael McGovern at Yale University; Michael Lambek and Andrea Muehlebach at the University of Toronto; Ben Lee at the New School; Mika Aaltola at the Finnish Institute of International Affairs; Terence Turner and Holly Case at Cornell University; Dominic Boyer and Jim Faubion at Rice University; and Michael Stewart at the University College London.

During a series of meetings in Toronto, Barcelona, and Budapest, Gavin Smith, Don Kalb, and Susana Norotzky graciously included me in conversations about the unfolding condition in Europe, particularly as the sovereign debt crisis took hold in central and southern Europe. Gavin and Don also provided vivid accounts of how the interplay of finance and politics was not only creating deprivation, but also implacable responses. By so doing, they gently reminded me of the commitment that sustained my earlier research in Europe.

Ivan Karp and Cory Kratz served as a steadfast audience during many years. They listened attentively to the ups and downs of this project, and they provided unflagging intellectual and moral support. I hope Cory recognizes the mark she and Ivan made on this project, and I only wish that Ivan had lived to read what resulted.

When I first expressed interest in undertaking this project to my then dean at the University of Otago, Robert Hannah, he seemed perplexed, even dubious. Within a short time, however, he became excited and intrigued. I am grateful for his very early support of the ideas developed herein. Initial funding for this project was provided by a grant from the dean of Harpur College, Jean-Pierre Mileur—funding which was crucial for its formulation and design. Dean Mileur also granted me two terms of academic leave to pursue the research at what turned out to be a very propitious moment. Fieldwork was funded with the generous support of the Wenner-Gren Foundation.

Students at Binghamton University who participated in my ethnography workshop and or who have taken my seminars—notably, Priscilla Bennett, Brian Escobar, Annemarie Fischer, Rui Gomes Coelho, Vinny Ialenti, Carmita Eliza D. Icasiano, Polly Ilieva, Changkyu Lee, Chris Loy, Jackson Malle, Alysa Pomer, Amy Robbins, John Rogers, Giusi Russo, Hande Sarikuzu, and Cheng Sun—contributed at various stages of this project, with the provocations of their own work and with their engagement with mine.

Priya Nelson expertly assisted David Brent at the University of Chicago Press in the production process of this book. I am particularly grateful for Ruth Steinberg's very careful and thoughtful copyediting of this text.

My friends have shown great patience during the long course of researching and writing this book. Robert Ku; Nancy Um; Eliot and Oliver, as well as Nat and Katherine Bouman; Harper and Otis in Binghamton; Sara Cicalo in New York; and Bob Reichlin, Amy Blakemore, and Chip Briscoe in Texas, have demonstrated kindness and understanding, for which I am enormously grateful.

My family has been steadfast in their love and support. The thoughtful attention and care that Mel Pipe, Mike Nyland, Jinna Zwanikken, Andrew Cohen, Sarah Prouty, and George Holmes have provided over the last few years has been invaluable. I have dedicated this book to Pamela Smart and Eli Holmes. They have participated directly and vicariously in every aspect of this research. Pam has reviewed numerous drafts of the text and worked tirelessly to endow it with descriptive and analytical clarity. Eli has lived virtually his entire life with the long and demanding parturition of this project. Together they sought to persuade me that for this project to succeed, I needed a life outside of my work. They did everything to make that possible and pleasurable. My gratitude is boundless.

CHAPTER ONE

Creating a Monetary Regime

I have said often enough that I am Mr. Euro. There is no doubt: we issue the currency and I sign the banknotes. My signature is on the notes. — Jean-Claude Trichet, President of the European Central Bank (2003–11)

This book is *not* about the financial crisis per se. Rather it is about the creation of a monetary regime—a regime impelled by a series of communicative experiments that predate the crisis and that have continued to be refined and modified in the teeth of the unfolding turmoil (Blinder 2004; Bernanke 2012). Indeed, this compendium of experiments—in which we are all participants, knowingly or not—has been instrumental in the management of some of the most vexing circumstances that arose in the wake of the failure of financial markets after the collapse of Lehman Brothers in September 2008 and in the ensuing debacle (Roitman 2013; Tett 2009).

Known narrowly and rather prosaically as "inflation targeting," these communicative experiments established the intellectual architecture and the regulatory mechanisms of a monetary system that I have defined in relationship to the concept of a "public currency," a term used in passing by Mervyn King, governor of the Bank of England (2003–13).[1] At the heart of this regime is a far-reaching premise: the public broadly must be recruited to collaborate with central banks in achieving the ends of monetary policy, namely, "stable prices and confidence in the currency."

I began this research with a focused examination of the protocols of inflation-targeting that have, as Alan Blinder (2004) asserts, revolutionized the practices of central banking. I followed the progressive unfolding of these innovative practices, which, I will argue, were recast as the moving parts of a new monetary regime, a regime predicated on distinctive analytical modalities that enlivened collaborative relationships between central bankers and diverse strata and segments of the public. The crucial piece of this puzzle was the reconceptualization of the audiences for these communicative experiments by which members of the public emerged as protagonists fully implicated in the management of monetary policy (Boyer 2012; Lucas 1997; Dewey 1927; Lippman [1927] 2002).

What Is a Central Bank?

One of the exercises that central banks have undertaken globally over recent years, under the sway of transparency, is to describe simply and explicitly their purposes and functions. This is how the Bank of England describes its roles:

Core Purpose 1—Monetary Stability

Monetary stability means stable prices and confidence in the currency. Stable prices are defined by the Government's inflation target, which the Bank seeks to meet through the decisions on interest rates taken by the Monetary Policy Committee, explaining those decisions transparently and implementing them effectively in the money markets.

Core Purpose 2—Financial Stability

Financial stability entails detecting and reducing threats to the financial system as a whole. Such threats are detected through the Bank's surveillance and market intelligence functions. They are reduced by strengthening infrastructure, and by financial and other operations, at home and abroad, including, in exceptional circumstances, by acting as the lender of last resort.

In pursuit of both purposes the Bank is open in communicating its views and analysis. (Bank of England, n.d., "Core Purposes")

I focus on the first of these core purposes, the arena of monetary policy—the means and methods by which money is supplied to the economy—because it has been at the center of the revolutionary innovations just alluded to among major central banks over the course of the last three decades.

Governor King summarizes concisely the central preoccupations of monetary policy—that is, the relationships among the quantity of money, interest rates, and prices, and how the public exercises a key role in these dynamic relationships:

Most people believe that economics is about money. Yet most economists hold conversations in which the word "money" appears hardly at all. Surprisingly, that appears true even of central bankers. The resolution of this apparent puzzle, is, I believe, the following. There has been no change in the underlying theory of inflation. Evidence of the differences in inflation across countries, and changes in inflation over time, reveal the intimate link between money and prices. Economists and central bankers understand this link, but conduct their conversations in terms of interest rates and not the quantity of money. In large part, this is because unpredictable shifts in the demand for money mean that central banks choose to set interest rates and allow the public to determine the quantity of money which is supplied elastically at the given interest rate. (Mervyn King 2002, 174)

The public, insofar as its members play the role alluded to by Governor King, participate with central bankers and financial markets in this relentless monetary drama.[2]

The area of financial stability (Core Purpose 2) is vitally important—most notably in central banks' role as lender of last resort—but this book does not systematically examine these regulatory functions. That said, many of the insights that I have developed to explore the operation of monetary policy are also relevant for addressing the challenges of maintaining the operational integrity of financial markets and the banking system.

Central bankers are members of an elite group of government appointees numbering in the dozens globally. For the purposes of this book, members of the monetary policy committees (MPCs), the officials charged with determining monetary policy of their respective central banks, are the individuals identified as "central bankers." These figures do not, however, merely carry out the procedures of a technocratic officialdom. Rather, they are in many cases the designers of this new monetary regime; it is they who have crafted its distinctive linguistic and communicative features. Further, they see their institutions and the ideas that animate them as inevitably works in progress; the ultimate status of their labor is, from their perspective, uncertain, and open to continual refinement and revision (Bernanke et al. 1999; Bernanke and Woodford 2005; Woodford 2012; Goodhart 2010; Grimes 2001; Mervyn King 2004).

Senior officials among these institutions typically know each other personally, they are generally aware of their respective policy positions, and in extreme circumstances they are fully prepared to coordinate policy interventions to address what are seen to be threats to the global economy and financial system. These figures share a broad understanding of the historical, theoretical, and methodological issues at stake in monetary policy as well as the technical issues involved in managing money and credit. That said, they work within national traditions of research, analysis, and decision making specific to each central bank and, as a legal matter, they are accountable to different national constituencies and various forms of legislative oversight. Although there is a broad consensus on state-of-the-art practices of monetary policy, central bankers do not speak with a single voice. Far from it. As we will see, within each of these institutions there are diverse perspectives and positions on policy and practices and a willingness on the part of senior officials to articulate them forcefully (Blinder 2004).

Central bankers have also assumed a symbolic role, as betrayed by Jean-Claude Trichet's curious assertion that he was "Mr. Euro." But this is more than mere celebrity or vanity. Trichet is asserting that central bankers must continually "speak," as it were, for their respective currencies and for the monetary institutions that regulate them: their spoken and written communications are obliged to model linguistically credible relationships with the public. This, I argue, is a defining feature of contemporary monetary policy.

I have expanded the category of central banker modestly to include other senior officials who participate in policy deliberations but are not necessarily members of MPCs, including senior members of the research staff as well as the bank personnel charged with communicating policy. Central banking also depends on intermediary groups of academics as well as networks of observers in business, finance, and journalism that can influence and interpret the information brought to bear on the formulation and communication of monetary policy.

In 2001 I began examining the intellectual routines that inform contemporary practices of central banking. After a preliminary visit to the New York District branch of the Federal Reserve, the project shifted to Frankfurt, headquarters of the European Central Bank and the Deutsche Bundesbank. Over the last decade, the project expanded and I have pursued research at the Reserve Bank of New Zealand, the Swedish Riksbank, and the Bank of England. In the background of the study is an ongoing assessment of the policies and practices of the United States Federal Reserve.

Most importantly, this book is concerned with a particular communicative aspect of work within central banks, namely, the drafting of technical reports, writing speeches, crafting presentations, compiling briefing documents, and composing policy statements (Elyachar, 2013; Smart 2006). I have included as often as possible the documents or excerpts of documents that are the basis of my research for the readers to appraise and interpret for themselves. Far from being routine records of past institutional matters, these documents were crafted for the purpose of shaping economic and monetary conditions prospectively, as instruments of persuasion (Riles 2001, 2006; Sunder Rajan 2006). In this regard, I followed initially the method developed by Bruno Latour in his classic study, *The Pasteurization of France* (1988). Latour demonstrated how a revolution in the science of bacteriology unfolded as a *communicative* phenomenon serialized in three journals: *Revue Scientifique, Annales de l'Institut Pasteur*, and *Concours Médical.* These journals not only reported contemporaneously on the development of scientific innovations, but they endowed the revolution with intellectual form and content. The communicative dynamics operating within the field of monetary policy are far more consequential insofar as markets themselves, as I will argue, are a function of language.[3]

For the purposes of this study I tracked the reports serialized in the *Monetary Policy Statement of the Reserve Bank of New Zealand*, the *Monthly Bulletin of the European Central Bank*, the *Monthly Report of the Deutsche Bundesbank*, the *Minutes of the Monetary Policy Committee of the Bank of England*, and the *Minutes of the Executive Board of the Sveriges Riksbank's Monetary Policy Meeting.* Using these and other documents, I show how the regular communication of central bank policy assessments plays a decisive role in the emergence and refinement of a monetary regime over and above the articulation of specific policy positions. My thesis here is that these statements are not merely expressing an interpretative account or commentary, they are *making* the economy itself as a communicative field and as an empirical fact.

I focus in the first instance on the research practices that inform these reports, and I further show how these documents seek to model relationships between these institutions and the public—relationships by which members of the public are interpellated as protagonists (Althusser 1971). Rather than the reception or efficacy of policy statements, which central banks believe they can measure quantitatively,[4] it is the crafting and modeling of collaborative relationships with the public that is, I will argue, the most radical feature of this monetary system. Treating the audience as protagonists is thus fundamental for understanding the remarkable communicative issues at stake in this text and, deeper still, for grasping the significance of the intellectual practices that constitute research in these institutions.

Analytical models—the "machineries of knowing," as Karin Knorr-Cetina (1999, 2007) terms them—that orchestrate research practices in these institutions must be viewed also as machineries of *relating*, capable of articulating policy in relation to both the distinctive and the shared circumstances of individuals and firms who are continually modeling and transacting economic relationships. The emerging monetary regime is predicated on distinctive modes of research and analysis. One of these modalities was particularly important: broadly, it encompassed analysis and interpretation of economic and financial phenomena fully in context and in something that approximates real time.

Central banks cultivate networks of interlocutors that generate knowledge—what amounts to ethnographic knowledge—about the *social* and *cultural* character of the economy animated by precisely the contextual and situational information that is typically stripped out from conventional macroeconomic and financial analysis. Conversations with and among these contacts constitute the communicative interchanges by which central bankers simulate the economy "in the wild," or "in vivo," as Michel Callon and his colleagues have termed it, in order to enter the arena of contemporaneous decision making by businesspeople and by the public.

Hundreds, and in some case thousands, of interlocutors linked informally to secondary and tertiary networks of countless other contacts are the circuitry of a vast communicative field across which "economic intelligence" is continually created. Diverse groups of contacts perform descriptive, explanatory, and interpretative labor, refining the conceptual nature of economic phenomena in real time. The efficacy of monetary policy rests, in part, on the representational enterprise of these contacts with which central banks must orchestrate the contingencies of economic stability and growth.

The concept of a public currency, *avant la lettre*, unfolded gradually in the text more or less as it did for me, as a cumulative outcome of the research experience that coalesced in the shifting situations and predicaments I observed. Similarly, my insights on language and, specifically, the linguistic modeling of economic phenomena, also unfolded in a manner that was inextricable from the details of the research—that is, from my own practices and those of my subjects. The project thus took form as an ethnographic exploration of multiple genres of collaboration worked out with George Marcus. I observed, as suggested above, how engaged and sophisticated research practices, indeed ethnographic practices, were operating in the scene of fieldwork independent of my project. The challenge I faced was to align my project at every turn with what were the remarkable experiments pursued by the personnel of these institutions, experiments that exceeded the bounds of monetary economics, broaching what are, I believe, the most profound questions of and for contemporary anthropology. This book thus represents a test case of what Marcus and I have advocated, an exploration of the intellectual strategies and struggles that constitute ethnographic practice in and of our time (Marcus 2007, 2008, 2012).

Epistemic Anxieties In Extremis

There is one final and related point. I stated emphatically at the outset that this text is not about the financial crisis. There is, however, a very important qualification to this assertion. As I noted above, the senior cohort of central bankers are not merely managers of the contemporary monetary regime, but its architects. They are keenly aware that monetary policy in general, and inflation-targeting in particular—their innovations—are fully implicated in the prehistory of the financial crisis.

Faith in what Jordi Gali and Oliver Blanchard termed "divine coincidence"—the consensus view that "strict inflation targeting is good, both for inflation, and for output"—established the general policy conditions that fueled the catastrophic risk taking and the regulatory complacency that laid the groundwork for the crisis (Blanchard 2008, 10–11).[5]

Claudio Borio, deputy head of the Monetary and Economic Department and director of research and statistics at the Bank of International Settlements (BIS), states concisely this tragic convergence:

> The crisis has shaken the foundations of the deceptively comfortable central banking world. Pre-crisis, the quintessential task of central banks was seen as quite straightforward: keep inflation within a tight range through control of a short-term interest rate, and everything else will take care of itself. Everything was simple, tidy and cozy. Post-crisis, many certainties have gone. Price stability has proven no guarantee against major financial and macroeconomic instability. (Borio 2011, 1)

Again, this text is not about the origins of the crisis, except to say that these issues—these intellectual failures of central banking—weigh on the thinking of all the figures who are the subject of this book, and, of course, on my own thinking (Miyazaki and Riles 2005; Miyazaki 2013; Riles 2011; Stoler 2008).[6]

CHAPTER TWO

Communicative Imperatives

It's all very different from the time, not so long ago, when the stated objective of the Bank's press officer was to keep the Bank out of the press, and the press out of the Bank." — Richard Lambert, member of the Monetary Policy Committee of the Bank of England (2003–06)

Many years ago I examined the economic dilemmas and cultural predicaments that had for centuries circumscribed the lives of a rural population in northeast Italy. During that work I encountered a question that perplexed my subjects and continues to perplex me. These rural folk, descendents of peasants who had lived for roughly a thousand years under a profoundly cruel and unjust agrarian system—enforced by a brutal regime of numerical accounting—had undergone a change in outlook. They became in the latter part of the twentieth century susceptible to a very un-peasant like sentiment. To their surprise, and to mine, they were experiencing something that might be construed as "hope," if not "optimism" (Herzfeld 1992; Holmes 1989; Kalb 1998; Miyazaki 2004; Muehlebach 2012; Narotzky and Smith 2006; Scott 1979; Smith 1999; Stiglitz 2009). This hope was predicated upon the totality of promises conferred on Italian citizens in the wake of the Second World War; the promises of welfare and dignity that underwrote the European social model reset expectations. The future no longer loomed merely as a matter of dread and despair; it had become for these people a subject with discernable features that could be reflected and acted upon. This curious shift in sentiments and expectations about the future set the course of my research to some of the most complex technocratic institutions in the world—central banks.

In the broadest terms, I examine how central banks seek to endow the future with discernible features and how these institutions underwrite representations of the future with faith and credit. To do this, I have aligned this text with a series of experiments, initially designed by the Deutsche Bundesbank and refined and formalized as policy by the Reserve Bank of New Zealand, that seek to influence future sensibilities—not merely sensibilities about the future but also sensibilities *in* the future—to shape the expectations that impel the most fundamental dynamic of market economies: the evolution of prices (Woodford 2001). The bridge to the ephemera of expectations, to sensibilities in the future, is constructed in part with language, through the technical modeling of what I am referring to herein as an "economy of words" (Holmes 2009).[1] Let me put this a little more technically. I am interested in how the economy is modeled linguistically and hence communicatively; how the economy can and must be understood as communicative action, which is performed socially and enacted prospectively; and how language can sustain belief and sentiment by means of what Kaushik Sunder Raja refers to as a "promissory vision" (2006, 115).

The logic guiding these experiments goes like this: If the behavior of prices is "expectational"—as Irving Fisher, J. M. Keynes, and Knut Wicksell initially proposed in the 1920s—then an anticipatory policy that projects central bank action into the future becomes a means to influence these sentiments (Woodford 2001, 2003). As "economic agents"—that is, you and I—assimilate policy intentions as our own *personal* expectations, we do the work of the central bank.

In plain terms, this is how this "self-fulfilling policy" is meant to work: If we fear that consumer prices will rise by 5 or 6 percent over the next few years, then we will continually calibrate our wage demands, for example, in anticipation of that expected rate of inflation and, by so doing, we will push prices, of which wages are a key component, upward. Alternatively, if we can be persuaded by a monetary authority that it will do everything in its power to restrain price inflation to something like a 2 percent rate per year for an extended period of time, then the public— that is, you and I—will be inclined to adjust our prospective demands for wages around the lower target and, thereby, stabilize price inflation going forward (Merton 1948; Hilgartner, Nelson, and Geltzer 2008).

The instruments developed to manage expectation are expressed most concisely in official statements (typically running between five hundred and a few thousand words) that the major central banks of the world publish every month or two in support of their interest-rate decisions— decisions that can stimulate, retard, or leave unchanged the pacing of economic activity. These "econometric allegories," as Alan Blinder and Ricardo Reis term them—in clear evocation of the persuasive labor these narratives are called upon to perform—draw on the full intellectual resources of these institutions: the research acumen, the judgment, and the experience of their personnel. They project a forecast of economic and financial conditions over a time horizon of approximately one to two years, along with an explanation of how the respective bank's interest policy will maintain consumer prices within an inflation target range of 1 to 3 percent (or around a single target, typically of 2 percent). A group of key theorists defined the elements of this experiment as follows:

> Inflation targeting is a framework for monetary policy characterized by the public announcement of official quantitative targets (or target ranges) for the inflation rate over one or more time horizons, and by explicit acknowledgement that low, stable inflation is monetary policy's primary long run goal. Among other important features of inflation targeting are vigorous efforts to communicate with the public about the plans and objectives of the monetary authorities, and in many cases, mechanisms that strengthen central banks' accountabilities for attaining those objectives. (Bernanke et al. 1999, 4)

This text is primarily concerned with the serialization, the periodic updating, of these econometric allegories—relentlessly and rigorously crafted in relation to data—and how sentiments and expectation that sustain the targeting framework are imparted through these communicative instruments (see Latour 1988, 1999).[2] Again, as we incorporate these statements of policy intentions as our personal expectations, we do the work of the central bank. As our expectations about prices become stabilized or "anchored" by virtue of these econometric allegories, we adjust our practices and thereby participate in the general development of consumer prices in the future. Narratives, articulated in concert with open market operations—the purchase and sale of government securities by which money is supplied or withdrawn from the economy—are the main tools of monetary policy (Bernanke and Mishkin 1997).

I focus on the creation and articulation of these econometric allegories during a particularly tumultuous period in the history of central banking, a time, as we will see, when shaping public expectations was crucial. During this period a very important, indeed radical, feature of the inflation-targeting regime was revealed in the course of central bank personnel grappling analytically with some of the most vexing problems in macroeconomics. The solutions they developed faced a double challenge imposed by the new commitment to transparency. They had to draw on state-of-the-art ideas in academic economics for their technical insights, but in addition they had to craft their solutions in a manner that made them plausible to the public; their solutions had to be rendered coherent communicatively in order to yield effective policy.

By virtue of these intellectual engagements, classic questions in monetary economics—pertaining to interest rates, inflation, employment, etc.— had to be rearticulated for the purposes of informing public expectations. Monetary economics under this regime becomes a strategic form of communicative action aligning it with what are essentially pedagogical and, thereby, behavioral aims. It is this second intellectual exercise that is the main concern of this text, but, of course, this second form of analytical labor anticipates or presumes a global communicative field in which we all participate in modeling economic phenomena. It also presumes very important shifts by which economic actors came to be conceived of as reflexive subjects who are capable of employing theory and parsing the ambiguities of data and the anomalies of information. In other words, monetary policy has assumed a phenomenological cast with each refinement of the inflation-targeting framework and, as we will see, the predicaments of economic actors, that is, our predicaments, became the fulcrum of policy.

From Predictive Science to Performative Art

The production of these narratives, in the first instance, provides access to the "epistemic culture" of central banks (Knorr-Cetina 1999)—to the research practices, to the policy deliberations, and to the organizational values that define the day-to-day operation of these institutions. These narratives thus function as instruments of far-reaching experiments in the formulation and communication of monetary policy, demarking the communicative imperatives that have sustained a "quiet revolution" in the practices of central banking (Blinder 2004). Again, my thesis here is that these statements are not merely *expressing* an interpretative account or commentary, they are *making* the economy itself as a communicative field and as an empirical fact. This constitutes an amplification of the performative hypothesis, particularly as delineated by Michel Callon and Donald MacKenzie. MacKenzie frames the hypothesis in this way: "Did finance theory bring into being that of which it spoke? Did its practical use

increase the extent to which economic processes or their outcomes re-
sembled their depiction by theory?" (2006, 253). Callon provides a framing of the interplay between these analytical and performative dynamics:
"Economics ... performs, shapes, and formats the economy, rather than
[merely] observing how it functions" (Callon 1998, 2). Performativity presumes, in my elaboration of the concept, the operation of the economy
as a communicative field in which the continual generation of economic
ideas and economic information—data—has currency. Where this information comes from and how it is serialized as technical narratives or allegories is a central preoccupation of this book.

The communicative imperatives that have "revolutionized" the practices of central banking over the last three or four decades then reside,
I will suggest, not merely at the level of institutional accountability or
public relations per se—insistence on transparency over this period
notwithstanding—but also at the level of data. Within central banks data
have at least three performative registers: as analytical, as representational, and as instrumental phenomena. Central bankers engage these
three registers more or less sequentially: data are grounded analytically in
conventional economic theory, reconfigured representationally to inform
policy decisions, and retransmitted instrumentally to target audiences—
the public—to influence behavior going forward.[3]

In the middle of the last century there was hope, faith even, that the
social and behavioral sciences—notably economics—might become pre-
dictive sciences. The overarching claim of this book is that from the van-
tage point of the early decades of this new century, economic theories
have been most consequential as a performative apparatus shaping economic institutions and economic thinking rather than underwriting a pre-
dictive science. I will argue in the next chapter that J. M. Keynes established the intellectual foundations of a performative economics in which
data and representations of data have persuasive authority. I will further
argue that central bankers have become agile practitioners of this performative art (Hawtrey 1970; Heikensten and Vredin 2002; Leeper, Sims, and
Zha 1996).

Quiet Revolution

I became interested in central banks in the early 1990s, at the time of the
drafting of the Treaty of Maastricht creating the European Union (1992).

I was struck by the few paragraphs of the treaty that proposed the creation of a monetary authority to manage a new and, at the time, unnamed
currency. This goal of European monetary union, the most far-reaching
agenda of the treaty, had by 1999 yielded a new institution, the European
Central Bank (ECB), charged with managing monetary affairs of what
became known as the "euro." My interest in the European Central Bank
and the Deutsche Bundesbank, which is now an integral part of the ECB,
has since expanded, as noted in the previous chapter, to include the Reserve Bank of New Zealand (RBNZ), the Sveriges Riksbank, the Bank of
England, and the United States Federal Reserve System.

Starting with Alan Blinder's insights on the quiet revolution that these
institutions have participated in, I have framed this book as an account
of how these famously secretive institutions—institutions that were in
some notable cases committed well into the 1990s to a mystique of secrecy as vital to their function—began to experiment with far-reaching
communicative practices under the aegis of transparency (Blinder 1998,
2004; Blinder et al. 2008). Tellingly, this communicative imperative is not a
matter of merely informing the market and the public about central bank
policies and practices, nor should it be mistaken for a conventional informational or public relations function of a government bureau or agency.
Rather, as indicated above, these narratives are generative of a communicative field within which and by which the economy is made, remade, and
unmade.

Blinder has reviewed some key elements of the revolution. He began
by quoting Karl Brunner's acerbic "Art of Central Banking" (1981) regarding the old regime of central bank communications. "Central Banking ... thrives on a pervasive impression that [it] ... is an esoteric art. Access to this art and its proper execution is confined to the initiated elite.
The esoteric nature of the art is moreover revealed by an inherent impossibility to articulate its insights in explicit and intelligible words and sen-
tences" (quoted in Blinder 2009, 1).

He, Blinder, then reviews his own interventions, drawn from his 1996
Robbins lectures at the London School of Economics, in which, far from
employing the mystified practices that Brunner describes, he asserts the
contemporary values of central bankers forthrightly articulating their
aims, means, and intentions:

> Greater openness might actually improve the efficiency of monetary policy ...
> [because] expectations about future central bank behaviour provide the es-

sential link between short rates and long rates. A more open central bank ... naturally conditions expectations by providing the markets with more information about its own view of the fundamental factors guiding monetary policy ... thereby creating a virtuous circle. By making itself more predictable to the markets, the central bank makes market reactions to monetary policy more predictable to itself. And that makes it possible to do a better job of managing the economy. (Blinder 1998, 70–72)

The third and arguably most important element of this abbreviated history is Michael Woodford's (2001) assertion that the essence of monetary policy is the art of managing expectations: "Successful monetary policy is not so much a matter of effective control of overnight interest rates ... as of affecting ... the evolution of market *expectations.* ... [Therefore,] transparency is valuable for the effective conduct of monetary policy." (quoted in Blinder 2009, 1). Woodford's assessment goes to the heart of the issues at stake in this text, namely, that the most powerful tools that central bankers possess are communicative.

Blinder further summarized the revolutionary significance of these ideas on the practices of central banking:

These new ideas from the academy had major impacts on actual central banking practice. Even the Federal Reserve, where then-Chairman Alan Greenspan once prided himself on "mumbling with great incoherence," has been increasing its communicativeness incrementally since 1994. And the Fed is far from a leader in this regard. Indeed, one might argue that the European Central Bank (ECB) has been more transparent than the Fed ever since it opened for business. The Reserve Bank of New Zealand and the Bank of England were early and enthusiastic converts to greater transparency and remain among the leaders in that regard, although Norges Bank and Sveriges Riksbank may now be in the vanguard. And there are many other examples. The attitudes that Brunner parodied have been put to rout. (Blinder 2009, 1)

The impact of the revolution can be measured ex post facto.[4]

Charts that trace the behavior of consumer prices illustrate and communicate the efficacy of the inflation-targeting regime and specifically the institutional efficacy of expectation management. The European Central Bank regularly publishes updated versions of the following chart to illustrate how the bank policy regime tamed prices both immediately prior to and subsequent to the introduction of the euro in 1999.

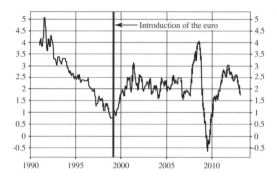

FIGURE 1. Inflation in the euro area (annual percentage changes, non-seasonally adjusted) as measured by the Harmonized Index of Consumer Prices (HICP).

The ECB's target is simple and explicit: "The primary objective of the ECB's monetary policy is to maintain price stability. The ECB aims at inflation rates of below, but close to, 2% over the medium term.... Inflation refers to a general increase in consumer prices and is measured by an index, which has been harmonized across all EU Member States: the Harmonized Index of Consumer Prices (HICP). The HICP is the measure of inflation which the Governing Council uses to define and assess price stability in the euro area as a whole in quantitative terms" (ECB 2013).

The declining percentage changes in consumer price inflation prior to 1999 (see figure 1) was, in part, anticipatory, the result of a carefully planned and executed communication policy that preceded the introduction of the euro transmitting the ECB's determination to pursue the ardent inflation-fighting policies of the Bundesbank. Expectations about prices were anchored in anticipation of the policies of a central bank that did *not* yet exist.

In late 2008, during a brief visit to the RBNZ, I noticed a modest terminological distinction. I noticed that people were referring to "the framework" rather than to the "inflation-targeting framework." I had assumed that the former term was just shorthand for the latter, and, perhaps, that is all it had been. However, in the midst of the financial turmoil ensuing after the collapse of Lehman Brothers, this tiny terminological shift came to seem significant. "Inflation targeting" emerged during this period as a far broader framework for addressing acute analytical problems—not merely inflation—that challenged fundamental conventions of monetary economics. Notably, it provided the communicative instruments for recruiting the public to participate in the labor of resolving the unfolding crisis (Krugman 1999).

Central bankers are keenly aware of how these experiments are based on a self-conscious use of language. One can find in their offices Deirdre McClosky's books on the rhetorical nature of economics, for example, or a volume of the Oxford English Dictionary open on the desks of personnel intent on linguistic concision and subtlety. But, as I have already suggested, I am also interested in deeper cultural issues at stake in this revolution that exceed the concerns of optimal monetary policy. Economic allegories designed to shape public expectations also addressed reciprocally the power and limitation of "data" and the vulnerabilities of a world that depends for its operation on the information that can or cannot be gleaned from quantitative models that conventionally for economists have constituted data (Gusterson 1997; MacKenzie 2006; Masco 2010).

Macroeconomics In Vivo

From the outset, my own intellectual practices were fully implicated in what I was studying. Specifically, I observed how "ethnographic" modalities were assimilated within the technocratic settings of central banking, settings in which the "subjects" themselves—central bankers—experiment creatively with the empirical challenges of gaining access to the contemporary situation, to the full range of ideas and insights animating economic action (Holmes and Marcus 2008; Westbrook 2009). In the messy flux of this "real world"—the economy in the wild or in vivo—is an abiding preoccupation of central bankers (Muniesa and Callon 2007).

Here is an example. Timothy Besley, while he was one of the nine members of the monetary policy committee (MPC) that formulates interest-rate decisions for the Bank of England, drew attention explicitly to the complementary relation between the intellectual practices of anthropologists and central bankers in an interview in May 2009[5]:

> Well you know I spend a lot of my time, and it is one of the great pleasures of being on the MPC, talking to businesses. Only last week I was out on the road 40 or 50 miles away from London talking to a number of businesses and it is really interesting when you kind of, if you like, almost take the anthropological approach, to the global crisis. You sit down perhaps with an entrepreneur, someone who is in a small business, could be a midsize business and they give you their own window on the global crisis and what is interesting about that is that each of them will have their own particular story of how it is hitting them. And while in the end we talk of these big macro trends it is really pretty fascinating to see how it plays out in a particular context. One thing you quickly

learn there is no single model of how the global crisis is evolving at that micro
level even though the big picture trends are familiar. (Besley 2009)

Professor Besley then made an ethnographic assertion, noting that during his sojourns in the field, what he was able to observe was the ebbs
and the flows of what he termed the "currency of confidence," a phenomenon that was not fully nor necessarily evident from his conventional purview as an economist. "We hear time and time again the currency of confidence is hugely important to people who run businesses. Something I
perhaps learned as an economist, we do talk about animal spirits and we
talk about the psychology of confidence but [it is] something I guess I
hadn't quite appreciated as much as I do now as I go on the road" (Besley
2009). Going into the field opened interpretative insights for Besley, insights on how the decisions he was making as a member of the MPC
shaped expectation, animating a currency of confidence. His conversations in the field permitted access to the motives and reflections of economic actors operating in various domains of business, allowing him to
engage the *creative* dynamics of the economy in vivo—dynamics not
merely or necessarily reducible to Adam Smith's invisible hand and Alfred Marshall's supply and demand curves (Mankiw 2006, 8).

Besley is drawing on the intellectual acumen of networks of situated
actors across the UK to creatively engage the foundational dynamics of
the economy rooted in learning and in experience (Riles 2000). Crucially,
he is not invoking an anthropological purview to illustrate an idiosyncratic practice of the Bank of England, but rather to gain purchase on
its core concern, the dynamics of confidence—the cumulative manifestation of those sentiments impelling and shaping expectations. The operation of the Bank of England's remarkable network of interlocutors—in
which the bank has invested substantial resources—is examined in detail in chapter 10. In particular, I examine how the bank actively aligns
its policy with the expertise of seven thousand contacts, and with their insight into the various predicaments they face. By so doing, the bank demonstrates how the efficacy of monetary policy rests on the enterprise of
these contacts—distinct from the abstract "rational actors" of classical
economic theory, but protagonists with whom the bank must orchestrate
the contingencies of economic stability and growth.

Thus, engaged and sophisticated ethnographic practices were operating in the scene of fieldwork independent of my project. I was thus able
to orient my work in a manner that drew on the collaborative possibilities offered by this salutary coincidence (Holmes and Marcus 2008, 2012;

Riles 2011). This unlikely convergence of intellectual pursuits around ethnographic modalities had, however, methodological significance exceed-
ing the intellectual practices of central bankers and the disciplinary conceits of anthropologists: it went directly to the nature and the operation
of quantitative data.

As we seek to render data increasingly precise, increasingly reliable, increasingly abstract, increasingly "scientific," we strip away information—
the social, historical, and cultural information—that is crucial for understanding key issues defining the contemporary world. This is hardly
a novel insight. It is a central preoccupation of Émile Durkheim in his
classic treatise, *On Suicide* ([1897] 1997), a study in which he explores
the process of denaturing phenomena by virtue of empirical scrutiny in a
manner that both informs and obstructs analytical understanding (Berger
and Luckmann 1967). This is a particularly relevant challenge for central
bankers, who are acutely aware of the limitations of the analytical tools
they employ and who understand implicitly the historically situated, socially constructed, and culturally encumbered nature of data. They have
assimilated ethnographic modalities—permitting alternative constructions and interpretations of information—to perform what I initially
thought were compensatory analytical maneuvers, but that I now am inclined to see as distinctive, though typically unmarked, intellectual practices that address the circumstances of contemporary knowledge production in technocratic settings (Fischer 2007; Masco 2009).[6]

Besley demonstrates in his brief aside how these alternative modalities can generate analytical perspectives and robust insights on fundamental issues of monetary economics. I will argue in subsequent chapters
that these struggles with the nature of data impel the continual creation
of the economy as a communicative field and as an empirical fact, albeit a
dynamic, unstable, and enigmatic fact. Besley's comment further reveals
how the economy must be understood as communicative action—as an
economy of words—performed socially and enacted prospectively.[7] These
ethnographic modalities, I will argue, circumvent classic problems with
technocratic knowledge (Hayek 1948a, 1948b; Riles 2011).

Public Currency

What is at stake in the cumulative experiments pursued by central banks?
The accretion of these experiments over the last three or four decades has
yielded a public currency. Complex communicative practices—informed

by continuous experimentation and learning—anchor (or tether) the operation of this currency. In other words, a simple governmental "fiat" is
not sufficient or, perhaps, even plausible:

> With paper money intrinsically almost worthless, what then determines
> whether a loaf of bread is worth one dollar or three dollars? The short answer,
> sweeping a lot of complications under the rug, is that in a paper-money system
> there is a need for some additional constraint on monetary policy, called a nom-
> inal anchor, to tie down the price level to a specific value at a given time. . . . An
> effective commitment to long-run price stability is just such a nominal anchor,
> since (given the current level of prices), a target rate of inflation communicates
> to the public the price level the central bank is aiming to achieve at specified
> dates in the future. (Bernanke et al. 1999, 19–20)

The nominal anchor that Ben Bernanke and his colleagues are referring
to represents an abstraction—a radical distillation—of a vastly more
complex intellectual and monetary regime that links the soundness of a
currency directly to the predicaments of the public, to their sentiments
and expectations.

The next chapter is devoted to laying out the theoretical groundwork of this research, notably explaining further how aspects of monetary policy operate performatively. I will also outline J. M. Keynes's formulations of monetary economics, showing how he sought to model the
economy communicatively and how he framed a performative economics
of sentiment and expectation.

Markets Are a Function of Language

The deepest question posed by Keynes's work is as follows: Is it money which causes the economy to misbehave? Or is it uncertainty which causes money to misbehave? Between these two views the theory of monetary policy is still poised. — Robert Skidelsky, John Maynard Keynes's biographer

In the eighteenth century the directors of the Bank of England erected a weather vane on the roof of the bank as a tool for monetary policy. A steady easterly wind indicated that within hours ships would be making their way up the Thames estuary, delivering their passengers and crews and disgorging their cargos along the wharfs of the great river. The rapid upturn of commercial activity that ensued created a demand for money that the bank would respond to by issuing more coinage. In the age of sail, the breeze carried information on future monetary conditions.[1]

In June 2010, I was in London talking to an official of the Bank of England, Gareth Ramsay. We were discussing a chart that projected gross domestic product (GDP) for the UK economy over the ensuing two years. It also happened to retrace the history of GDP since 2006, depicting the scale of the economic decline that marked the onset of the crisis. The chart, a "fan chart," is unusual insofar as it portrays graphically the MPC's judgment of GDP growth in a manner that explicitly addresses uncertainty:

Nobody can predict the future evolution of the economy with absolute certainty. It is more realistic for forecasters to recognize that uncertainty when describing their projections. Consequently, the forecasts for GDP growth . . . are always presented in probability terms. And the fan charts are graphical representations of those probabilities. . . .

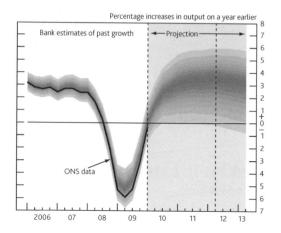

FIGURE 2. Bank of England GDP fan chart (from *Inflation Report, May 2010*). The black line traces the Office of National Statistics (ONS) estimates of GDP employing a standard, linear representation of data.

The width of the coloured bands is an indication of how uncertain the Committee is about the prospects for inflation. [Narrower, darker banks represent the central part of the forecast distribution, and the fan around this path captures the degree of uncertainty around the central estimate.] The Committee uses the experience of past forecast errors to inform its judgment. But the MPC does not mechanically extrapolate those errors in order to calibrate its uncertainty for each forecast. Rather it makes a subjective assessment, based on the economic conditions prevailing at the time. . . .

Given the lag between the change in the official interest rate and its full impact on inflation, the forecast represented by the MPC's fan chart is a key input to policy decisions. But it must be emphasized that there is no mechanical link between either the central projection or the distribution of inflation at the forecast horizon and the setting of monetary policy. (Bank of England 2002, 48–49)

The Bank of England is proud of its fan charts because they communicate overtly how their policy stance is intended to influence economic activity over time as well as the limitations inherent in the forecasting exercise. That said, it was hard not be impressed with how this simple chart summarized the course of an astoundingly complex historical event (see Tufte 1983, 1990, 1997).

We were discussing the uncertainties about evaluating recovery in the UK going forward when Mr. Ramsay made a small observation about the chart. He noted that the fan chart also projected backwards—that is, it depicted both the past and future probabilistically.[2] The scale of the downturn and the then current state of the UK recovery were not entirely clear in June 2010, and they, like the future, could only be expressed probabilistically. The dimensions of the crisis we were living through were understood only imperfectly and imprecisely.

In the Wild

Representations of the economy—notwithstanding a general willingness to invest mathematical representation with empirical weight—are fragile cultural constructions. Mr. Ramsay's aside reminded me that the personnel of central banks, while seeking to address pragmatic issues of monetary policy, were quite self-consciously engaged in the challenges of representation. Specifically, they struggled with the representational forms—the models—that define our economic predicaments. The Bank of England's fan chart, and countless other technical depictions, are not merely abstractions of economic phenomena; they are representational forms that are, as I will show, fully within the economy and intrinsic to its operation.[3] In the wild there are no externalities.

The analytical practices for depicting and simulating economic phenomena have a fundamentally communicative nature. Economic data are not merely discrete distillations. Rather, within these institutions data are continually refined and reinterpreted as dynamic communicative idioms. This insight is, of course, blindly self-evident: all representations are communicative. What I am arguing, however, is perhaps less obvious: that these representational practices are also constitutive, and that, indeed, they are vital to creating the economy as an empirical fact which is communicative at the very core of its operation (see Latour 2005; Poovey 1998; Rabinow 1986). As MacKenzie, Muniesa, and Siu note: "Michel Callon . . . proposes considering economics not as a form of knowledge that depicts an already existing state of affairs but as a set of instruments and practices that contribute to the construction of economic settings, actors, and institutions" (2007, 3–4). And, "It is this kind of interweaving of 'words' and 'action'—of representations and interventions—that the concept of 'performativity' is designed to capture" (5). There is one decisive distinction in the case of central bankers: they are fully aware of the performative nature of monetary theory, and they are fully dedicated to exploiting

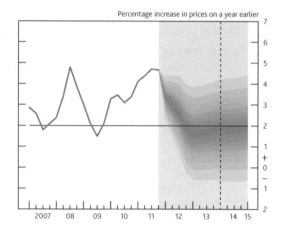

Percentage increase in prices on a year earlier

FIGURE 3. Bank of England February 2012 CPI fan chart

this potential (Lucas 1997). Performative action is overt in these settings, designed explicitly to be persuasive and efficacious.

Figure 3, like many Bank of England charts, illustrates more than mere projections; it is a performative instrument. The course of consumer price inflation from February 2012 through 2015 is projected to decline from over 4 percent to very close to 2 percent. Rather than a forecast of some natural phenomenon (like the weather), CPI inflation is something over which the Bank of England seeks to exercise control. The chart is a declaration of sorts that the bank will do all that it can within its power to achieve the target, and this is the basis of its performative efficacy. By projecting its policy intention, the bank seeks to shape expectations going forward such that the market and the public will adjust their behavior in anticipation of the bank's potential moves. The chart, then, should be understood as a policy instrument designed to influence the course of price behavior prospectively, rather than serve as a pure, probabilistic representation of future conditions. The dark reddish lines thus trace paths of persuasion.

Performativity Revised

In what follows, I begin my renovation of the performative thesis in relation to the unusual exigencies of contemporary knowledge production within and among central banks. The representational genres of the targeting regime—to overcome the limitations inherent in econometric projections and to address circumstances that arise at the limits of calculation and measurement—have created something distinctive: communicative experiments that I will show reconfigure the parameters of performativity. Here is what I mean.

Central bankers are, as noted earlier, attentive to the intellectual challenge of escaping abstract formulations of economic conditions in order to enter the arena of contemporaneous decision making by businesses and by the public. They are acutely aware, too, of the planning and circumspection that enliven thought and action at every level of production, distribution, and consumption, and of the extent to which central bank pronouncements become a crucial element of that planning. In this economy in vivo, words perform the decisive function of creating context—simulating countless situations—that frame data series, statistical measures, and econometric projections. The shifting and fugitive dynamics of global markets, their operation as seen from innumerable perspectives, are made available to us through language and, more specifically, through agile constructions of linguistic scenarios that are susceptible to continuous modification and elaboration.

Crucially, words model the purposeful and the persuasive. Unlike the processes of abstraction that characterize conventional economic analysis that strips away "extraneous" detail, the economy in vivo retains information, retains circumstantial conditions, retains perspectives, and retains experience as relevant analytical material. Expectations are alive in this economic scene and open to refinement and modification going forward. Unprecedented circumstances can be addressed descriptively, new ideas and new metaphors can be generated, and contestation can be treated as inherent at every level in this communicative field. The economy in vivo, insofar as it is not framed as an aggregated totality, is discernable from the standpoint of situated subjects. Learning and circumspection are integral to the practice of these actors and the plasticity of economic categories is manifested in every aspect of their own linguistic modeling.[4]

Economic actors can be unruly; they can learn about the world and act upon it with little regard for monetary authorities or economic theory. Their expectancy can succumb to the irrational; their sentiment can become inflected, as Keynes noted, with animal instincts. The challenge for central banks is to shape expectations with persuasive narratives informed by a continuous stream of data and analyses and articulated in a measured and consistent fashion. To address this challenge these institutions cultivate an experimental ethos focused not on the lab, but performed in vivo within and across the economy at large:

> These experimental activities are research activities in the sense that they aim at observing and representing economic objects, but also—and quite explicitly—in the sense that they seek to intervene on these economic objects: to seize them, to modify and then stabilize them, to produce them in some specific manner. To experiment is to attempt to solve a problem by organizing trials that lead to outcomes that are assessed and taken as starting points for further action. Experimentation is action and reflection. (Muniesa and Callon 2007, 163)

The experimental ethos that operates within these settings has a relentless character. Analytical insights are in motion; they are continuously refined in order to address the shifting nature of markets and economic phenomena.

My version of performativity rests on the premise that the experiments orchestrated by central banks unfold in collaboration with the public across a communicative field in which research, broadly conceived, is ubiquitous and enacted by reflexive, thinking subjects. Experimentation is performed in both directions, as it were, by policymakers and by the public (Miyazaki 2013). As I will show, in the shadow of the formal economic and monetary analysis performed by central banks, there is an alternative means of knowledge production, often unmarked—a complex epistemic system that draws directly on the intellectual acumen of economic actors fully implicated in the day-to-day operation of the economy. These actors are members of the same "metaphysical club," as Louis Menand terms it; they share "not a group of ideas, but a single idea—an idea about ideas." The founders of this club—O. W. Holmes Jr., William James, Charles Peirce, and John Dewey—believed that "ideas are not 'out there' waiting to be discovered, but are tools—like forks and knives and microchips—that people devise to cope with the world in which they find themselves. They believe that ideas are produced not by individuals, but by groups of individuals—that ideas are social. They believed that ideas do not develop according to some inner logic of their own, but are entirely dependent, like germs, on their human carriers and the environment. And they believed that since ideas are provisional responses to particular and unreproducible circumstances, their survival depends not on their immutability but on their adaptability" (Menand 2002, xi–xii). This experimental stance, as we will see in the next chapter, characterizes the alternative means for thinking and acting upon our shared predicaments; it underwrites the relational knowledge upon which an emergent monetary regime depends.

Ceteris Paribus

A tiny group of actors—central bankers—thus engage the analytical problems of the economy in the wild, problems that are essentially anthropological in character. I have developed the notion of an "economy of words" to encompass, inter alia, how these figures model linguistically, and hence communicatively, economic phenomena operating at the limits of calculation and measurement. These linguistic practices are by no means indifferent or antagonistic to the realm of numbers. Far from it. In the first instance, they are shaped by the analytical predicaments (as suggested by the fan charts) posed by various forms of statistical measurement and quantitative analysis.

There is one economist-cum-anthropologist-cum-linguist who is particularly important for this text, who during his entire career focused fully on engaging analytically and shaping empirically the economy in vivo. I draw on the work of J. M. Keynes at many points in this text, albeit for some unfamiliar reasons. In a famous and rather playful aside in *The General Theory of Employment, Interest, and Money*, he models linguistically a chain of dynamic relations while capturing their indeterminate nature:

> We have now introduced money into our causal nexus for the first time, and we are able to catch a first glimpse of the way in which changes in the quantity of money work their way into the economic system. If, however, we are tempted to assert that money is the drink which stimulates the system to activity, we must remind ourselves that there may be several slips between the cup and the lip. For whilst an increase in the quantity of money may be expected, *ceteris paribus*, to reduce the rate of interest, this will not happen if the liquidity-preferences of the public are increasing more than the quantity of money; and whilst a decline in the rate of interest may be expected, *ceteris paribus*, to increase the volume of investment, this will not happen if the schedule of the marginal efficiency of capital is falling more rapidly than the rate of interest; and whilst an increase in the volume of investment may be expected, *ceteris paribus*, to increase employment, this may not happen if the propensity to consume is falling off. Finally, if employment increases, prices will rise in a degree partly governed by the shapes of the physical supply functions, and partly

by the liability of the wage-unit to rise in terms of money. And when output has
increased and prices have risen, the effect of this on liquidity-preference will be
to increase the quantity of money necessary to maintain a given rate of interest.
(Keynes [1936] 2007, 155)

If we venture out of the closed system of *ceteris paribus*, uncertainties
proliferate and we can assert that all things are virtually never equal, that
indeterminacy is built into every economic relationship, and that every
representational model must account for the slip between the cup and the
lip, as the unrelenting spirit and fact of the economy *in vivo* (Nelson and
Katzenstein 2010; Skidelsky 2009; Tett 2009). In *our* world, in *our* time,
where *ceteris paribus* does not necessarily obtain, where the rational and
the irrational coexist or may be entirely inseparable, where knowledge
is imperfect and experience can or must inform judgment—it is in *that*
place that the anthropologist has something to say (see Callon and Law
2005; Collier 2011; Elyachar 2005; M. Fisher 2012; Guyer 2004; Ho 2009;
Lépinay 2011; Maurer 2000, 2005; MacKenzie 2006; Muehlebach 2012; Miyazaki 2013; Riles 2011; Roitman 2004, 2013; Rudnyckyj 2010; Tett 2009;
and Zaloom 2006).

In the wild, our economic lives are impelled by diverse motives and
purposes that can and often do exceed the bounds of formal rationality.
Keynes was familiar with this spectrum of volatile motives that he glossed
as "animal spirits":

> Even apart from the instability due to speculation, there is the instability due
> to the characteristic of human nature that a large proportion of our positive
> activities depend on spontaneous optimism rather than mathematical expec-
> tations, whether moral or hedonistic or economic. Most, probably, of our de-
> cisions to do something positive, the full consequences of which will be drawn
> out over many days to come, can only be taken as the result of animal spirits—
> a spontaneous urge to action rather than inaction, and not as the outcome of a
> weighted average of quantitative benefits multiplied by quantitative probabili-
> ties. (Keynes [1936] 2007, 161–62)

George Akerlof and Robert Shiller have probed the etymology of these
thoroughly human "animal spirits": "In the original use of the term, in its
ancient and medieval Latin form *spiritus animalis*, the word *animal* means
'of the mind' or 'animating.' It refers to a basic mental energy and life
force" (2009, 3). They further note that these animating sensibilities can

drive profound economic shifts as they continually coalesce as stories, as economic allegories: "The idea that economic crises . . . are mainly caused by changing thought patterns goes against standard economic thinking. But the current crisis bears witness to the role of such changes in thinking. It was caused precisely by our changing confidence, temptations, envy, resentment, and illusions—and especially by changing stories about the nature of the economy" (4). Though I am, of course, in full agreement with their etymological account, I disagree with Akerlof and Shiller on how animal spirits are manifest. Specifically, I will show how these "changing stories" and "thought patterns" don't just reside within the minds of individuals, as Akerlof and Shiller would have it, but are wired in, as it were, to vast communicative fields in which ideas and information are malleable, continually configured and reconfigured by networks of interlocutors modeling the crisis in diverse settings and shifting contexts.

I have been making an argument in this chapter, albeit implicitly, that is fundamentally opposed to the assumptions of behavioral finance of which Akerlof and Shiller are key theorists and proponents. My revision of the performative thesis is framed not only in relation to the work of Muniesa and Callon (2007) but as a critical alternative to the assumptions of behavioral finance. My emphasis is on knowledge-production, how analytical accounts are not mere empirical abstractions of economic behavior operating under the purview of academic observers, but fully within the scene of economic life and integral to its operation. Further, as argued above, these analytical stories are made, remade, and unmade continuously. And they are ubiquitous; they are manifestations of an experimental ethos built into the structure of the economy enacted and communicated in concert among thinking subjects.

My basic premise is that to understand the economy at large, it must be viewed as operating across an intricate communicative field, traversing what amounts to an ethnographic scene. I am pushing against analyses that abstract "economic behavior," stripping away precisely the contextual information, the rich variety of sensibilities and expectations, the volatile contradictions as well as the representations and misrepresentations that not only impel, but are the substance of economic and financial phenomena. Markets are a function of language, of analytical regimes that operate fully and emphatically in context.[5]

There is one more orientation, perhaps the most important one, which constitutes a defining preoccupation for central bankers: the future (Guyer 2007; J. Friedman 2008; Marcus 2012; Miyazaki 2006b; Munn 1992;

Rabinow 2008; Rabinow et al. 2008; Sunder Rajan 2006). Central bankers face a paradigmatic technocratic challenge; they must make decisions on interest rates in the present with data that are typically belated and with the knowledge that their policy interventions will only have measurable outcomes at some indeterminate time in the future. Anthropologists have generally found it difficult to say much about the future and future-oriented cultural practices. Addressing this discrepancy forms one of the defining issues of this book. Again, I argue that the bridge to the ephemera of expectations, to sensibilities in the future, is constructed with language through the technical modeling of an economy of words.[6]

Analytical Field

Jean-Claude Trichet provided a glimpse of the intellectual dilemma facing central banks at the limits of calculation as they seek to operate within a dynamic analytical field that is in part their own creation, yet in profound ways beyond their control. Trichet, while president of the ECB, addressed why under these conditions words matter:

> Because the economy is never at rest: agents have to catch up with the continuous change in their environment. When shocks [unanticipated events such as wars, natural disaster, sudden shifts in commodity prices, financial disruptions and so on] are moderate, or the underlying evolution of the economic structure proceeds at a slow pace, imperfect information and learning do not excessively complicate our interactions with the private sector. But there are times in which stormy perturbations and accelerated structural change make uncertainty more acute. These are times in which a perpetual process of learning on the part of economic actors can have implications for the overall stability of the system—to some extent independent of the monetary policy regime that is in place. (2005, 11–12)

Skillfully composed narratives, with supporting data and charts, serve as analytical bridges to the near future—instruments for guiding economic activity by recasting historical and contemporaneous data to project economic conditions prospectively. These carefully calibrated communications, informed by a keen technical expertise and crafted by a small group of individuals working within central banks, are, however, not merely projections of economic activity in the future, they are, again, themselves instruments for shaping and defining that future. Public statements are now

viewed as essential to central bank operation, as a major practitioner dryly
noted: "Informing the public about the central bank's objectives, plans,
and outlook can affect behavior and macroeconomic outcomes" (Bernanke 2007).

When the governor of the Reserve Bank of New Zealand—or the
monetary policy committees of the European Central Bank, the Bank of
England, the Fed, the Bank of Japan, the Indian Central Bank, the Bank
of Canada, or the Swedish Riksbank—decide to raise or lower interest
rates, or decide to do nothing, they are acting within a remarkable intellectual tradition. Again, one figure looms large in this tradition, J. M. Keynes,
whose contributions to monetary economics in general, and the practices
of central banking in particular, exemplify this intellectual tradition.

Keynes's involvements, prior to, during, and immediately after the First
World War, with the cultural luminaries of Bloomsbury, with the political
and economic intricacies of financing the war effort, and with the drafting
of the Treaty of Versailles (and ultimately his famous denunciation of that
treaty), were closely related to his analytical breakthroughs. Keynes was
explicit that his theoretical breakthrough in the 1920s was predicated on
the creation of a new "language": a language that, I think, owed as much
to his association with Bloomsbury as to his work with the British Treasury and the Bank of England (see Maurer 2002b).

Robert Skidelsky's magisterial three-volume biography of Keynes
captures not just this intellectual history but provides a precise assessment of the operation of Keynes's theory—its analytical authority and its
limitations—and Keynes's struggle to find a language for money and for
monetary policy:

> The break with the past was sudden. New ideas came flooding in, and de-
> manded expression. From 1924 Keynes knew what he wanted to do and, in very
> broad terms, why. But he still needed to find a language to make a persuasive
> composition of his thoughts. Part of this language was assembled in the 1920s. It
> was a language of political economy. He tried to explain why a modern indus-
> trial society could not stand a policy of *laissez-faire*. He developed an imagery
> of fluids and sticky masses to explain the contrast between old and new forms
> of industrial life, and to pinpoint the need for a new type of statesmanship. The
> building of an economic theory of the treacly economy was much more diffi-
> cult. He came to realize that the economics he had been taught simply assumed
> away the *Sturm und Drang* of actual economic life: the unexpected craters in
> the roads, the grinding and jamming of the gears, the seizure of the engine....
> The steps in Keynes's struggle for language can be seen clearly in retrospect.

Yet the danger in partial excavation is that it removes the language from the context. Much of the new language was developed in lectures and journalism, which were themselves largely a reaction to immediate events or reflection on states of affairs or debates which would be fresh in the minds of his audiences or readers, but are remote from ours. (Skidelsky 1992, 174)

Keynes's evocative accounts yielded an analytical tableau—in many respects congruent with an ethnographic framework—to be communicated to a public, an elite public of politicians, bankers, academics, businessmen, and journalists who populated his analytic landscape, thereby making its features susceptible to policy interventions.

The possibilities and limitations of economic method and theory were thus grounded on particular historical circumstances of the early twentieth century. Keynes knew well that the economic and financial landscape was populated by protagonists capable of thinking and acting critically within and upon the then contemporary world. He sought not merely to debate, to persuade, and to otherwise influence these subjects, but to learn from them. "The economist's task was to discern the form or style suitable to the age—a matter of aesthetics and logic. . . . Keynes always stressed the crucial importance of 'vigilant observations' for successful theory-construction—theory being nothing more, in this view, than stylized reorientation of the dominant tendencies of the time, derived from reflection on the salient facts" (Skidelsky 1992, 221).

In tandem with his effort to render "experience" meaningful as "theory," Keynes also delineated a pedagogical idiom—communicated in the language of monetary theory and the vernacular of finance—by which economic phenomena could be made meaningful as a public discourse, as the instrument for intervention. Crucially, this language and pedagogy were emphatically future-oriented, focused in particular on the evolution of expectations. Within this pedagogic habitus the repertoire of skills and intellectual acumen we associate with the university professor—Keynes's economist-king—has become a model, if not *the* model, for the role of central banker (Krugman 2007; Skidelsky 1992).

Monetary Theory

The critique of the "quantity theory of money," which was at the heart of the Cambridge School of Economics, established the analytical agenda for the monetary reform movement of which Keynes was a central figure:

The quantity theory of money was a theory of the price level. It stated, quite simply, that prices vary proportionately with the quantity of money and that the quantity of money determines the price level. The greater the supply of money, the lower its value would be; which is the same as saying that the higher the prices would be of the goods and services it buys; and vice versa. The value of money, like any other commodity, depended on the laws of supply and demand. But it was a peculiarity of money that there was no demand for it as such—merely a demand for what it could buy. (Skidelsky 1983, 214)

What Keynes observed during a stint at the India Office in Whitehall, where he oversaw the operation of the Indian Central Bank from afar, was that demand for the rupee fluctuated seasonally. This very modest insight opened the way to a critique of the theory of money. "In the short run, changes in the *speed* with which people spend their cash—what economists call the velocity of circulation—can change prices independently of changes in the quantity of cash. What happens according to Keynes is that they speed up their spending when prices rise or are expected to rise, and slow it down in the reverse cases" (Skidelsky 1992, 156).

Keynes further recognized that central banks could intervene and regulate the demand for money and the level of prices:

The novelty in Keynes's book [on Money] . . . was his concentration on the variability of the "demand for money" for spending leading him to emphasize the control of this demand by the central bank as the key to stabilizing prices. The suggestion was that the same stock of money could support a lower or higher level of prices and business depending on how much people wanted to spend in a given period. The technical factor which made this possible was the ability of the banking system to *create credit or deposits*. A smaller or lesser quantity of credit could be built on an inverted pyramid of notes. As the notes, when spent, came back into the banking system, it could go on creating credit without infringing on its reserve requirements. . . . Thus prices were to be controlled by regulating not the quantity of notes but the terms of which credit could be obtained—that is, the rate of interest or cost of borrowing—so as to balance changes in the demand for purchasing power. (Skidelsky 1992, 162)

By regulating the cost of borrowing, a central bank could influence the level of prices in the economy as a whole. How does this work?

The Bank of England described in an official report in the early inflation-targeting era how this process unfolds: "Decisions about that official interest rate affect economic activity and inflation through several channels, which are known collectively as the 'transmission mechanism' of monetary policy" (Bank of England 1999, 3). The bank's research staff further described the four transmission channels:

> First, official interest rate decisions affect market interest rates (such as mortgage rates and bank deposit rates), to varying degrees. At the same time, policy actions and announcements affect expectations about the future course of the economy and the confidence with which these expectations are held, as well as affecting asset prices and the exchange rate.
>
> Second, these changes in turn affect the spending, saving and investment behaviour of individuals and firms in the economy. For example, other things being equal, higher interest rates tend to encourage saving rather than spending, and a higher value of sterling in foreign exchange markets, which makes foreign goods less expensive relative to goods produced at home. So changes in the official interest rate affect the demand for goods and services produced in the United Kingdom.
>
> Third, the level of demand relative to domestic supply capacity—in the labour market and elsewhere—is a key influence on domestic inflationary pressure. For example, if demand for labour exceeds the supply available, there will tend to be upward pressure on wage increases, which some firms may be able to pass through into higher prices charged to consumers.
>
> Fourth, exchange rate movements have a direct effect, though often delayed, on the domestic prices of imported goods and services, and an indirect effect on the prices of those goods and services that compete with imports or use imported inputs, and hence on the component of overall inflation that is imported. (Bank of England 1999, 3)

The substance of this concise overview (which the entire report expands upon) is, of course, fundamentally important for understanding monetary policy, but for the purposes of this project the genre itself is also critical. By that I mean this more-or-less textbook summary was efficacious, insofar as it educated the public or, more precisely, elite representatives of the public, about the workings of what was a new monetary framework. Indeed, the report was prompted in response to suggestions made by an oversight committee, the House of Commons and the House of Lords Select Committee on the Monetary Policy. From the standpoint of a public currency, what is significant is the capacity of the report to model the technical operation of the transmission mechanism linguistically, in something like standard English, and in a manner that can serve the communicative, educative, and persuasive ends of monetary policy.

By raising or lowering the interbank lending rate, the US Federal Reserve's "federal funds rate," the Reserve Bank of New Zealand "official cash rate," the ECB's "main refinancing operation rate," or the Bank of England's "bank rate," or by doing nothing at all, central bankers regulate the amount of credit available to the banking system. By regulating thereby the cost of credit, they influence the pacing of economic activity. But this latter task requires a convincing explanation and justification to be effective. In short, it demands a story. And this is where the operation of central banks flirts with the uncanny.

Central banks must publicly justify their action in reference to an evolving account of present economic conditions, but also in relationship to forecasts of future conditions across a series of time horizons. More challenging still, they must signal implicitly or communicate explicitly their future course of action in reference to alternative scenarios derived from these forecasts. In the current jargon, decision-making within central banks has become "forecast dependent." The research staffs of central banks thus assume a pivotal position in this new framework. The circumstances that defined the onset of the financial crisis put extreme demands on this pedagogic and narrative framework as conventional monetary policy became of limited value.

"Monetary policy *à outrance*"

Keynes anticipated the circumstances of late 2008 in 1930. He also designed a radical solution:

> In the *Treatise [on Money]*, Keynes had already arrived at the conviction that, *if contraction were once allowed to gather momentum*, the type of monetary policy measures conventionally used by the Bank of England up to that time would be inadequate to correct the situation rapidly enough. A belated Central Bank action, he urged, must take the form of 'open-market operations to the point of saturation' or a 'monetary policy *à outrance*' as he termed it. He was careful to point out that such a policy would mean that the Central Bank would incur losses on its open market operation over time. (Leijonhufvud 1968, 20)

Keynes recognized that a strategy of massive and timely monetary intervention, a "monetary policy *à outrance*," could thwart a catastrophic economic decline; he also fully understood that as a practical matter the policy was at the time unworkable. His experience working closely with senior officials of the Bank of England led him to conclude that the bank's leadership would not permit its balance sheet to be used in such an unorthodox fashion. He understood too that putting huge liabilities on the bank's balance sheet to support demand and thwart an economic catastrophe would be viewed as unsound or worse. This insight, however, presaged another solution: the fiscal policy measures Keynes advocated in *General Theory of Employment, Interest, and Money*:

> The suggestion that the Old Lady of Threadneedle Street should run her affairs in this manner was—if possible—received with even more horror in 1930 than the "unsound" Keynesian fiscal policy recommendations in later years. Keynes' experiences with the Bank of England representatives, when he was a member of the Macmillan Committee, demonstrated quite clearly the uselessness of investing his influence and energy in pressing for this type of monetary policy. If the Central Bank could not be made to take losses for the general welfare, the government must. (Leijonhufvud 1968, 20)

In 2009 the Bank of England faced some of the same grim challenges that it had in 1930. It's governor and senior officials did not, however, labor under the same inhibitions as their predecessors. The Bank of England described the dilemmas posed by the crisis, and the bank's plan to address them, via the "unorthodox monetary" strategy of "quantitative easing":

> Significant reductions in Bank Rate to date have provided a large stimulus to the economy but as Bank Rate approaches zero, further reductions are likely to be less effective in terms of the transmission to market interest rates and the impact on demand and inflation. And interest rates cannot be less than zero.
>
> The [bank] . . . therefore needs to provide further stimulus to support demand in the wider economy. It boosts the supply of money by purchasing assets like Government and corporate bonds—a policy sometimes known as 'Quantitative Easing.' Instead of lowering Bank Rate to increase the amount of money in the economy, the Bank supplies extra money directly. This does not involve printing more banknotes but rather the Bank pays for these assets by creating money electronically and crediting the accounts of the companies it bought the assets from. This extra money supports more spending in the economy to bring future inflation back to the target.
>
> In essence, when spending on goods and services is too low, inflation will fall below its target. With Bank Rate already at a very low level, a further measured

stimulus is needed through an increase in the quantity of money. (Bank of England, n.d., "Quantitative Easing Explained")

Thus, as the crisis unfolded, monetary policy interventions shifted from the price of money—regulated by interest rates—to the quantity of money. As the risks of inflation were superseded by the perils of deflation, the major central banks of the world—most prominently the US Federal Reserve System—employed their balance sheets to create massive quantities of money out of thin air to avert what was widely perceived to be a looming economic catastrophe (Bernanke 2002a, 2009a). To make these monetary interventions work, central banks had to inform the public; they had to shape public expectations, but expectations not merely about consumer prices, but about the operation of monetary policy more generally. Confidence became a paramount concern.

Central bankers had to endow the future—in extremis—with discernible features, and underwrite representations of the future with faith and credit. In so doing, they faced the metaphysical problems of imparting confidence at a moment when their standard tools of analysis and persuasion were of questionable value. Akerlof and Shiller (2009, 12), echoing (perhaps unknowingly) Søren Kierkegaard, described how monetary policy in the midst of the crisis depends on leaps of faith:

> The dictionary says that it [confidence] means 'trust' or 'full belief.' The word comes from the Latin *fido*, meaning 'I trust.' The confidence crisis that we are in at the time of this writing is also called a *credit crisis*. The word *credit* derives from the Latin *credo*, meaning 'to believe.' . . . The very meaning of trust is that we go beyond the rational. Indeed the truly trusting person often discards or discounts certain information. She may not even process the information that is available to her rationally; even if she has *processed* it rationally, she still may not *act* on it rationally. She acts according to what she *trusts* to be true. (Akerlof and Shiller 2009, 12)

Again, I have no issue with their etymology, but as I have suggested above, confidence and leaps of faith that impel action unfold fully in our world and in our time by means of innumerable conversations. Like religion, confidence can give rise to powerful cognitive states, but it is a dynamic communicative phenomenon enlivened by diverse and often contradictory emotions and not merely or necessarily a psychological disposition that can be abstracted from the settings in which it is articulated. My view of confidence is further aligned with the implicit assumptions of inflation targeting and the monetary regime it has given life to. By that I mean it presumes that economic actors function as reflexive subjects who are, as noted in the previous chapter, capable of employing various species of theory and who seek to parse the ambiguities of data and the anomalies of information. These actors further constitute a diverse public with whom central bankers are compelled to establish a communicative relationship upon which confidence and trust, among other things, can be constructed and sustained.

In the next chapter I begin to examine how this communicative relationship emerges out of research processes. Working with language, central bankers have refined an alternative economics, aligned with analytical practices operating naturalistically within the economic and monetary fields and fundamental to their operation. The following chapter also recounts the circumstances that prevailed during the earliest episode of my research.

CHAPTER FOUR

Apprehensions

"*Anecdote*: Secret, private, or hitherto unpublished narratives or details of history.... The narrative of a detached incident, or of a single event, told as being in itself interesting or striking...." — *Oxford English Dictionary*

I was early for my appointment and I walked in the direction of Saint Paul's Chapel on Broadway. It was an overcast mid-December afternoon and crowds were moving under the scaffolding that ringed abandoned office buildings. Workers on their lunch break and sightseers pressed toward the spotlights that ringed the site, illuminating the spectacle. Tour buses lined up next to media trailers and construction vehicles as street venders hawked souvenirs.

Saint Paul's Chapel was brightly lit for the shifts of work crews who were its temporary occupants. In the street in front of the churchyard were posted countless snapshots of the victims along with poignant expressions of loss and grief memorialized by family members, friends, and acquaintances. On the walls blocking off the view of the recovery efforts were posted thousands of colorful banners and handwritten signs from schoolchildren, police and fire departments, and various official and unofficial groups and individuals, sent from every corner of the country, expressing solidarity with the plight of victims' families and with the people of New York. A few blocks away occasional Christmas lights and decorations began to normalize the scene in the financial district. I turned down Maiden Lane and walked toward a fortress-like building with heavy iron barred windows that housed the New York District Branch of the Federal Reserve System. I had traveled to New York in late 2001 to interview officials of the research division of the bank.

I had been reading beginning in the late-1990s as much as I could about

the creation of the new European Central Bank and the impending introduction of what came to be known as the "euro," but I also followed the
public statements of a group of other central banks, most notably the periodic reports of the United States Federal Reserve System, "the Fed," specifically the statements of its Federal Open Market Committee (FOMC).

The FOMC consists of twelve members—the seven members of the
Board of Governors of the Federal Reserve System; the president of the
Federal Reserve Bank of New York; and four of the remaining eleven Reserve Bank presidents, who serve one-year terms on a rotating basis. The
rotating seats are filled from the following four groups of banks, one bank
president from each group: Boston, Philadelphia, and Richmond; Cleve-
land and Chicago; Atlanta, St. Louis, and Dallas; and Minneapolis, Kansas
City, and San Francisco. Nonvoting Reserve Bank presidents attend the
meetings of the committee, participate in the discussions, and contribute
to the committee's assessment of the economy and policy options in what
is essentially a consensus-building process.

The FOMC holds eight regularly scheduled meetings per year. At
these meetings, the committee reviews economic and financial conditions, determines the appropriate stance on monetary policy, and assesses
the risks to its long-run goals of price stability and sustainable economic
growth. The committee is charged under law "to oversee open market operations, the principal tool of national monetary policy" (FRB, n.d.). This
legal authority over the management of monetary policy, exercised primarily through the setting of interest rates, makes the committee one of
the most—if not *the* most—powerful single institutions governing financial markets.

In reports that summarized the meetings of the FOMC in late 2000 and
early 2001, reference was made to a particular kind of data that seemed
incongruous. These statements justified changes in policy based on what
was referred to as "anecdotal" data. It was the usage of this single term
that prompted my trip from New Zealand, where I was living at the time,
to Lower Manhattan.

Uses of the Anecdotal

The key analytical dilemma faced by central bankers can be stated as follows: Central bankers must act in the present, in real-time, with (quantitative) data that are from the moment they are reported historical and, to a

greater or lesser degree, outdated. Furthermore, their regulatory actions influencing interest rates only have clear and measurable impact on the economy in the future across a time horizon of many months. How central bankers deal with this predicament of the timeliness of their data is, of course, key to the formulation of effective monetary policy, but there is far more at stake.

Jean-Claude Trichet described this dilemma in relation to estimates and subsequent revisions of the "output gap"—a fundamental metric, notoriously difficult to calibrate, that measures the difference between potential and actual GDP:

> The first estimates of the output gap are typically available during the reference year, and are then revised over subsequent years. It is important to note that the final estimate is not available for a very long period of time: 1999 estimates, for example, were still revised by non-negligible amounts in 2004. Revisions are also large: they can often affect the sign [their positive or negative value], as well as the magnitude of estimates. In the case at hand, for example, the revised output gap measure available to us today is positive in almost all estimates from 1999, 2000 and 2001, but it was estimated to be negative in real time.... Uncertainty is even higher for output gap projections, which are the only measures of output gap existing at the beginning of each year. For example, the real-time estimates of the output gap for 2005 published in spring by the European Commission, the IMF and the OECD, differ on average more than 25% from the output-gap projections these institutions made at the end of 2004. And if we add to the real-time measures of the output gap for 2005 the average size of the revisions observed in the past, we can conclude that it may ex post turn out to be anything between −3.6% and +0.8%. (Trichet 2005)

Thus, a fundamental measure of whether or not the economy is in an "inflationary" or "recessionary" mode can in real time yield erroneous information that is open to literally years of revisions and recalculations. What do central bankers do when faced with this kind of intellectual problem?

In late 2000 and early 2001 the "dot.com boom" had collapsed and a presidential election yielded enormous uncertainty about the political fate of the nation. Beginning on June 30, 1999, the FOMC had begun to raise incrementally the federal funds rate from 5 percent to 6.5 percent over the course of six meetings. This "tightening move" was intended to thwart inflationary pressures that appeared to be building in the economy at the time. By May 2000, the members of the FOMC believed that they had stabilized prices and stopped their tightening. Over the next six meetings during 2000, they left rates unchanged at 6.5 percent.

In December 2000, however, there was evidence, though often far from unequivocal, beginning to emerge indicating that the economy was losing momentum. The members of the FOMC were facing the prospect that their tightening strategy had worked too well and the economic slowdown they had engineered might turn into a more serious downturn. The members of the FOMC sought to address these circumstances in their December meeting. They decided, yet again, to leave the Fed's policy rate, the federal funds rate, unchanged. They did, however, assert in their accompanying statement that the risks to the economy had shifted, signaling that the potential for an economic slowdown had increased: "The drag on demand and profits from rising energy costs, as well as eroding consumer confidence, reports of substantial shortfalls in sales and earnings, and stress in some segments of the financial markets suggest that economic growth may be slowing further" (FRB 2000a). The "asymmetrical" assessment of risk (on the down side) hinted at an impending policy shift.

Then, a mere fifteen days later, the FOMC made the following surprise announcement after an unscheduled telephone conference call among its members:

> The Federal Open Market Committee decided today to lower its target for the federal funds rate by 50 basis points to 6 percent. . . . These actions were taken in light of further weakening of sales and production, and in the context of lower consumer confidence, tight conditions in some segments of financial markets, and high energy prices sapping household and business purchasing power. Moreover, inflation pressures remain contained. Nonetheless, to date there is little evidence to suggest that longer-term advances in technology and associated gains in productivity are abating.
>
> The Committee continues to believe that, against the background of its long-run goals of price stability and sustainable economic growth and of the information currently available, the risks are weighted mainly toward conditions that may generate economic weakness in the foreseeable future. (FRB 2001a)

The FOMC continued over the ensuing two and a half years to reduce the Fed funds rate to 1 percent. No one could have anticipated that this brief statement would presage one of the most convulsive episodes in the history of monetary policy. It was, however, the fifteen-day period spanning the end of 2000 and the beginning of 2001 that initially caught my attention, and, specifically, a few asides in the summary minutes of the meeting suggesting that "anecdotal evidence" was a persuasive element in the decision making. What I didn't know at the time was that the conversations during the FOMC meeting in December had, in fact, centered on the specific problems posed by anecdotal evidence for decision making. Only with release of the confidential transcript of the meeting (after a multi-year embargo) was this confirmed.

Adjectives

Fifty people were present at the closed FOMC meeting that began at 9 a.m. on December 19, 2000, in Washington, DC, that preceded the conference call and subsequent announcement of the lowering of the Fed funds target rate. All voting members of the committee were present, as were alternate members of the committee as well as a contingent of senior officials of the twelve Federal Reserve banks. Senior economists from the Division of Research and Statistics and the Division of Monetary Affairs and other key staff of the Federal Reserve were also in attendance.

The meeting began with presentations by senior economists reviewing current financial and economic conditions in the US and in other major economies. These presentations updated and elaborated on two briefing documents: "Current Economic and Financial Conditions" (marked "Confidential"), also known as the Green Book; and "Monetary Policy Alternatives" (marked "Strictly Confidential"), also known as the Bluebook. They had been prepared by the Fed staff and circulated to members of the committee about a week before the meeting. The Green Book presents the forecasts that are generated by the Fed's macroeconomic models, and the accompanying presentations seek to convey candidly the thinking of the staff in their preparation of economic forecasts and the revisions of those forecasts. Parsed in these discussions are various scenarios developed by staff economists projecting economic and financial conditions—notably, economic growth, growth in money and credit, conditions in labor markets, interest rates, exchange rates, and core inflation—over the course of the ensuing six to twelve months.

The Bluebook scripted a very specific policy agenda, on this occasion offering three recommendations on the setting of the Fed funds rate—raising it by 0.25 percent, lowering it by 0.25 percent, or leaving it unchanged. It also proposed a draft statement for the public, which included a sentence setting target interest rates and a much-scrutinized sentence assessing the "balance of risk" to the economy. Significantly, in addition to laying out alternative recommendations and the rationales for each scenario, the staff also appraised the potential reception of each policy stance by the markets and the public. These presentations were followed by questions and answers by members of the committee and detailed discussions on the setting of the federal funds rates. A third briefing document, entitled "Summary of Commentary on Current Economic Conditions by Federal Reserve District," known as the Beige Book, also informed these discussions and provided summaries of "anecdotal reports" for each of the twelve district banks.

Vice Chair William McDonough (New York Fed) outlined the particular situation the committee faced in mid-December 2000: "Available official and private data make clear that the expansion is slowing to a pace below trend growth. Inflation seems quiescent, but it is not decreasing. Anecdotal evidence, however, is overwhelming that the economy is slowing faster than the available data indicate, and the anecdotal information is more forward-looking. The economy in my view is likely to grow at a slower pace than we had hoped to achieve through our policy tightening" (FRB 2000b, 58–59). The other senior member of the committee, Chair Alan Greenspan, was more precise about the significance of the anecdotal data and the urgency of their message: "I've been hearing the same sort of adjectives that all of you have heard used to describe everything that is going wrong. And indeed we ought to be very careful to recognize that if one could put hard numbers on the anecdotal data we now have, we would not be looking at a 2 percent plus growth rate in GDP. It would be closer to zero. How one reads that evidence is a question, which we have to consider" (FRB 2000b, 71–72).

Other members of the committee were more cautious, expressing their ambivalence about these data. President Michael Moskow (Chicago Fed) interjected: "I agree that the anecdotes point to a much lower rate of growth than do our models at this time. But they are anecdotes, and I think we'd all like to see some more evidence in the data and other information we receive that would help clarify the situation" (FRB 2000b, 76).

Two other members of the committee linked their caution to the public reception of their decision. President Cathy Minehan (Boston Fed) noted: "I just think we ought not to let all the strength that's still in the economy be forgotten in the face of what are largely anecdotal and expectations-related data. They could turn if the market receives what we do today very favorably" (FRB 2000b, 78). Governor Roger Ferguson also weighed in, bringing the politics of expectation into the conversation: "The markets will not think us foolish for not jumping based on what is anecdotal evidence, but we are warning them—or in some sense maybe comforting them—that we are awake and alive and if things work out in a certain way, we're prepared to respond" (FRB 2000b, 82).

The subsequent, unscheduled meeting of January 3, 2001, started at 11 a.m. and ran about an hour.[1] The conference call opened with a statement by Chairman Greenspan reviewing new information that had become available over the prior fifteen days, notably Labor Department statistics for a pending announcement of increases in unemployment along with a range of anecdotal evidence suggesting increasing problems in the economy. President Alfred Broaddus of the Richmond Federal Reserve Bank noted: "There has clearly been a very negative turn in sentiment. I'm seeing it in our District. I'm getting phone calls that I don't normally have to field" (FRB 2001b, 9). Vice Chair McDonough was more emphatic: "I believe that the markets and the leaders of major firms in the world are at or near a point of psychological crisis. The pessimism about what is likely to happen in the economy is at a point where it can start feeding upon itself, which could make the extent of the slowdown in the expansion greater than would be in the interest of the country" (FRB 2001b, 6–7).

Most of the discussion during the brief meeting was not concerned with the pending decision regarding the unusually large interest rate reduction being contemplated—which was on a scale of the reduction taken in the midst of the 1987 stock market crash—but with the reception of the decision. Governor Lawrence Meyer was emphatic that the committee had the opportunity "to reset the psychological tone and expectations" of the markets and of the public on the health of the economy and the committee's readiness to intervene (FRB 2001b, 18). The members of the committee thus shifted their orientation becoming, as it were, the audience for their own decision; they stress-tested their decision on themselves. They also reviewed the commentary they would be asked to give once the decision was made public. Chairman Greenspan recommended strategic dullness: "I would suggest to you that your inclinations to be thoughtful, conceptual, and interesting be suppressed. [Laughter]" (FRB 2001b, 30). Despite Greenspan's only half-joking aside, the committee was deeply interested in the "structures of feeling" they were aligning and fashioning. Keynes's animal spirits of "fear" and "greed" preoccupied them; but they were also intent on framing more subtle sentiments, more nuanced apprehensions.

In Extremis

This brings me to Lower Manhattan in late 2001. On that afternoon, I spoke to the individual charged with gleaning information from a network of informants, a network that he personally developed, on the unfolding economic conditions within the jurisdiction of the New York District Branch of the Fed. Again, similar reports are drafted for each of the twelve districts of the Federal Reserve System just prior to the FOMC meeting, summarizing qualitatively the particular economic circumstance in each district. The twelve reports are compiled, and a summary statement is added, yielding the Beige Book, a spiral-bound report that runs about forty double-spaced pages with, at that time, a beige cover. As the discussion at the FOMC meeting attests, the overt purpose of these anecdotal reports was to overcome or circumvent lags attendant on virtually all the quantitative measures and data series that the Fed depends on. But, of course, there is a deeper process operating under the sign of the anecdotal: the social mediation of economic information (Latour 1999, 2005).

The material that follows was drawn from a conversation with Jason Bram, the analyst who conducted the research and drafted the Beige Book entry for the New York District. Significantly, there is no formal protocol specified by the Fed for how this analysis should be undertaken. Rather, the research divisions of each of the twelve district banks pursued this work independently—and, in fact, competitively—to provide a descriptive tableau of the US economy. Mr. Bram, working with a small staff, began calling his contacts about a week before the report was due and drafted the actual document at the last possible moment to make it as contemporaneous as possible.

Bram thus cultivated highly developed "contacts" with interlocutors who oversaw daily transactions within strategic spheres of the economy. These interlocutors—typically bankers, manufacturers, real estate brokers, and retailers—transact loans, book orders (and cancellations), and track store sales minute to minute, hour to hour. Since they operate in real time, they provide the closest possible approximation to a contemporaneous engagement with the economy.

The Beige Book entry for the New York District was completed on

September 10. In the immediate aftermath of the attacks the following day, a group of senior personnel of the New York Fed were brought together to assess the economic impact of the disaster. From their homes, since the Maiden Lane building housing the bank was closed for two weeks, these personnel called their contacts, individuals who had decisive purviews on various sectors of the New York area economy. From these accounts a confidential report, along the lines of the Beige Book entries though significantly more detailed, was drafted and sent to Washington, which became a basis of the government's initial response to the economic consequences of the disaster.

In redrafted form, the document became the substance of the October 24 Beige Book entries. In Bram's restrained prose, elements of the disaster are tightly summarized. What gives this account its power and its insights—its rich engagement with situated, reflexive interlocutors—is edited out from the report, as the following short excerpt shows:

> Home sales in and around New York City have slowed drastically since the last report, and both apartment prices and rents have fallen by an estimated 10 percent. In general, contacts note that the high end of the market has been the most affected. Contrary to initial post-attack expectations, Manhattan's office market has not tightened—availability rates at the end of September were slightly higher than a month earlier. Hotels, taxi drivers, and Broadway theaters experienced a steep falloff in business in mid-September, but activity has reportedly recovered somewhat in the weeks since. Finally, bankers again report weaker loan demand, tighter credit standards, and moderately higher delinquency rates in the latest survey, taken in early October. (FRB 2001c)

Bram described his autodidactic method in terms that are familiar to an anthropologist. "It's sort of an art, you have to know the people you are talking to." "I can't put it into a formula, it is very opportunistic." "It is very wide open." "As you do it—I have been doing it for four or five years—you learn. When you start out you ask [a retailer] about sales and inventories. But then [I learned] you have to know how retailers think [to interpret these numbers]. . . . It's a very subjective thing, you have to learn what kinds of questions to ask." "You try to find common threads." Though Mr. Bram's method lacked a formal disciplinary identity, it yielded a refined analytic engagement with complex economic activity and human behavior. At a moment when all quantitative data had been rendered suddenly outdated, given radically changed conditions, a systematic analysis of anecdotal narratives provided a critical means for engaging the fraught nature of the contemporary. With a few pages of text an unprecedented circumstance of enormous complexity was endowed with discrete contextual and situational features and rendered coherent for policymakers.

During the unscheduled FOMC meeting held by conference call late in the afternoon of September 13, 2001, another channel of anecdotal information was mentioned. Two members of the committee, President Minehan (Boston) and President Jack Guynn (Atlanta), referred to information drawn from consultations they had with their district boards the prior day. These boards constitute an official network of informants, and they were in continuous contact with senior officials of each district and of the branch banks of the Fed as the crisis unfolded. They are also regularly consulted in the preparation of the Beige Book, as are the individuals who are part of the more informal networks of interlocutors cultivated by the research divisions of the district banks.

Analytical Tableau

Each of the twelve district banks and their twenty-four branch banks has its own board of directors, with nine appointed members for the district banks and either five or seven members for each of the branch banks. Members are appointed for three-year terms and they are specifically charged with gleaning precisely these kinds of finely tuned anecdotal accounts of very detailed facets of the US economy. Indeed, the directors are classified in terms of the nature of their expertise and their specific professional activities. Three directors of the nine-member district-bank boards, designated "Class A" directors, represent the stockholding member banks in the region, and are typically senior bank executives.[2] Three "Class B" directors (appointed by the district bank) and three "Class C" directors (appointed by the Board of Governors of the Federal Reserve System) are chosen as representatives of the "public," and they are *not* permitted to be officers, directors, or employees of any bank; rather, they are chosen "with due, but not exclusive, consideration of the interests of agriculture, commerce, industry, services, labor and consumers"(FRB 2011). The boards of the branch banks are similarly divided between appointees named by the district banks and those named by the Board of Governors.

Apart from formal oversight responsibilities managing the operation of the twelve district banks, board members serve as strategically positioned interlocutors who report on a regular basis on the conditions of key sectors and often geographically localized and highly focused aspects of the economy (Granovetter 1985; Riles 2006). The group (in 2010) of two hundred and seventy or so district and branch board members encompassed a diverse cross-section of public and private organizations. Members included ranchers, executives of agribusinesses, food processors, managers of farm cooperatives, credit unions, utility companies, software firms, construction companies, defense contractors, hospitals, and biotech firms. There were partners of law firms, hoteliers, real estate developers, operators of fast food chains, retailers, manufacturers, executives of insurance companies, employment agencies, accounting firms, brokerages, logistics providers and freight forwarders, even college professors. Also, management consultants, resort operators, publishers, managers of environmental service firms, executives of oil exploration companies, union leaders, university administrators, officials of various public authorities, and mangers of charities and philanthropic organizations.

The professional experience and purview of board members also varied considerably, from those operating within fully global mega-corporations to executives whose expertise has a more regional or even local provenance, as illustrated in the following examples. The composition of the board for the 2nd District—covering New York State, the twelve northern counties of New Jersey, Fairfield County in Connecticut, Puerto Rico, and the US Virgin Islands—included the chairmen and CEOs of JPMorgan Chase, Adirondack Trust Company, and Banco Popular Inc. (Class A); the chairmen and CEOs of GE, Pfizer, and Loews Corporation (Class B); and the presidents of the New York State AFL–CIO, Columbia University, and the Partnership for New York City (Class C). As one moves across the country, the composition of the boards reflects the complexity and regional specificity of the US economy. The eastern portion of the 10th District lies in the Great Plains and includes Oklahoma, Kansas, Nebraska, and the western third of Missouri. The western portion of the 10th District lies along the Rocky Mountains and consists of Colorado, Wyoming, and the northern half of New Mexico; it has among its members the president of Agee Energy, the chairman of the board of the Mill Creek Lumber and Supply Company, and the governor of the Chickasaw Nation. The board of the 11th District, covering Texas, Northern Louisiana, and southern New Mexico, includes the founder of Southwest Airlines and the chief executives of Anadarko Petroleum Corporation and J.C. Penney Company.

These men and women, typically senior managers, have access to an extraordinary range of proprietary data—hard quantitative data—but they are also in conversations with clients, customers, and colleagues: auto executives walk showroom floors talking to potential car purchasers; bank executives converse with prospective borrowers about the state of their businesses and their outlook for the future; manufacturers discuss with their customers their future needs in order to plan capital expenditures; union leaders appraise the labor market as they negotiate contracts. By gleaning knowledge from these interlocutors, the Fed gains access to those profound and elusive forces guiding the economy: the expectations and sentiments that take social form across the intricate, geographically diverse communicative tableau of the United States. Contextual and circumstantial knowledge are modeled dynamically with language (Maurer 2005b; Riles 2011; Westbrook 2009).

Plasticity

Why model the economy anecdotally? Earlier in this chapter, I quoted President Jean-Claude Trichet to illustrate the abiding issues posed by quantitative data in the formulation of monetary policy, and specifically problems surrounding the timeliness of such data. I have sought to demonstrate how and why central bankers employ anecdotal modalities to perform what I had initially thought were compensatory analytical maneuvers. Subsequently, I have come to recognize these modalities as a bridge to decisive intellectual practices that address far more consequential issues at the heart of technocratic knowledge (Riles 2011). Anecdotal data reveal a central, albeit largely unmarked epistemology in which economic phenomena must be modeled linguistically. Why?

The network of interlocutors not only generate the circumstantial and comparative information that enables central bankers to develop a fine-grained understanding of the situations that they are charged with regulating, they also challenge the constitution of particular economic and/or financial phenomena—how we define and represent them—which in the midst of a crisis becomes as important as how we measure them. The shifting nature of employment, unemployment, productivity, investment, savings, trade, deficits, surpluses, sales, inventories, etc., etc.—the relationship between and among these concepts—demands continuous interpretative scrutiny. The conceptual integrity of data, their empirical value, is continually questioned epistemologically. The Fed refers to the operation of the network as "economic intelligence," acknowledging that these diverse groups of interlocutors are performing descriptive, explanatory, and interpretive labor in vivo, refining the conceptual nature of economic phenomena and contextualizing their domains of operation.

The Fed has thus designed an intricate system that continuously generates knowledge about the *social* and *cultural* character of the economy, shaped by precisely those subjectivities that are typically not represented in quantitative analysis. Members of the FOMC are not detached observers, nor should they be; they are deeply implicated and fully invested in the apprehensions of vast networks of informants—protagonists—who animate the economy. The knowledge glossed by anecdotal evidence constitutes the communicative interchanges by which members of the FOMC simulate the economy in the wild, modeling its fugitive characteristics linguistically. Under the guise of anecdotal data, the representational labor vital to the operation of the economy is performed and its radically communicative nature is imparted. The currency of confidence is created and articulated across this ever-shifting and uncertain communicative field (Callon 1986; Latour 1987, 2005; Law and Hassard 1999).

The Fed has developed an intellectual apparatus operating in vivo, a performative apparatus composed of interlocutors who are not merely representing economic conditions: they are actively participating in the creation of those conditions. The two hundred and seventy interlocutors that make up this formal apparatus are, of course, linked informally to secondary and tertiary networks (of their own making)—networks composed of countless other contacts who do not merely have intellectual access to a vast communicative field but who are the circuitry of that field.

This performative apparatus poses one more question that is central to the analysis of this book: what is the nature and status of the public in this monetary regime? As we have seen, the "public" has a precise legal status in the classes of membership of the district and branch boards. Overtly, the system operates to serve the interests of public accountability, encompassing, on the one hand, the role of members in the election of district bank presidents and, on the other, their oversight of the formulation and outcomes of specific bank policies. If we, however, view the network as an intellectual apparatus, the public interest emerges somewhat differently, as intrinsic to the bank's operation. Insofar as the members of the FOMC are deeply engaged in conversations with networks of interlocutors—inclusive of the district and branch boards, and beyond—they are operating in concert with the public, wired into their communicative field, and aware of their unfolding predicaments. Further, as hinted at in the FOMC transcripts, they, the members of the committee, are also masterful at modeling linguistically the opportunities and challenges facing various segments of this public; they routinely scrutinize policy to see, in the first instance, if it is credible, persuasive, and convincing to themselves, in an effort to anticipate how central bank communications will be received. As I pursued the meaning of anecdotal data, the communicative imperative of contemporary monetary policy began to gain clarity, most notably as a means of modeling dynamic *relationships* with the public.

Loose Ends

Many questions arose at the margins of this early episode of research. Some were incidental, some tangential, and some weighty. Three are worth mentioning here.

First, I was curious about how inflation targeting came to be incorporated as an official policy of the Federal Reserve System. An aside by Alfred Broaddus, president of the Richmond Fed, during the December 2000 FOMC meeting, was intriguing. He suggested the Fed take advantage of a change in the legislation governing the system's periodic reports to Congress as an opportunity to formally introduce "inflation targeting." Greenspan rather briskly tabled the idea. Only in January 2012 did the FOMC announce a formal inflation target: "2 percent, as measured by the annual change in the price index for personal consumption expenditures, is most consistent over the longer run with the Federal Reserve's statutory mandate" (FRB 2012a).

Second, there was during this period a growing attention to why inflation had been quiescent during the 1990s, while unemployment remained low. This era of "great moderation" began to draw scrutiny, notably as to why unemployment was falling below a level, "the natural level of unemployment," at which inflation, at least in theory, was supposed to accelerate (Freidman 1968; Phelps 1968). The argument that was developing held that productivity gains facilitated by technological innovations were altering basic structural conditions, permitting extended periods of low inflation and low unemployment (Bordo and Orphanides, forthcoming).

Inflation targeting was also credited with aiding in the moderation of consumer price inflation.

Third, and most importantly, on November 10, 2001, a 995-page diplomatic treaty, by which the People's Republic of China became a full member of the World Trade Organization, was signed. No doubt, we were all still preoccupied with the aftermath of the 9/11 attacks, but in late 2001 something like 1.3 billion souls were quietly added to the global economy. China, after extended negotiations, agreed to abide by rules governing economic and trade matters in order to gain full participation in the global system of trade and commerce. Hardly a dog barked.

China's ascendency, nonetheless, reverberated throughout this research, albeit in a manner that was often hard to describe, let alone measure. As we will see in chapter 10, one of the most important insights to emerge from the Bank of England's network of contacts in the 1990s was the insistence, initially resisted by economists, that global pricing was changing as a result of Chinese manufacturing. The China story was of course immense and unprecedented, challenging assumptions of how the global economy operated and just about every means and method for analyzing it.

The next two chapters examine the historical circumstances that prompted the development of inflation targeting as well as the institutional issues at stake in formalizing the targeting framework as operational protocols for central banks.

CHAPTER FIVE

Kultur

First of all, the Bundesbank stands for a culture of stability. — Jens Weidmann, President of the Bundesbank

In the East End of Frankfurt along the banks of the Main stands a huge abandoned structure, the Großmarkthalle, the city's historic wholesale market. In March 2002, the European Central Bank agreed to purchase the site from the city and an international urban planning and architectural design competition, chaired by Lucas Papademos, former vice president of the ECB (2002–10), was launched to select a plan for the central bank's new headquarters.

On a winter afternoon in early 2005 I visited the Frankfurt City Museum to view the three finalist models in the design competition. The winning design concept, by the Viennese firm of Coop Himmelb(l)au, had been announced a few weeks earlier by President Jean-Claude Trichet. The press release that announced the winner praised the Coop Himmelb(l)au design as best meeting "the functional and technical requirements specified by the ECB, and has features that reflect the ECB's values and transforms them into architectural language." Papademos had noted in a statement accompanying the earlier announcement of the finalists (on February 20, 2004) that the jury had been looking for a "visible icon" that expressed a very particular constellation of communicative values. He went on to describe the distinguishing features of the Coop Himmelb(l)au design:

> Their design concept was viewed by the Jury as a powerful image, reflecting the values of the ECB, such as transparency, communication, efficiency and stability. It is also an appealing and sophisticated design, which is easily readable and establishes a strong and unique identity in Frankfurt's skyline. The high-

rise is a sculptural hybrid of two towers connected by an atrium. We felt that this multi-purpose atrium reflected the values of transparency and communication. We believe this project to be compatible with the City's urban design concept for the whole river Main area. The Großmarkthalle itself is well preserved, both in terms of external visibility and its interior architectural articulation. (ECB 2004)

The design gave physical expression to the philosophy governing inflation targeting. Crucially, it sought to symbolize how the communicative practices like those operating within these institutions could be transformed into a public discourse mediated by transparency (Garsten and Montoya 2008, 79–96; Grossman, Luque, and Musiena 2008, 97–116).

The text drafted by the winning firm to accompany its architectural plan was explicit that the building's architecture aspired to create a dramatic cultural statement:

> Starting from a research base of urban sightlines and cones of vision, we proposed a polygonal-shaped double slab tower in the east-west orientation. The narrow side of the tower profile is a solitary figure seen from all of downtown Frankfurt's major viewpoints. . . . Its form and presence becomes an unmistakable fixture on the Frankfurt skyline. . . . By reinforcing the dynamic internal communication culture of the ECB the solution will create an unprecedented symbol in the urban context, representing the public dimension of the ECB within Europe and the world. (ECB 2009)

In the city museum, where the three finalists' scale architectural models were moved after their initial presentation and display across the Main at the architectural museum, I had a chance to view closely these efforts to materialize ECB values.

I found the winning design to be arresting. Each of the main towers of the Coop Himmelb(l)au design had a distinctive translucence that addressed the key design brief of ECB: the transparency that was to be emblematic of the new European order. At the same time, each tower was anchored or otherwise linked to the dramatically renovated Großmarkthalle, a symbol of the old economy of trade and commerce. The glass towers were to my naive architectural eyes most captivating. Unlike the modernist skyscraper, in which a building's structural elements are exposed, these towers seemed to be suspended by an invisible hand, as it were, their load-bearing elements obscured (ECB, n.d., "New Premises").

Why all this glass? The translucent design is intended to symbolize the free movement of ideas and information, countering the (historically correct) suspicion that central banks are resolutely secretive. It invites scrutiny, acknowledging that monetary policy operates in the world in collaboration with markets and the public, and that communications mediate this collaborative operation. For all its translucence, the transparency signaled by the building is more than merely ephemeral; it forms a significant load-bearing element of an intellectual regime, a constellation of values, ideals, and practices encompassing a Kultur. The architecture of the new ECB headquarters conveys an insistence that the soundness of the euro must be conceptualized and managed across a vast communicative field within which confidence is continually shaped and modeled as a public discourse. The euro was designed from the outset as a public currency with emphatic communicative features.

Money Targets

It is only a slight exaggeration to say that the reason for all this glass, all this signaling of transparency, can be traced back to information contained in a technical publication of the other great financial institution in Frankfurt, the Deutsche Bundesbank. Broached for the first time in the bank's publication of December 5, 1974, is a target for the growth of money—8 percent—for the following year: a target that would serve as the bank's nominal anchor (Issing 1997). Articulating this target number publically was meant to exert leverage on the development of prices in Germany in the face of the eclipsing of the last vestiges of the Bretton Woods agreement, in March 1973, and the destabilizing oil shocks in the early 1970s.[1]

A little over a year after the end of the global monetary regime of fixed exchange rates pegged to gold and to the dollar, the Bundesbank began to tether expectations about the value of the Deutsche mark to a publicly announced target for the growth of money. After the tightly defined monetary rules of the post–World War II era governed by Bretton Woods, central banks had to find new means, a discretionary means, to exercise their responsibility for managing the value of money—namely, "to provide a nominal anchor for national fiat currencies to replace the gold standard" (McCallum 2008).[2]

By announcing targets for money growth, the Bundesbank began experimenting with discretionary monetary policy. Crucially, the bank began enlisting the public as an active participant in what became its "Kultur" of inflation fighting. The bank not only worked out what were to become the key features of inflation targeting, it also began to experiment fully with the performative nature of economic ideas and theory (MacKenzie, Muniesa, and Siu 2006; MacKenzie 2006; Muniesa and Callon 2007).

The 1957 design of the Bundesbank Act, particularly Article 3, mandated the "safeguarding of the currency," and thus the achievement of price stability, as the overriding priority of monetary policy. The episodes of hyperinflation in the 1920s—incited by reckless, indeed staggering, increases in the printing of money—that had rent asunder the German social fabric and political order, opening the way for the destructive enthusiasms of National Socialism, established the exigencies of monetary policy. An inflation rate averaging 322 percent per month over a fifteen-month period from August 1922 to November 1923, fueled by an increase of currency in circulation by a factor of 7.32×10^9, provided an emphatic countermodel to what the Bundesbank sought to establish in the postwar era (Salemi 2008).

Fighting inflation was thus not merely a technical matter of avoiding "suboptimal economic performance," but a profound societal preoccupation that was key to the reconstruction of the postwar Federal Republic. The leadership of the Bundesbank knew that they could invoke the memory of a searing history to recruit the German people in their inflation-fighting campaign. But the inflation fighting agenda was also buttressed by a theory—an abbreviated account of monetarism—providing a macroeconomic allegory that could render the relationship between monetary policy and price stability plausible and coherent to the citizens of Germany. Monetarism, as a public allegory, had a deceptively simple articulation: control the growth of money and you control inflation. Or, more formally, in Milton Friedman's classic statement first articulated in "The Counter-Revolution in Monetary Theory": "*Inflation is always and everywhere a monetary phenomenon* in the sense that it is and can be produced only by a more rapid increase in the quantity of money than output " (M. Friedman 1970, 24; italics in original).

The bank's institutional independence demanded a new, "nonpolitical," basis of accountability, and the "scientific principles" of macroeconomics and monetary theory fulfilled this role. Data were the idioms of credibility predicating the monetary regime on an analytic question: Do broad measures of the supply of money in the present contain information on the evolution of prices in the future? As we will see, the rel-

evance of this question for macroeconomic adjustments shifted over time
and became increasingly open to doubt.

Symbolic Capital

The leadership of the Bundesbank, the Direktorium, had determined
that in order to confer a stable value on the German currency, an evolving story about the present and the near future, rendered credible to the
public by virtue of the artful and consistent communication of the central bank's officialdom, was needed. Soundness came to be mediated by
an explicit anchoring of Bundesbank policy in a macroeconomic allegory
focused on a broad measure of money, central bank money (CBM), and
its relationship to changes in prices. Protagonists within the Bundesbank
began to interpret systematically the dynamics of prices as a function of
central bank communication. They knew that an intellectual regime was
needed to legitimize these communications, and thus to influence the evolution of expectations (Knorr-Cetina 2007).[3]

There was a particular reason for the Bundesbank to embrace monetarism in the early 1970s. The authority of Keynesian monetary and fiscal activism—namely, its efficacy in managing the business cycle—was in
doubt; the inverse relationship between unemployment and inflation—
known as the Phillips curve—had faltered. The apparent policy trade off,
"less unemployment at the cost of a finite boost in inflation," was undercut
by the experiences of the 1960s, in which inflation and unemployment
appeared to develop simultaneously (Tobin 1999–2010). The Keynesian
framework had offered policymakers the promise that permanent levels
of lower unemployment could be achieved by accepting a higher rate of
inflation, and vice versa. The outcomes of these activist policies in the
1960s and 1970s were dismal; not only did they fail to deliver their promised benefits, "they helped to generate the inflationary pressures that
could be subdued only at high economic costs" (Bernanke et al. 1999, 11;
Bordo and Orphanides, forthcoming). These costs were manifest in the
deep recessions and attendant unemployment of 1973–74 and 1981–82.
Milton Friedman provided an alternative analysis that appeared to explain these new circumstances and provide a policy framework to respond
to them. "Friedman convinced the economics profession in 1968 that if
monetary policy persistently attempts to bring unemployment below 'the
natural rate of unemployment' (the rate corresponding to Keynes's "full

employment"), it will only boost the inflation rate explosively. Friedman's further conclusion that monetary policy should never concern itself with unemployment, production, or other real variables has been very influential" (Tobin 1999–2010). Friedman made another important assertion about the nature of monetary policy, notably that its effects on the real economy "set in only with lags that are both long and variable (that is, varying from episode to episode in essentially unpredictable ways). Consequently, Friedman argued that monetary policy, though powerful, is not a tool that can be used with precision" (Bernanke et al. 1999, 12).

Robert Lucas Jr. (1976) introduced another powerful critique, focusing on the role of expectations. The Lucas critique has been stated in terms of a metaphorical shift:

> There is an important difference between rockets and the people who make up an economy, which is that people try to understand and predict the actions of their "controllers" (the policy-makers), while rockets do not. More specifically, Lucas showed that the optimal control methods may be useless for guiding policy if they do not take into account the possibility that the public's expectations about the future will change when policies change. The public's expectations about the future, including expectations about future policy actions, are important because they affect current economic behavior. Consequently, Lucas argued, policy-making takes on elements of a strategic game between the policy-makers and the public. Analyzing such a game is a considerably more difficult problem than guiding a rocket. (Bernanke et al. 1999, 12)

Lucas, by introducing something that approximates reflexive subjects who could assimilate the same models as policymakers and thus anticipate their intervention, appeared to make control of the economy with any degree of precision perilous (Soros 1994, 2008).

Another source of uncertainty identified by Friedman was the "tendency of the public and politicians in modern democracies to take a myopic view of public policy issues. Given the pressures of frequent elections and the almost instantaneous reporting of poll results, it is difficult for politicians to appreciate that watchful waiting is sometimes the best policy" (Bernanke et al. 1999, 13). Policy discretion—in this case, the latitude to overmanipulate monetary policy—exercised by politically exposed central bankers would, in Friedman's view, inevitably undermine the credibility necessary for sustainable and consistent management of money and credit, and thereby the control of prices.

The Bundesbank thus began to experiment in the 1970s with its new framework, announcing prospectively very specific goals for monetary policy and explicit outcomes for these interventions. By so doing, the bank created a system of accountability aligning its actions directly with public interests in a manner that was overt and transparent. Each year the banks' performance was exposed: Did Bundesbank policies successfully control prices and thus retain the soundness of the Deutsche mark? A single measure of consumer prices, the German all-item consumer price index— itself an important innovation in the creation of a public currency— served as a standard for all to see (Strathern 2000).

Pragmatic Monetarism

The load-bearing elements of the bank's monetary framework, forged as technical issues in macroeconomic theory, were translated into a series of pragmatic institutional imperatives that animated the Bundesbank's Kultur of inflation fighting. The framework depended on a public recruited to the task of anchoring the value of money, but a public that could also serve as an intellectual foil compelling officialdom at the bank to think through fundamental questions in monetary economics. Crucially, these deliberations allowed abstract, theoretical matters to reemerge as a substantive basis of collaboration with various segments and strata of German society. In thinking through its relationship to the public, the bank's leadership refined and focused its internal practices of research and policy formulation for the purposes of creating a communicative field, a field within which the bank's narratives could circulate, and thus influence expectations.

Supporting the simple articulation of a numerical target for the growth of money for the coming year required an active pedagogy. Technical issues in economics and monetary theory were recrafted to speak directly to the German people. Initially these communications were directed to only a very tiny group of experts in business and finance, but increasingly these pedagogic narratives sought or acquired a broader audience as the bank turned from technical issues of money to consumer prices. The Bundesbank selectively revealed the data and the analysis informing the banks decision making retroactively. Acute attention to the rhetorical nature of policy in shaping expectations was a central preoccupation imparting an educative dynamic to monetary policy and to the symbolic economy of the Deutsche mark (Brenneis 1999). If, as Lucas suggested, the public can learn to anticipate policy moves, then central banks can respond by establishing a pedagogic framework that conveys not just information but a shared formula for interpreting monetary policy over time. Persuasion was built into the regime. What were the lessons that the bank sought to convey?

The central dictum of this pedagogy was reducible, again, to Friedman's (1970) famous assertion that *"inflation is always and everywhere a monetary phenomenon"* which could be recast as a comprehensive rule for monetary policy, and that, "irrespective of current macroeconomic conditions, the stock of money should be made to grow month by month, and indeed, so far as possible, day by day, at an annual rate of X per cent, where X is some number between 3 and 5" (quoted in McCallum 2008; italics are Friedman's).

Under this rule, measuring the growth or contraction of the supply of money was a key intellectual challenge:

> Strictly defined, the use of a money growth target means that the central bank not only treats all unexpected fluctuations in money as informative ... but also, as a quantitative matter, changes the interest rate or reserves in such a way as to offset these unexpected fluctuations altogether ... and thereby restore money growth to the originally designated target rate. (B. Friedman 1995, 5–6)

The Bundesbank used a measure of money that captured these dynamics in a very simple numerical form. "The quantity equation states that the sum of real output growth and the inflation rate is equal to the sum of money growth and the change in (appropriately defined) velocity" (Bernanke et al. 1999, 57–58). The Bundesbank thus "derives the target growth rate of the change of monetary aggregates ... by estimating the growth of the long-run production potential over the coming year, adding the rate of price change it considers unavoidable ... and subtracting the estimated change in trend velocity over the year" (57–58). An explicit target for money growth was derived that would support long-term economic expansion consistent with what were deemed acceptable increases in prices. By holding to this target through the management of short-term interest rates, the central bank insured, according to this framework, the soundness of money. "This approach allows the Bundesbank to claim that it is not making any choice about the business cycle when it sets policy. It also de-emphasizes any public discussion of its forecasting efforts for the real economy, further distancing monetary policy from the conversations of expected fluctuations in output and employment. Thus the quantity approach serves to take certain items off the monetary policy agenda . . . by limiting the list of central bank responsibilities" (58). In other words, the strategy radically delimited the focus of policy interventions, at least in terms of how it was revealed publicly.

The Bundesbank made its projections of prices prior to the formulation of its money supply target in the last quarter of each year. A rate of growth of the German all-item consumer prices index was calculated and plugged into the quantity equation to derive its targets for money creation for the following year. This target made it clear that controlling the supply of money was pursued in the interest of price stability consistent with the growth potential of the Germany economy in the medium term. By the mid-1980s, the bank had shifted its projection of "unavoidable" inflation to "a medium term prices assumption of 2%" (quoted in Bernanke et al. 1999, 58). Inflation was thus designed into the monetary system, consistent with the growth potential of the German economy.[4]

The targeting of money growth is, in fact, difficult, and the Bundesbank modified its regime to account for these difficulties. Most notably, it shifted the measure of money it was targeting (from CBM to M3) as well as shifting from a fixed target to a target range of ±1–1.5 percent for money growth.[5] There were also actual deviations from targets, significant deviations, during the German reunification in 1991 that the bank carefully explained and justified. What the Bundesbank achieved over time was "confidence that it can explain target deviations and re-definitions to the public as reflected in the design of its reporting mechanisms" (Bernanke et al. 1999, 60). It is not mere explanation of the information transmitted to the public that is at stake, but, again, a matter of active pedagogy designed into the monetary regime by which the Bundesbank gained the confidence of the German people. An intellectual regime thus came to legitimize the bank's statutory independence, and research underwrote its credibility.

Confidence and credibility were also cultivated through networks of key figures in business, government, trade unions, and the news media, with whom wage- and price-setting information and economic data more generally were continually exchanged. Vigorous rounds of speechmaking by senior officials of the bank, the regular publication of technical reports and data series, and the scrupulous attention to the Bank's institutional independence and its constitutional accountabilities further enhanced this

credibility at every turn; however, the bank's leadership formulated policies attuned to unfolding political situations in Germany and in Europe.
These officials did not hesitate in correcting any "misunderstandings" of
the bank's positions among political, business, and labor leaders, nor were
they shy about expressing their rancor in very personal terms to participants involved in wage- and price-setting negotiations, or to political leaders involved in determining German budgetary, regulatory, and taxation
policies, if their actions threatened the soundness of the German currency.

Let me be clear, the Bundesbank was by no means perfect. It was capable of misjudgment, miscalculation, lack of candor, and various policy
infelicities. The bank's experiment in transparency was, by current standards, far from optimal (Nergiz and Eichengreen 2009). The Bundesbank
did not publish forecasts, nor did it publish any substantive accounts of
its policy discussions. It was not forthcoming about the range of data and
analytical models it employed in its policy deliberation. Indeed, we know
now that the Bundesbank was employing more comprehensive analytical agendas than would be required solely for the care and feeding of the
quantity equation. The bank was scrutinizing rigorously just about every
data series, every statistical report relevant to the performance of the
German economy, and carefully considering every alternative outcome of
its policies and practices:

> *Monetary targets were never the actual target of or even sole guide to policy....*
> [T]he announced monetary targets were never slavishly followed.... It is well-
> known that annual target ranges were missed around fifty percent of the time
> in Germany in the 1980s and 1990s. Far more significantly, the Bundesbank has,
> by its own account and as seen in the historical record, taken into account a
> much broader range of information than just money when setting policy. When
> inflation and monetary forecasts have diverged, the Bundesbank has responded
> to the former. Moreover, the Bundesbank has responded to a number of short-
> run shocks and challenges even when they have not directly affected inflation
> or money. (Posen 1997; emphasis in original)

As Adam Posen makes clear, the bank had two targets—money and
inflation—and as theoretical faith in monetarism ebbed, targeting inflation itself took precedence and money was relegated to a secondary role.

A former board member of the Bundesbank and founding member of
the Executive Board of the ECB, Otmar Issing described how the aims of
monetary analysis shifted as the latter institution assimilated them. Mea-

sures of money thus served as a basis for cross-checking analysis rather than as a meaningful standard in its own right. "Real-time extraction of signals of medium-term inflationary or deflationary pressures from monetary developments" served as the means for overcoming the "limited reliability of other indicators, such as the output gap, and the unavoidable limitations of economic analyses, such as macroeconomic projections" (Issing 2005).

Collaborative System

Over four decades, the bank built a Kultur that represented far more than a mechanism for setting targets for the growth of money and credit. Managing inflation, and thus insuring the soundness of the Deutsche mark, was achieved by means of a communicative system for endowing the future with discernable features. The Bundesbank created a framework for managing expectations by aligning its actions directly with public interests in a manner that was overt, if not entirely transparent. The load-bearing elements of the Bundesbank monetary framework depended not solely (or necessarily) on a quantity equation, but on macroeconomic allegories by which the public was recruited to the task of anchoring the value of money. The careful parsing of abstract, theoretical matters in monetary economics in a manner that was coherent and plausible to the German public served as a basis of an institutional collaboration that drew on and shaped distinctive cultural sentiments. Again, what was framed as an experiment in monetary policy was, in fact, a far broader historical and anthropological experiment implicating German society in its entirety (Herzfeld 1992, 2004). Notably, the Direktorium was fully aware of the audacious scope of its endeavor. They understood that they were imparting novel communicative features to the Deutsche mark; they understood too that confidence is always and everywhere mediated by culture, a communicative culture that made the near- and medium-term future plausible for the German public. How did this work?

Inflation fighting anchored cognitive balance sheets for individuals and households, for family owner-managers of the Mittelstand, for executives of large industrial manufacturers, for labor unions, for small exporters as well as for technocrats planning public expenditures, and so on. Expectations about the development of prices became manifest in real plans for budgets, for investment, for stocking inventories, for expanding or contracting employment, and, above all, for negotiating wages, for setting prices, for computing various commercial interest rates. The willingness of the German people to act in relationship to their expectations ratified and stabilized the future, conferring on it basic contours, if not precise characteristics. Faith—albeit contingent, informed by data, and contextualized within econometric allegories—allowed for planning and allowed for the diverse expectations of every segment of German society, if not for every individual, to yield action. The acumen of the bank's officialdom— notably, figures like Hans Tietmeyer, former president of the Bundesbank (1993–99)—shaped and modeled the economy linguistically in a manner that could align the bank's agenda with the plans and the expectations of the public. Economic reality was made and tested continually by shocks and uncertainty—not least of which were those attendant on German reunification—and relentlessly revised in concert with the German people.

Measures of money, whether CBM or M3, became persuasive instruments, less for their analytical precision than for their ability to sustain a consistent, if not entirely candid story about the evolution of prices that could facilitate planning and action:

> Monetary targets are seen by the Bundesbank as the main source of accountability and transparency because they commit the Bundesbank to having to explain policy with respect to a benchmark on a regular basis. Moreover, that explanation of policy to the public is given at length, and with respect to the whole economy (not just monetary developments). This is an explanatory impulse beyond the deceptively uninformative question of whether or not a specific target was met at the prescribed time. (Posen 1997)

As I suggested earlier, these data had a pedagogic nature serving a deeper "explanatory impulse." The pedagogic practices of the bank imparted faith in a broader story that tied the German people to a shared economic fate. The historical task of constructing narratives about the present and near future, accounts susceptible to revision and updating in relation to data, provided the cognitive model for planning and action that could be calibrated from countless perspectives. The Kultur of inflation fighting thus anchored a broader story about the German state and its ability to manage the future by aligning its citizens' expectations with national interests. Again, this was not merely about managing animal spirits of fear and greed and quelling speculative excesses, but rather about more subtle sentiments, more nuanced aspirations by which monetary policy underwrote an emerging constitutional order.

The Kultur of inflation targeting anchored a communicative field in which the economy undergoes incessant analytical scrutiny and linguistic modeling by countless actors, ratifying the conviction that monetary policy operates in the world, in vivo, in collaboration with markets and the public, and that transparency sustains this collaborative operation. By means of subtle cultural intermediations sentiments and expectations became overt bases for planning and for action. The gradual accretion of this experiment over the course of two decades established the Bundesbank's symbolic capital, its store of confidence, but it also provided an emphatic example of how to design a European Central Bank (Scheller 2004).

ECB Habitus

From the earliest negotiations on ECB's institutional design, the incorporation of the Bundesbank's Kultur was central to underwriting the credibility of the new institution and the new currency it was designed to manage, the euro. Transferring the Bundesbank's credibility to the ECB was key for the new project. Within the first decade of its operation, the ECB had gone considerably further than merely announcing targets for money growth. Indeed, with a few notable exceptions, virtually every aspect of the introduction of the euro and the operation of the new central bank was conceptualized as operating within a tightly managed public discourse. The ECB tries to be explicit about what it means to orchestrate monetary policy transparently:

> Transparency means that the central bank provides the general public and the markets with all relevant information on its strategy, assessments and policy decisions as well as its procedures in an open, clear and timely manner.
>
> Today, most central banks, including the ECB, consider transparency as crucial. This is true especially for their monetary policy framework. The ECB gives a high priority to communicating effectively with the public. . . .
>
> Transparency helps the public to understand the ECB's monetary policy. Better public understanding makes the policy more credible and effective. Transparency means that the ECB explains how it interprets its mandate and that it is forthcoming about its policy goals. (ECB, n.d., "Transparency")

By communicating its goals in an explicit and consistent fashion, the central bank seeks to continually shape market expectations in advance of the need to take those disruptive and often painful actions attendant upon the conventional exercise of monetary policy. The cultural challenge of operating in the near future is, at least in theory, resolved through monetary policy that focuses on the management of expectations:

> The ECB publicly announces its monetary policy strategy and communicates its regular assessment of economic developments. This helps the markets to understand the systematic response pattern of monetary policy to economic developments and shocks. It makes policy moves more predictable for the markets over the medium term. Market expectations can thus be formed more efficiently and accurately.
>
> If market agents can broadly anticipate policy responses, this allows a rapid implementation of changes in monetary policy into financial variables. This in turn can shorten the process by which monetary policy is transmitted into investment and consumption decisions. It can accelerate any necessary economic adjustments and potentially enhance the effectiveness of monetary policy. (ECB, n.d., "Transparency")

Transparency, then, is not merely about candor, openness, or, more generally, democratic accountabilities. It can be instrumental in defining future-oriented behavior. The basic argument of this text is that a distinctive kind of knowledge is being "created" in or mediated by central banks, knowledge that exceeds what is typically understood as "economic." The architecture of the new ECB headquarters conveys an insistence that the soundness of the euro must be conceptualized and managed across a communicative field within which confidence is continually shaped and modeled as a public discourse.

The full armature of the monetary regime embraced by the ECB drew also on another parallel experiment that was worked out in New Zealand by a group of young economists working at the Reserve Bank of New Zealand. Like the Bundesbank, the model developed by the RBNZ was rooted in a cultural project, not merely a narrow exercise in monetary economics. That said, the same issues in economic theory preoccupied the designers of the two monetary experiments, and certainly the Kiwis were cannily aware of the Bundesbank's innovations (Brash, forthcoming; Grimes 2001). The case of the RBNZ is particularly apposite in relation to our present circumstances because its experiments unfolded in the midst of a fiscal, financial, and constitutional crisis. The radical institutional redesign of the bank in what were dire circumstances fully defined the key elements of the inflation targeting regime, yielding the fundamentals of an ardently public currency.

CHAPTER SIX

Temporality

Montague Norman [former Governor of the Bank of England] famously said a central bank should "never explain, never apologize." Montague Norman was wrong. — Alan S. Blinder, Vice Chair of the Federal Reserve System (1994–96)

As I walked through the political and bureaucratic precincts of Wellington on my way to an interview with an official of the Reserve Bank of New Zealand (RBNZ), I was distracted. It was a blustery early austral spring afternoon; the camellias, rhododendrons, japonicas, and an occasional cherry tree were beginning to bloom on the hill leading up to the city's botanical gardens. Flags on the Beehive—the New Zealand parliament building—and other government offices were fluttering at half-mast to mark the death of the Maori Queen, Dame Te Atairangikaahu, whose funeral was taking place that afternoon on a hill overlooking the Waikato River. In the morning, her eldest son, Tuheitia Paki, had been named her successor to lead the Kingitanga movement founded in 1858 to unify the disparate tribes of the Maori, the indigenous peoples of New Zealand.

Television coverage was extensive, with anthropologically informed commentary and analysis of the meticulous Maori ceremonialism and the elaborate visual display that was mobilized for the occasion. The Queen's virtues, her grace, her beauty, and her accomplishments as a major figure of indigenous cultural activism were carefully recounted. Her life coincided with the intricate and, in many respects, still rancorous, postcolonial history of New Zealand.

I crossed the wet street from the parliament grounds to The Terrace, the steel-and-glass building that houses the central bank of New Zealand, to study a far more austere cultural transformation: the experiments that, again, have come to epitomize a "revolution" in central banking that commenced in the 1980s. By the time of my visit, in August 2006, virtually all the major central banks of the world had adopted, to a greater or lesser degree, the innovations initially tested in Wellington. On the one hand, I was interested in the particular historical and political circumstances that had impelled the unlikely innovations in central banking that took place in New Zealand in the 1980s. On the other, I was interested in the specific experiments that addressed analytical issues in monetary policy, most notably the intertemporal problem that continually insinuated uncertainty about central bank credibility over time. Mervyn King, in "The Institutions of Monetary Policy" (2004) , stated this challenge concisely: "A public monopoly [exercised by central banks] means that the demand for money today depends upon expectations of collective decisions about the supply of money tomorrow. The key question for a public currency is how do we prevent the government (ourselves) from abusing its issuing power in the future" (quoted in Singleton et al. 2006, 138). I was interested in how the RBNZ had worked out a series of institutional protocols to project its credibility into the future and resolve the problem identified by Governor King.

While most New Zealanders' attention was focused on the pomp and circumstance of Te Atairangikaahu's funeral and on recollections of events, deeply etched on their consciousness, that have defined their bicultural nationhood, I was preoccupied with this other coincident transformation that very few New Zealanders were fully cognizant of, even though all of them were in fact participants in its technical protocols and its symbolic operation. This transformation was framed by forward-looking sentiments that imparted very different cognitive purviews and very different structures of feelings than those that were informed by indigenous identity or colonial history. It required instruments of unapologetic explanation.

1984

The RBNZ was founded in 1934 and modeled on the Bank of England. Until 1989, it had been charged with serving a number of broad economic objectives, including the management of inflation, employment, the exchange rate, and the balance of payments. And, as was typical for the time, the bank was assumed to operate in secret, its decision making opaque, and these decisions were understood to be subject to governmental directives: "In the case of monetary policy, ministerial directions to the Reserve Bank typically were secret and priorities shifted frequently. Monetary policy was often aimed at a number of sometimes conflicting objectives" (RBNZ 2004). The Reserve Bank of New Zealand Act of 1989—what has come to be known as the framework—represented a major revision of the 1930s legislation, formulated in response to a series of sweeping transformations unfolding in New Zealand during the 1980s, but also in response to a very particular political incident that ensued in the midst of the national election, the snap election, of 1984.[1] The New Zealand experiment arose from a harrowing crisis in the value of the New Zealand dollar.

The election of July 1984 was notable for the effort by the government headed by the National Party leader Robert Muldoon to maintain its control of an economic system based on government planning, regulation, protectionism, and price controls, and the effort of a newly elected Labour government under the leadership of David Lange to undertake reform and restructuring. The circumstance of the crisis is instructive on a number of levels, not least because it illustrates why a left-of-center party (with far-left elements) would embrace a wide-ranging liberal program of transformation and a particularly emphatic variant of "audit culture," and further, how monetary issues would be both provoked and sustained by this kind of programmatic reform (Strathern 2000). The crisis came, in fact, even before the newly elected government had a chance to take power.

A key political actor, Roger Douglas, who became the architect of the liberalization of New Zealand society that ensued, recalled the onset of the crisis as follows:

At 9 pm on Sunday 15 July, the day after the 1984 election, the Reserve Bank [of New Zealand] announced that the foreign exchange market would cease operating until further notice. The massive run on foreign currencies during the four weeks leading up to the election had drained the Bank of foreign reserves and left the local market short of New Zealand dollars to carry on the usual day-to-day business of borrowing and lending. Since the snap election had been announced almost $1.4 billion had left the country, as much as the Reserve Bank usually handled in foreign exchange transactions in a year. The general market view was that the New Zealand dollar would be devalued and there was a rush to move funds off shore. The situation looked so bad that many of the foreign banks with whom the Reserve Bank had standby lines of credit found reasons to refuse the Bank's requests for loans.... On 18 July, four days after the general election and three days after the Reserve Bank had ceased trading in foreign exchange, David Lange announced the New Zealand dollar would be devalued by 20 per cent and most of the controls on interest rates introduced by the previous Government were removed.... The strict regulations of a fixed exchange rate and foreign exchange controls had not stopped speculation and we had been very fortunate in managing to honour our foreign obligations throughout the crisis ... [and] the adjustment, although sudden and expensive, was unavoidable. New Zealand had come very close to insolvency. (Douglas and Callan 1987, 136–37)

The crisis stemmed from conditions rooted in the structure of the New Zealand economy, which for more than a decade had struggled with slow economic growth, high unemployment, high rates of inflation, widespread industrial inefficiencies, and a looming internal deficit in excess of 9 percent of GDP (in 1983–84) (Douglas and Callan 1987, 36, 47). There were also problems as to how these complex and entangled issues had been communicated to the public, to say nothing of efforts by members of the Muldoon government, most notably by Prime Minister Robert Muldoon himself, to obscure, obfuscate, and dissemble in their public communications on these matters. As suggested above, few people understood how dire the situation was in the early 1980s and how close New Zealand was to insolvency.

Douglas became finance minister in the new Labour government and initiated the reforms of the Reserve Bank as an element in his comprehensive restructuring of public finances and the management of the entire state sector in New Zealand. With remarkable speed, the Labour government removed all controls on foreign exchange, floated the New Zealand dollar, and enacted legislation that initiated "financial liberalisation, corporatisation and then privatisation of state-owned enterprises, public sector reform, welfare reform, labour market liberalisation and trade liberalization" (Bollard and Karagedikli 2006, 3–4). This sweeping program, that came to be known as "Rogernomics" (in recognition of Roger Douglas's driving force in this), is remembered with a deep sense of ambivalence, if not loathing, by many New Zealanders. Those New Zealanders— and by no means only those on the left—who believed that their national identity was rooted in a shared economic experience felt their solidarity profoundly compromised by this wide-ranging program of reform. That said, hard economic facts, that just about everyone acknowledged once they were revealed, allowed the reform and restructuring not only to continue but to become fully entrenched in New Zealand society.

One of the most arresting facts, for the discussion here, was the cumulative rate of inflation for the prior decade, as reported by Peter Nicholl and David Archer in "An Announced Downward Path of Inflation":

> New Zealand experienced double-digit inflation for most of the period since the first oil shock [of 1973]. Cumulative inflation (on a CPI basis) between 1974 and 1988 (inclusive) was 480 per cent. A brief, but temporary, fall in inflation to below 5 per cent occurred in the early 1980s, but only as the result of a distortionary wage, price, dividend and interest rate freeze. Throughout the period, monetary policy faced multiple and varying objectives which were seldom clearly specified, and only rarely consistent with achievement of inflation reduction. As a result of this experience, inflation expectations were deeply entrenched in New Zealand society (quoted in Bernanke et al. 1999, 88).

Establishing price stability became a central issue in the reform program and a central intellectual preoccupation of the new government and the Reserve Bank. The experiment in inflation targeting arose inadvertently and in tandem with another major focus of the reform project that emerged in the guise of a personnel matter.

The issue at hand at the time was how to conceptualize a sweeping scheme for the management of the newly established State Owned Enterprises (SOEs), but the impact of this agenda went much further. Douglas introduced to New Zealand a highly focused audit regime to bring public expenditures under strict control. Under the new arrangement, public-sector managers were given greater latitude to manage their organizations, but the reforms held them "directly accountable for outputs— i.e., the measurable products or services that each agency was mandated or contracted to deliver" (Sherwin 1999, 1). The Labour government thus imposed an austere business model on the entire public sector, and this became a key issue in the subsequent deliberations in 1986–87 on how to draft an "employment contract" for the governor of the Reserve Bank. Specifically, the problem that Labour's leadership struggled with was how to conceptualize measurable "outputs" for a central bank that would enable the minister of finance to audit the performance of its governor?

Murray Sherwin, a former deputy governor of the RBNZ, reflected on the issues involved in working out this key dilemma of outputs:

In the Reserve Bank's case, it was difficult to define meaningful outputs. There were suggestions that some form of monetary base measure might be appropriate, but this concept failed when it proved impossible to identify a stable relationship between this particular output and the sort of ultimate outcome— price stability—our political masters were seeking from an independent central bank. (Sherwin 1999, 72)

What was decided was that "the Reserve Bank would be held accountable not for outputs, but primarily for the judgments it reached in pursuing the desired outcome itself." The overriding goal of the Reserve Bank, then, became "to formulate and implement monetary policy directed to the economic objective of achieving and maintaining stability in the general level of prices" (Sherwin 1999, 73). To this end, the employment contract for the governor of the Reserve Bank stated an inflation goal explicitly as a contractual obligation.

During the latter phase of these discussions, Roger Douglas, in a shrewdly calculated intervention, defined the key aspect of the experiment—the "nominal anchor"—the articulation of a numerical goal as the inflation target:

> Without consulting officials, or, apparently, his parliamentary colleagues, Douglas announced in a TV interview on 1 April, 1988 that policy was to be directed to reducing inflation to "around 0 or 0 to 1 percent" over the following couple of years. This was as much a surprise to the Reserve Bank as it was to the community generally. Douglas was aiming, with this announcement, to influence inflation expectations and by that means to reduce the inevitable costs of disinflation. With the input of advice from officials over the subsequent few weeks, that initial announcement crystallized as the 0 to 2 percent inflation target to be achieved by the early 1990's. (Sherwin 1999, 73)

The announcement of this key element of the new monetary regime was communicated directly to the public prior to full review or intervention of government experts. Rather than a rash outburst, this pronouncement was artfully conceived, as Douglas theatrically made the public party to the new regime.

Within the new legal framework—which was approved by the New Zealand parliament without a single opposing vote—a provision specified that it was the governor's contractual obligation to keep the level of prices in New Zealand to an explicit target over a specified period of time or his/her continuing employment was, at least in theory, in jeopardy. A single individual was thus made personally accountable for the evolution of price levels within the entire economy.

Equally radical was the degree to which the governor and the Reserve Bank were endowed, by virtue of the new legislation, with remarkable political independence. The talk at the time was of "Muldoon-proofing" monetary policy—that is, immunizing the governor from political influence and manipulation. By virtue of the new framework, the Reserve Bank achieved a high degree of operational autonomy and independence mediated by stark and explicit accountabilities: "So the Act provides the Bank with independence once the PTA [Policy Target Agreement] between the Minister and Governor has been signed. The Governor has no obligation to consult with the Minister, the Treasury, or with the Board of the Reserve Bank, when implementing monetary policy" (Bollard and Karagedikli 2006, 6).

Strict protections ensuring the independence of the governor's decision making were thus central to this program of reform. The "Governor cannot be dismissed because, in achieving price stability, he or she has irritated the government of the day, or because the timing of his or her decisions has been politically inconvenient" (RBNZ 2004). The employment contract, known as the Policy Target Agreement (PTA) negotiated between the Governor of the Reserve Bank and the minister of finance was signed by both parties and made public. The terms and provisions of the PTA were widely reported on in the press, communicating the political (and academic) conviction that "monetary policy has a single goal and whether that has been met or not is transparently obvious" (Sherwin 1999, 77).

In the language of a government employment contract, the Policy Target Agreement, a radical cultural field with far-reaching consequences, was "designed." As in the case of the Bundesbank, a communicative field was created. The RBNZ, however, had added a number of distinctive features and legal protocols by which the governor would be held accountable and the terms of a public conversation were defined. The economy was endowed with a legal pretext for a language; it was up to the officials of the Reserve Bank to model linguistically the nation's economic predicaments in a manner that could be scrutinized by the public. A real sense of drama was inserted into this unusual arrangement making the governor's job contingent, in part, on his/her skill at crafting a language and using it to construct a persuasive message to influence, if not master, the forces driving inflationary expectations over time.

Research Culture

Though the proximate causes of the remarkable institutional reforms pursued by the Reserve Bank in the 1980s were emphatically political, the innovations that resulted addressed basic questions in monetary economics. Perhaps the most radical and consequential aspect of the Kiwi experiment, as suggested above, tackled the issue of time: How does a central bank transmit a credible message about its intention into the future? The efforts to engineer an institutional procedure to assess the performance of the governor also happened to address this key conundrum in monetary economics.

Mervyn King, in "The Institutions of Monetary Policy" (2004), noted, "The core of the monetary policy problem is uncertainty about future social decisions resulting from the *impossibility* and *undesirability* of committing our successors to any given monetary-policy strategy" (quoted in Singleton et al. 2006, 134). In parliamentary democracies in which the central bank executes policy at the behest of a minister of the elected government of the day, as had been the case with RBNZ, time was an abiding problem. Central-bank policy positions were contingent on the viability of a government whose longevity was, to a greater or lesser degree, in doubt, conditional on its ability to remain in power. Elections could intervene, a new government could be formed, and new monetary goals established.

Furthermore, the potential for monetary policy to serve as a political instrument, as in the case of the Muldoon government, put central banks potentially at the service of short-term political objectives. Echoing Milton Friedman, King explains: "Without full government commitment to future policies, private sector agents cannot rely on the government to stick to its stated intentions; instead they form expectation that the government will follow policies that are optimal in the short term but suboptimal ... over the longer term. In such cases, the inflation rate may remain consistently higher than desired, without any offsetting economic advantages" (quoted in Singleton et al. 2006, 148–49).

The inability of central banks to formulate policy that was consistent over time thus hampered the capability of these institutions to influence prices. How was the dilemma resolved? Following an internal bank presentation by Arthur Grimes in 1987, a consensus began to emerge:

> The discussion that followed concluded that the government could escape the time consistency problem if it allocated a single inflation objective to an independent central bank, while separate arms of government retained responsibil-

ity for other economic policy objectives such as full employment. The prescription was in keeping with Mervyn King's observation that "suitably designed . . . monetary institutions can help to reduce the inefficiencies resulting from the time-inconsistency problem." (Singleton et al. 2006, 149)

The document drafted by Grimes and the discussion it stimulated represented another key aspect of the evolution of central banking in the post–Bretton Woods era—the need for an intellectual regime that would continually engender economic research and the generation of new ideas and techniques to inform monetary economics. In the New Zealand case, there were a few special circumstances:

> From the early 1960s onward, the Reserve Bank was one of New Zealand's most important centres of economic research. The Bank's relative contribution to economic thinking and research was greater than that of central banks in larger countries, where there were also well-funded universities and private research organizations. One of the Bank's tasks was to filter the latest economic thinking from abroad. Another was to generate new knowledge about the New Zealand economy. Both of these activities influenced the advice tendered, often in collaboration with Treasury, to the government. In addition, the Bank's research work created external benefits, since many of its findings were made available to other interested parties. (Singleton et al. 2006, 70)

Central banking required a continuous intellectual engagement with the shifting nature of the economy, its institutional contexts, and its regulatory environment, as well as a means to address the changing significance of economic data and the theories by which these data were analyzed. The Reserve Bank's unusual breakthrough in the 1980s was to translate this intellectual labor into a public discourse and thereby tether monetary policy to ideas that were continually created and refined by bank personnel, notably the development of instruments for forecasting the future performance of the New Zealand economy. Economic research thus had to serve as an instrument of persuasion, and not merely produce "objective" representations of economic facts.

Here is an off-handed abridgment of how that process unfolded: "The ideas that its economists exchanged in the course of informal discussion were filtered and repackaged, often several times, in order to persuade the Governors, directors, the government, and the public. This often involved simplifying concepts smoothing over qualifications. The message was tailored to meet the need of both the recipient and the occasion" (Singleton et al. 2006, 70). The continual refinement of the thinking of Reserve Bank personnel in terms of an audience or, rather, a series of audiences, had a reciprocal effect. It made the leadership of the bank, like their counterparts at the Bundesbank, sensitive to how they were creating a communicative field that could be utilized to align the policy goals of the bank with expectations of the public. In what has come to be known wryly as the Reserve Bank's "Open Mouth Operations," the consistent and repeated articulation of inflation targets, insofar as they were convincing, altered inflation expectations themselves (Guthrie and Wright 2000). Words thus came to mediate the evolution of prices in New Zealand. The Reserve Bank took up "the role of shaping general inflationary expectations through a vigorous external communications programme that stressed the Bank's commitment to the targets and the Governor's personal accountability for achieving them" (Sherwin 1999, 75). This was the unusual and unlikely legacy of the tumultuous events of 1984 in New Zealand.

Forecasting

The communicative strategy of the Reserve Bank was buttressed by two additional elements: the publication of the bank's macroeconomic forecasts and an implicit statement of the bank's policy responses to these forecasts, its "reaction function." This latter innovation is unusual insofar as it folded the Reserve Bank's own strategy or plan of action into its forecast. The research function was thus integral to the communicative action of the bank, transmitting and legitimizing evolving policy intentions in relationship to the data the Reserve Bank had on hand and the projections generated by the bank's forecasting models. Forecasting was the formal means by which the future was given discernable, though typically provisional, features.

Forecasting required a specification of the time horizon over which policy was projected. Again, monetary policy affects inflation with increasing power for up to six to eight quarters after a change in the Official Cash Rate (OCR), the RBNZ policy rate; this lag restates the classic risks involved in engaging the future via monetary policy:

> If we wanted to control inflation, say, within a six-month time frame, this would require very large changes in our policy instrument, the Official Cash Rate

(OCR). Given the magnitude of the interest rate change required to offset any inflationary pressures, the real economy would have to undergo abrupt adjustment. In the extreme, policy could induce a recession, which would then require the policy rate to be lowered if the impending fall in inflation were to be similarly managed within a six month time frame. This "instrument instability" associated with a lag mismatch would involve considerable variability in real GDP growth. It would also involve considerable variability in the exchange rate (to the extent the short term interest rates affect the exchange rate), and indeed, the short horizon would implicitly rely on the direct exchange rate channel to inflation, . . . given the quicker pass-through from the exchange rate to inflation. So, one element of a flexible approach to inflation targeting is to match up the policy horizon to the instrument lag. (Bollard and Karagedikli 2006, 13)

Aligning the forecasting models of the central bank with its midterm policy horizon reduced the "instrument instability" and thereby reduced the potential magnitude and frequency of policy interventions. The time-horizon issue also alters in an unlikely way the forecasting function of the Reserve Bank, recasting its research as foundational to the communicative action of the bank.

Fundamentally, targeting inflation over the medium term requires a credible projection of output and prices that is publicly articulated in order to link policy intentions with public expectation. The forecasting exercise allowed the central bank to both communicate and legitimize evolving policy intentions in relation to the data, to the technical projections generated by the bank's forecasting models. The Kiwi innovation went even further. Again, in addition to their macroeconomic forecasts, the Reserve Bank makes explicit how monetary policy will be orchestrated to address future economic developments:

> Policy inclinations and biases are explicitly stated in response to the projected evolution of prices and output of the New Zealand economy. Since 1997, the Reserve Bank of New Zealand has been publishing projected tracks for interest rates and exchange rates consistent with achieving our inflation target, i.e. implicitly forecasting our policy response to our forecasts. The extent of inflationary or disinflationary pressure that we believe will be present over the period ahead can be read directly from the extent to which the policy instruments are projected to adjust. Through this device, we provide a numeric representation of the extent of our policy bias, not only over the period until the next decision point, but also over the next two years or so. (Bollard and Karagedikli 2006, 11)

This completes the communicative arc of the New Zealand experiment, revealing it's overriding aim: "The obvious advantage of being so explicit in our forecasting, and in the connection of policy actions to those forecasts, is that the economic agents can learn to anticipate our policy interests" (Bollard and Karagedikli 2006, 11).

The outcome of this experiment was dramatic. "What has happened under inflation targeting is a drop, not just in our absolute inflation rate, but also in our relative inflation rate. Compared to OECD averages, New Zealand's inflation has moved from very much at the top end of the spectrum to the mainstream," and this strategy for reducing inflation was achieved without incurring the costs of conventional monetary policy interventions. Moreover, it had the additional benefits of smoothing out the business cycle and reducing the probability of periodic economic downturns or recession (Sherwin 1999, 77). Thus the soundness of the Kiwi dollar was underwritten by the efficacy of the targeting experiment, which turned monetary policy inside out, taking its secrets and making them public.

But for the purposes of my broader arguments concerning the crafting of a public currency, these innovations were far more consequential. They harnessed a particularly potent aspect of an economy in vivo: its susceptibility to linguistic mediation, that is, its latent communicative nature. The designers of the new regime imparted to the New Zealand economy not merely distinctive communicative features but carefully parsed pedagogic aims. Again, the foundational instrument in the communication of bank intentions was and is the Policy Target Agreement. What follows is the first of these agreements in its entirety, drafted shortly after the passage of the new legislation:

Policy Target Agreement (March 1990)

In terms of section 9 of the Reserve Bank of New Zealand Act 1989 (the Act), the Minister of Finance (the Minister) and the Governor, of the Reserve Bank of New Zealand (the Governor) agree as follows:

1. Inflation Targets

Consistent with section 8 of the Act, the Reserve Bank should formulate and implement monetary policy with the intention of achieving price stability by the year ending December 1992. An annual inflation rate in the range of 0 to 2 per cent will be taken to represent the achievement of price stability. The inflation rate should be kept within that range for the remainder of the Governor's current term of office, which ends on 31 August 1993, and conditions at that date should be consistent with the maintenance of sustained price stability thereafter. In pursuing this target, and subject to the caveats below, the Bank's implementation of monetary policy should be designed to achieve a steady reduction in the annual rate of inflation (exclusive of the direct impact of the July 1989 GST increase) throughout the period to December 1992. Each policy statement released by the Bank under section 15 of the Act should contain a projected path for inflation over the following five years.

2. Measurement of Inflation

Section 8 of the Act requires the Bank to direct monetary policy towards the stabilisation of the "general level of prices." In pursuing this objective, the Bank will monitor price movements as measured by a range of price indices. However, it is considered that the primary measure of prices used to calculate the inflation rate for the purpose of these targets should relate to the prices of goods and services currently consumed by households. Unfortunately, the All Groups Consumers Price Index (CPI) is not an entirely suitable measure of these prices since it also incorporates prices and servicing costs of investment-related expenditures, notably in the housing field. The New Zealand CPI is unusual amongst OECD consumer price indices in including components for both the purchase price of dwellings and the cost of mortgage finance. For this reason, while the CPI will, for practical purposes, be the measure of inflation used in setting the targets, the Bank is to prepare an alternative measure of consumer prices based on an internationally comparable approach, so as to provide a basis for assessing the impact of investment-related housing costs on the CPI. In particular, the Bank's adjusted index will replace the current expenditure based measure of housing costs in the CPI with a measure based on imputed housing rentals. The Bank shall publish this index on a quarterly basis and is to ensure that the calculation of the index is verifiable by reputable external sources.

3. Variations to Targets

A. If an Order-In-Council comes into force under section 12 of the Act, the policy targets in this document cease to have effect and must be replaced by new targets within 30 days of the making of the order in accordance with section 12(7) of the Act.

B. These targets may also be varied at any time by agreement between the Governor and the Minister in accordance with the provisions of section 9(4) of the Act. The following specific instances will trigger a renegotiation of these targets in accordance with these provisions:

(i) The Bank shall notify the Minister if, in 1992 or 1993, there is, or is likely to be, a divergence of at least one half of one percentage point between the annual inflation rate of the CPI and of the Bank's internationally comparable measure of consumer prices. Within 30 days of this notification, the Governor may choose to renegotiate new policy targets so as to take account of the effect of the deficiencies in the construction of the CPI.

(ii) Any decrease or increase in GST, or any material change in other indirect taxes, will automatically lead to a renegotiation of these targets where the change is expected to impact directly on the 1992 or 1993 annual inflation rate. In general, a material change in indirect taxes will be interpreted as one which has a positive or negative impact on the price level of at least one half of a percentage point within a one year period. It is intended that the targets will be renegotiated on the basis of allowing the direct effect of the change to impact on the price level, with no accommodation of second round effects. Following a GST change, or following what the Bank estimates to be a material change in other indirect taxes, the Bank shall inform the Minister in writing of its estimate of the direct effect of the change on the price level. If necessary, new policy targets shall be set within 30 days of this estimate being received by the Minister.

(iii) A significant change in the terms of trade arising from an increase or decrease in either export prices or import prices will trigger a renegotiation of the policy targets, where the Bank indicates to the Minister in writing that it estimates the change will have a significant direct impact on the 1992 or 1993 annual inflation rate. In informing the Minister that a significant change has occurred, the Bank should provide an estimate of the direct price effects of the terms of trade change on the price level. Following the provision of this estimate, new policy targets shall be set within 30 days. The intention of this provision is to enable some or all of the direct price effect of a significant terms of trade change (whether positive or negative) to be accommodated but it is not intended to accommodate any second round influences. Thus it is intended that any terms of trade change will have, at most, only a transitory effect on the inflation rate.

(iv) In the case where some other crisis situation, such as a natural disaster or a major disease-induced fall in livestock numbers, is expected to have a significant impact on the price level, the same procedures should be followed as in the case of a terms of trade change.

C. It is intended that section 9(4) of the Act will not be utilised to alter the policy targets in response to any domestically sourced inflationary shock other than the particular cases already considered. In particular, increases in wages or profit margins that are inconsistent with these targets will not be accommodated by the Bank and will not give grounds for automatic renegotiation of the policy targets.

4. Implementation

Sections 10 and 14 of the Act set out certain considerations that the Bank must take into account when implementing monetary policy; provided, in accordance with section 13 of the Act, that these considerations do not limit the Bank's obligation to meet its monetary policy objectives. Within this context, considerations that the Bank should take into account when formulating and implementing monetary policy shall include the following:

A. The Bank must take into account the effects of its actions on the efficiency and soundness of the financial system. Where it considers that its actions may have a materially adverse effect on the efficiency or soundness of the system, it must inform the Minister. Following the provision of this advice to the Minister, the Governor and the Minister may review whether the existing policy targets remain appropriate, and may fix new policy targets in accordance with section 9(4) of the Act.

B. Where the Bank considers that the actions of any other party (including the Government) may have an adverse effect on the achievement of the policy targets, or may increase the economic or social costs of achieving the policy targets, or may prejudice the efficiency or soundness of the financial system, the Bank shall consult with that party in an attempt to change that party's actions as necessary to reach the desired policy outcomes at minimum cost.

C. The policy targets are established on the basis of the current institutional structure of the financial sector, particularly in relation to the settlements process within the banking sector. If the Bank considers that the institutional structure has changed or is likely to change in a manner which will prejudice the Bank's ability to implement monetary policy, it shall inform the Minister. If the institutional changes continue to hamper the implementation of policy, the Minister and the Governor may set new policy targets in accordance with section 9(4) of the Act.

Signed on Friday, 2 March 1990, by the Minister of Finance, the Hon. David Caygill, and the Governor of the Reserve Bank of New Zealand, Dr Donald T. Brash. (RBNZ 1990).

Obviously, the provisions of the PTA were not instantly assimilated by the New Zealand public as a template for economic planning and action. Rather, the PTA was a starting point, an awkward and overly tech-

nical starting point, for what has become a regular series of communications that over time achieved an ever greater refinement of aims and
ever greater concision in their articulation of these macroeconomic allegories. The appointment of the economist Don Brash as the first governor
under the new regime and the first signatory of a PTA was also intended
to promote this agenda. Brash was known as a deft communicator, and his
implementation of the new framework was in many respects key to the
overall success of the inflation targeting experiment (Brash, forthcoming).
Thus, by the last decade of the twentieth century, the basic architecture
of a new monetary system was in place and the economy had attained a
subtle voice imparting an intertemporal architecture to a public currency.

CHAPTER SEVEN

Simulations

All agents inside the model, the econometrician, and God share the same model. — Thomas Sargent, American economist

The central banks that I have studied typically have museums attached to them. I have a particular fondness for the Geld Museum of the Deutsche Bundesbank in Frankfurt, with its handsome curation of the history of coinage and banknotes along with elegantly designed exhibits that explain the nature of money and the operation of central banks. A colleague at the Bundesbank suggested that on my next visit to the museum I should try an interactive electronic display that simulates the role of a central banker, illustrating how monetary policy influences the economy over time. I followed his advice.

The simulation was ingenious. It provided a careful explanation of the policy tools available to central banks—basically, the manipulation of short-term interest rates that determine the availability of money and credit to the German economy—and how these monetary interventions are meant to work, along with the contingencies and the constraints associated with each policy move. Then it presented a series of economic scenarios and asked the participant, in the role of the central banker, to select an appropriate policy stance. What made the simulation particularly intriguing (and rankling) was that, as it played out over time, the implications of each of one's prior decisions was transmitted to the German economy. Thus, at each subsequent stage of the simulation, one was compelled to take a policy stance that responded to new conditions in the economy—specifically, price inflation and economic growth—that one had had a hand in creating. Beyond evoking mild mortification, this simulation of path dependence demonstrated, even on this very elementary level, the complexities faced by central bankers in their role in stabilizing the economy and thus fostering balanced growth while restraining inflation.

Between 2004 and 2008 I made repeated trips to Frankfurt to study the creation of a currency from scratch, as it were, which was the goal of European Monetary Union (EMU). I spent my time going back and forth between the Bundesbank and the European Central Bank, examining this issue that had first caught my attention a decade earlier, during my research on European integration and the drafting of the Maastricht Treaty. The European Central Bank, established under the terms of the treaty to regulate the new currency, incorporated from its inception the experiments in inflation targeting formulated by the RBNZ and the communicative innovations developed by the Bundesbank. The Bundesbank provided another historical precedent. It had only a few years earlier navigated the monetary union attendant on German reunification—an episode that had compelled the bank to address and to explain to its citizens the communicative issues that animated its currency.

The ECB's constitutional mandate "to maintain price stability" was in itself not unusual for a central bank. The technical innovation pursued by the ECB was the formulation of two targets as part of its "twin pillar" approach to anchoring monetary policy: a target for money growth (M3) and a target for consumer prices (HICP). The ECB was thus perpetuating fidelity to the Bundesbank's "pragmatic monetarism" while incorporating the new developments in inflation targeting. But from the outset, what was being pursued by the ECB was far more radical, more intricate, and, inevitably, more inelegant: the creation of a public currency.

Early episodes of research in Frankfurt were conducted at a time when appraisal of the euro and the monetary authority that managed it flirted with the triumphal. One such monthly statement drafted by the executive council of the ECB and presented by President Jean-Claude Trichet is excerpted below. In what follows, I work back from statements like this one to the technical regime—the forecasting and the simulation exercises—upon which they were based, to reveal how inflation targeting was, in the first instance, contingent on forecasting models. Unsurprisingly, decisions on interest rates were arrived at and justified based on forward-looking projections. What is particularly interesting is that these forecasting models and the theories upon which they draw are themselves rife with contradictions and inherent limitations. These gaps and incongruities produced, as we saw earlier and as we will see further iterations of in what

follows, a space for alternative and unlikely analytical practices. Most notably, as I will show, the theoretical search for microfoundational bases of
macroeconomic theory produced an unexpected series of challenges that
lent themselves to ethnographic inquiry.

Objectivity

Twice a month, the president of the Bundesbank traveled across town to
meet at the Eurotower, the temporary headquarters of the ECB, with the
governors of the euro-area national central banks (NCBs), along with the
six members of the executive board of the ECB. This group—the Governing Council—is the main decision-making body of the ECB. These senior officials represent distinctive economies and societies as well as diverse traditions of data collection, analysis, and decision making. At these
gatherings, however, they operate, in theory, with a degree of formal independence from political accountability to their respective national constituencies. Instead they are constrained by a collegial ethic of consensus-
building and unanimity in which policy discussions are "data driven."
What constitutes compelling data and how data are generated and communicated, is, however, more complex and more consequential than one
might expect.

Typically, at the first of their monthly meetings the members of the
Governing Council assessed monetary and economic conditions and took
decisions on key interest rates and the supply of liquidity available to the
banking system. At their second monthly gathering they discussed issues
related to the management of the other main functions of the ECB and
the Eurosystem. These included foreign exchange operations, management of the foreign reserves of the euro member states, and the smooth
operation of the euro payment systems, known as TARGET 2, through
which money circulates as encrypted bundles of electrons.

Unlike the US Federal Reserve, the Bank of England, or the Sveriges
Riksbank, however, the minutes of these meetings remained, and remain,
secret, though a comprehensive review and assessment of the decisions on
monetary policy is presented by the president at a news conference immediately after each meeting. Trichet's statements on behalf of the Governing Council of the ECB have typically been conversational in tone. They
were delivered prior to a question-and-answer session with the financial
press in Frankfurt, and conducted often with the then vice president of

the ECB, Lucas Papademos, or other senior officials of the ECB or the EU in attendance.

The transcript I have excerpted below pertains primarily to the dual analysis that informs the ECB's projections of and about the futurity of prices from the perspective of mid-2006. In retrospect, this was a relatively uneventful, if not tranquil, moment in the turbulent second half of the decade. The overall statement runs about fifteen hundred words and summarizes the circumstances of hundreds of millions of people living within the eurozone. Periodically, the Governing Counsel relocates it's meeting outside of Frankfurt. In the case of the deliberations on June 6, 2006, the meeting was held in Madrid. President Trichet began the news conference with an account of the interest rate decision, in a manner that was concise and, by and large, self-explanatory. The conversational tone, however, masks a carefully scripted story that drew on the full intellectual and rhetorical resources of the bank:

> At today's meeting, we decided to increase the key ECB interest rates by 25 basis points [to the bid rate of the main refinancing operation of 2.75%]. This decision reflects the upside risks to price stability over the medium term that have been identified through both our economic and monetary analyses. The further withdrawal of monetary accommodation will thus contribute to ensuring that longer-term inflation expectations in the euro area remain solidly anchored at levels consistent with price stability. As stressed on previous occasions, such anchoring is a prerequisite for monetary policy to make an ongoing contribution towards supporting economic growth and job creation in the euro area. Overall, also after today's increase, the key ECB interest rates are still low by historical standards, liquidity is ample and our monetary policy remains accommodative. Given the outlook for price developments and the dynamism of money and credit growth in the euro area, we will continue to monitor closely all developments to ensure price stability over the medium and longer term. (ECB 2006)

Trichet then remarked briefly about the data-dependent nature of the Governing Council's decision—specifically, the economic analysis that constituted the first of the bank's dual mandates:

> Allow me to explain our assessment in greater detail, starting with the economic analysis.
> All the main indicators of economic activity that have recently become

available are positive. According to Eurostat's first estimate, on a quarter-on-quarter basis, real GDP grew by 0.6% in the euro area in the first quarter of 2006, compared with 0.3% in the previous quarter, with domestic demand making a significant contribution. The expected re-acceleration of real GDP growth in the first months of 2006 has thus materialised, confirming our view that economic growth is broadening and becoming more sustained. This assessment is further supported by information on activity in the second quarter—such as various confidence surveys and indicator-based estimates—which continues to be encouraging.

Looking further ahead, the conditions are in place for growth in the euro area to remain close to its trend potential rate, despite the impact of the rise in oil prices. Growth in the economies of the euro area's main trading partners remains robust, providing support for euro area exports. Strong investment growth is expected to continue, benefiting from favourable financing conditions, corporate balance sheet restructuring, and gains in earnings and business efficiency. Consumption growth should continue to strengthen gradually over time, in line with developments in real disposable income, as the labour market situation gradually improves.

This outlook is also reflected in the June Eurosystem staff macroeconomic projections, which provide additional input into our analysis of the prospects for economic activity. The projections foresee average annual real GDP growth in a range between 1.8% and 2.4% in 2006, and between 1.3% and 2.3% in 2007. The growth projections for 2006 are broadly unchanged from the ECB staff projections of March 2006, while those for 2007 are slightly lower, reflecting mainly the recent rise in oil prices. Most recent forecasts by international organisations and private sector institutions give a broadly similar picture. It is the Governing Council's view that risks to these projections for economic growth are broadly balanced over the shorter term, while longer-term downside risks relate mainly to potential further oil price rises, global imbalances and protectionism.

Turning to price developments, according to Eurostat's flash [preliminary] estimate, annual HICP inflation increased to 2.5% in May, compared with 2.4% in April and 2.2% in March. Although no detailed information is available as yet, this increase probably stems from energy price developments. In the months to come and in 2007, inflation rates are likely to remain above 2%, the precise levels depending on future energy price developments. While the moderate evolution of labour costs in the euro area is expected to continue in 2007—also reflecting ongoing global competitive pressures, particularly in the manufacturing sector—indirect effects of past oil price increases and the announced changes in indirect taxes are expected to have a significant upward effect on inflation. Against this background, it is crucial that the social partners continue to meet their responsibilities.

Further input into our assessment of the outlook for price developments is provided by the June Eurosystem staff projections. Annual HICP inflation is projected to lie between 2.1% and 2.5% in 2006, and between 1.6% and 2.8% in 2007. Compared with the March 2006 ECB staff projections, these ranges imply a slight upward shift to the profile for HICP inflation in 2006, largely reflecting the assumption of higher oil prices.

In the view of the Governing Council, risks to the outlook for price developments remain on the upside and include further increases in oil prices, a stronger pass-through of past oil price rises into consumer prices than currently anticipated, additional increases in administered prices and indirect taxes, and—more fundamentally—stronger than expected wage developments due to second-round effects of past oil price increases. (ECB 2006)

The story that Trichet told was the outcome of the continuous conversations that routinely emanate from the bank's research directorates, incorporating the full range of technical resources available to economists and policymakers from within the ECB, the member central banks, international organizations, and from financial institutions and other private research organizations. For the purposes of this chapter, I will show how the research personnel of the Bundesbank serve as one important source of the technical arguments that imparted form and content to Trichet's story. But first a brief aside on the perils and promises of economic modeling and the role of models in shaping the judgments that inform policy decisions.

Micro-Foundations

Fundamental to the research function of central banks is high-level quantitative analysis "constructing systems of equations—models—to capture the forces most relevant in the complexities of the economy" (Galí et al. 2004, 7). These econometric instruments serve, as we saw in the last chapter, as a basis of the forecasting exercises employed for policy formulation, and in that role they serve as the framework of disciplined discussions and interpretations (Clarida, Galí, and Gertler 1999; Rotemberg and Woodford 1997). The design of these models also serves the specific analytical prerequisites of inflation targeting.

Forecasting models employed by central banks are mathematical representations of the dynamic characteristics of the economy. They are also instruments that generate representations of the economy prospectively, and as such they serve the needs of policy formulation, framing *interpretative* discussions and establishing arguments for specific policy positions. By so doing, they provide a means for the delineation of analytical scenarios at the limits of calculation and measurement. The refinement of econometric analysis over the last three decades has focused on the "micro-foundational" basis of macroeconomic phenomena, which means that some of the most contentious issues in the history of economics abide in the architecture of these instruments.

Here is how N. Gregory Mankiw described the analytical problem that has established historically the agendas of and for business cycle modeling:

> Economists attracted to the Keynesian approach to the business cycle have long been discomfited by the issue of microfoundations. Indeed, a 1946 article by [Lawrence] Klein, one of the first to use the term "macroeconomics," begins as follows: "Many of the newly constructed mathematical models of economic systems, especially business-cycle theories, are very loosely related to the behavior of individual households or firms which must form the basis of all theories of economic behavior." (Mankiw 2006, 8)

Mankiw then alluded to the theoretical challenge that the models sought to bridge:

> All modern economists are, to some degree, classical. We all teach our students about optimization, equilibrium, and market efficiency. How to reconcile these two visions of the economy—one founded on Adam Smith's invisible hand and Alfred Marshall's supply and demand curves, the other founded on Keynes's analysis of an economy suffering from insufficient aggregate demand—has been a profound, nagging question since macroeconomics began as a separate field of study. (Mankiw 2006, 8)

Whether or not Keynesian macroeconomics can be made compatible with neoclassic mircoeconomics depended initially on a division of analytical labor:

> Early Keynesians, such as [Paul] Samuelson, [Franco] Modigliani, and [James] Tobin, thought they had reconciled these visions in what is sometimes called

the "neoclassical–Keynesian synthesis." These economists believed that the classical theory of Smith and Marshall was right in the long run, but the invisible hand could become paralyzed in the short run described by Keynes. The time horizon mattered because some prices—most notably the price of labor—adjusted sluggishly over time. Early Keynesians believed that classical models described the equilibrium toward which the economy gradually evolved, but that Keynesian models offered the better description of the economy at any moment in time when prices were reasonably taken as predetermined. (Mankiw 2006, 8–9)

The rationale for econometric modeling has undergone a series of revisions to address ongoing reformulations of these two theoretical agendas. The current situation is characterized by a particular though uneasy theoretical rapprochement: "Today, many macroeconomists coming from the new classical tradition are happy to concede to the Keynesian assumption of sticky prices as long as this assumption is imbedded in a suitably rigorous model in which economic actors are rational and forward-looking. Because of this change in emphasis, the terminology has evolved, and this class of work now often goes by the label 'dynamic stochastic general equilibrium' theory [DSGE]" (Mankiw 2006, 8).

These DSGE models are aligned with the analytical conventions of inflation targeting that, as the Bank of England notes, serve as "the primary organisational framework to process the various judgments and assumptions made by the [Monetary Policy] Committee" (Harrison et al. 2005, 5). Pursuing this notion of an "organizational framework," and what that has meant operationally, reveals the extent to which the models operate as instruments with an interpretative nature providing access to the performative dynamics of the monetary regime.

The disciplined and rigorous nature of the models, and the forecasting exercises more generally, conferred credibility and coherence to the adjudication and communication of policy. Models systematically align the thinking of bank personnel with a comprehensive account of the economy—one, as we will see, that allows for multiple and potentially conflicting interpretations. Central banks are explicit about the operation of these models, the criteria and tradeoffs that influenced their construction, as well as the contingencies that drive their ongoing revision and modification. The Bank of England, for example, uses "numerous economic models to help produce these projections. No model can do everything—*all* models are imperfect, precisely because they are simplifications of reality. And each projection is a judgment of [policymakers] rather than a mechanical output from any model" (Harrison et al. 2005, 5).

DSGE

The Bundesbank's Macro-Econometric Multi-Country Model: MEMMOD (2000) illustrates the distinctive innovations of the DSGE models[1]:

> Such models fully and consistently reflect the fact that agents in the economy base their actions to a large extent on expectations about the future—a factor that is not incorporated (or incorporated only to a limited extent) in traditional models. This aspect, in turn, has far-reaching consequences for economic policy analysis and our current understanding of how monetary policy works. Shifts in policy can cause changes in behaviour and alter parameters once assumed to be constant. Insights derived from the past are then inadequate for correctly assessing the future implications of current economic policy measures. (Deutsche Bundesbank 2008, 32)

Here is a basic example of the kind of insights these models can generate in relation to the key policy concerns of the Bundesbank, consumer prices, and changes in GDP over time. A hypothetical interest rate shock—a 1 percent (100 basis points) increase over two years—is imposed on the German economy, and this is the kind of prospective story the model would generate:

> Consumer prices lie 0.56 percent below baseline in the second and third years after the end of the shock. We observe a fast transmission of price effects in import prices due to the euro appreciation. German export prices react more sluggishly and only dominate the import price effects in the medium term.
>
> The short-run effects of the interest rate rise on real GDP are −0.28 percent in the first year and −0.33 percent in the second year, driven by the reduction in investments, exports and, to a smaller extent, private consumption. In the medium run, owing to the strong fall in prices, real disposable income rises, which results in a positive deviation of real private consumption from its baseline values. The subsequent increase in final demand in turn leads to a rise in real investment. Overall this results in a positive real GDP effect from the second year after the end of the shock. If a longer horizon of ten years were considered, however, the effect of the temporary interest rise on real GDP would van-

ish in the long run. Real imports increase in the first year because of the reduction in import prices. In the subsequent two years, the decrease of the deflator of final demand dominates the behavior of real imports. Because of the sluggishness of real imports, their decline continues until the end of the fourth year.

The initial reduction in output has a negative effect on the labour market with a fall in employment and a rise in the unemployment rate. In the longer run both return to their baseline values. On the fiscal side, government expenditures as a percentage of GDP temporarily rise by more than the receipts do, so the government debt increases. (Hamburg and Töder 2005, 127–29)

This stylized exercise demonstrates the dual temporality of the model, whereby the interest rate shock imparts a series of short-term Keynesian responses to GDP (in this case, negative) followed by neoclassical responses to medium- and longer-term growth (in this case, with positive GDP outcomes). This capacity to simulate the effects of shocks over time fits well with the forward-looking requirements of inflation targeting.

In addition to telling a story about the effects of interest rates on consumer prices and the implication for GDP across various time horizons, the model also projects the effects of the interest rate shock on exchange rates, investment, exports and imports, private consumption, and the labor market, as well as government expenditures and debt. Further, there are a series of other "real" shocks that the model can address—notably, fiscal policy, demand, and oil shocks.

For the moment, it is important to note again that central banks employ numerous models. The models are calibrated and solved for shocks of different magnitudes and of different durations. The databases on which the models run are continually updated, which means that subsequent simulations quarter to quarter, even with the same hypothetical shock, will potentially generate somewhat different projections. By calibrating interactions among economic variables with mathematical rigor and running various simulations, the models can elaborate alternative scenarios on the operation of the German economy prospectively. Solving the model, however, demands considerable interpretative skill.

Interpretative Economics

Many economists working in central banks are skeptical, at times scathing, about the forecasting capabilities of these sequences of equations

(Blinder 1998, 7–8; Solow 2010).[2] They are viewed, at best, as crude simplifications of the boundless complexity of economic phenomena. Indeed, during the financial crisis, the models were notably deficient in this role of projecting a calculable future as fluctuations of the economy exceeded the models' steady-state assumptions. That said, the models, particularly the DSGE models, retained, counterintuitively, an ethnographic efficacy that was important for addressing interpretative or heuristic issues. Models put at the service of evaluating policy questions had a different nature than models put at the service of generating discrete forecasts: models might fail in pursuit of the latter goal and yet have value in furthering the former aim.

Despite misgivings about these instruments, there is a consensus in central banks regarding the value of these models in framing and disciplining what are essentially interpretative discussions about how changes in a particular set of variables propagate across diverse sectors of the economy. The efficacy of these instruments resides, for example, in their capacity to evaluate how various economic events are transmitted along distinctive channels to the economy at large, rather than to generate precise and accurate forecasts. Put simply, the models play a decisive role in orchestrating wide-ranging discussions by which data are rendered informational. These forecasting exercises—which represent perhaps the most formidable analytical practices employed by these institutions—are generative of a "thick description" of, in this case, the German economy, an interpretative exercise that seeks to capture the interplay of its moving parts (Geertz 1973).

How does this work? In interviews with econometricians at the Deutsche Bundesbank, I learned how macroeconomic simulation attained a communicative dynamic. Indeed, the description of the interactive museum exhibit that opened this chapter is misleading: simulations were far from a mechanical process of inputting data to a sequence of equations for the purpose of yielding a discrete policy stance. Rather, it was a process that continually required reflection and judgment to generate multiple scenarios which could sustain the appraisal of various contingencies. Further, the museum simulation is also misleading in another obvious respect. In the post-1999 era of the euro, the president and leadership of the Bundesbank no longer make interest rate decisions for Germany. Rather, their very rigorous engagement with research is for the purpose of making a persuasive argument that could sway the decision making of the Governing Council of the ECB. Quantitative and linguistic modeling of the economy have, thus, unfolded more or less in tandem.[3]

Making an Argument

In preparation for his meeting across town at the ECB, Axel Weber, then president of the Bundesbank, met with his research staff to review their analyses and their projections. Germany was emerging from an economic downturn early in the decade; hence, the exercise was particularly consequential, as policymakers sought to discern the evidence of sustainable recovery. A small group, half a dozen or so, responsible for the management of the bank's MEMMOD, discussed how they modeled the economy communicatively.

In the week running up to the policy meeting at the ECB, Weber met regularly with the modelers. Rather than a straightforward briefing, the group participated with Weber—who is an economics professor—in what amounted to a seminar. They repeatedly ran the models with different assumptions. The discussions drew on just about every source of information this small group had available to it, which of course amounted to the full research capabilities of the bank. Their discussions were framed by their thorough understanding of the performance of the German economy over time and by a range of "qualitative" reports gleaned from networks of contacts in business, finance, and government. They also drew into their interpretative discussions what they understood to be the contingencies governing specific data series, the nuances of key statistical measures, as well as the idiosyncratic properties of the model itself. What emerged from the discussions were not merely artifacts of elaborate (and obscure) quantitative analysis, but a prospective representation—a linguistic model—informed by qualitative information concerning the German political economy and the economic condition among Germany's key trading partners too. These deliberations simulated the economy performatively, yielding arguments, scenarios—macroeconomic allegories—by which the economy was rendered susceptible to policy interventions.

The repeated interchanges between policymakers and the researchers fostered a systematic evaluation of a range of scenarios in relation to a spectrum of contingencies. The ambiguities in the data—whether they were artifacts of statistics, theory, or other aspects of data collection and quantitative analysis—were parsed discursively. Abstract projections were rendered meaningful as layer upon layer of information was added to the analysis. Further, as suggested earlier, the modelers went through this exercise on a monthly and quarterly basis; hence, what emerged over time was a serialized story, open to multiple iterations and capable of sustaining continued learning and interpretation. The heuristic exercises generated arguments for policy positions rather than merely producing a forecast or testing a theory (Morgan 2012, 1–43).

As we have seen, the DSGE and other models can sustain discussions covering the theoretical and the methodological assumptions that inform contemporary understandings of how the economy works across diverse spheres and sectors. Moreover, the discussions are not about a single picture—one representation of facts—but simulations represent multiple stylized scenarios. That said, unprecedented and unforeseen circumstances continually lurk in ways that are, at least in the present, undetectable—in forms that are incalculable. DSGE models, thus, trace the *limits* of knowledge, and yet, it is precisely at this analytical boundary that it seems to me that a decisive threshold is crossed.

The limitations of the models establish the point at which monetary policy becomes more than a mere technical intervention. In this alternative guise, models no longer serve merely as a detached forecasting mechanism, but also as templates for discerning the constellation of human predicaments that link policymakers to various constituencies, sectors, and strata of the public over time. Starting from a pragmatic policy question rather than solving a series of equations, reveals the collaborative dynamic of monetary policy. Models—these "machineries of knowing," as Knorr-Cetina (2007) terms them—can be, as proposed in chapter 1, viewed as machineries of *relating*, capable of articulating policy in relation to the shared circumstances of individuals and firms who are themselves continually modeling and transacting economic relationships.

The policy question early in the new century could be stated simply: Were the prevailing circumstances propitious for the German Mittelstand (the dynamic small- and medium-sized enterprises) to lead a German and a European economic recovery? While it was the abiding concern of the Bundesbank, it is a problem that is hardly noteworthy in and of itself. It was an issue that was also widely discussed in the media and by political and financial observers of the German and European economies. What caught my attention was simpler still. Acknowledging the circumstances of these firms also acknowledged (if only inferentially) that the creative labor for resolving countless recessionary predicaments was ultimately in their hands. The effort to model the predicaments of the Mittelstand, or any other group for that matter, hinted at a means to bridge ethnographically macro- and microeconomic analysis, providing analytical purchase on the creative acumen by which the economy is made, unmade, and remade.

Models, particularly the DSGE models, demark what I began to think of as an interpretative threshold across which issues of forecasting and policy formulation take a decisive turn. The empirical imperative—the data-driven orientation to policy—could be superseded by communicative imperatives oriented to the refinement of a particular relationship with the public. Policymakers were compelled to listen and to speak persuasively to the circumstances of a diverse public, to articulate meaningful stories in order to credibly and consistently shape confidence. Monetary policy embedded in and anchored by these interpretative narratives became the means to create and to model *relationships* with the citizens in terms of *their* economic circumstances and preoccupations. DSGE and other models served as templates for simulating these dilemmas linguistically. The load-bearing capacities of the resulting narrative relationships were, as we will see, tested as the decade wore on. I also began to see the monetary story, rather than the inflation target per se, attain increasing and, ultimately, decisive significance as the forecasting capacities of the models were compromised in the latter part of the decade.

Symbolic Economy

Trichet turned in his June 6 statement to the second pillar employed by the bank, monetary analysis, to "cross-check" the economic analysis and as a means, a controversial means, to ostensibly assess the future behavior of prices[4]:

> Turning to the monetary analysis, the Governing Council again had a thorough discussion of underlying developments in money and credit. In a context of already ample liquidity and very strong monetary and credit growth, the annual growth rate of loans to the private sector has increased further in recent months to reach double-digit levels. Credit growth has also been broadly based across sectors. Borrowing by households—especially for house purchase—and by non-financial corporations has been growing very strongly. At the same time, monetary growth has risen further over the past few months, with the annual growth rate of M3 standing at 8.8% in April.
>
> The rapid rate of monetary growth continues to be driven mainly by the expansion of its most liquid components. Thus, the latest developments confirm that the stimulative impact of the low level of interest rates remains the dominant factor behind the current high trend rate of monetary expansion, which signals inflationary risks over the medium to longer term. The further accel-

eration of monetary and credit growth in this environment of already ample
liquidity points to increased upside risks to price stability at longer horizons.
Monetary developments, therefore, require careful monitoring, in particular in
the light of strong dynamics in housing markets. (ECB 2006)

The ECB's "second pillar" of monetary analysis is, again, the legacy of
the Bundesbank's policy innovations. But the focus on money and credit
is enigmatic. A lengthy official publication of the ECB encompassing an
exhaustive review of the role of money, edited by two of its then senior
officials, Lucas Papademos and Jürgen Stark, concludes: "The changing
patterns of influence with which money acts upon the economy and price
formation—at times more directly through expansions or contractions in
purchasing power, at other times in a more roundabout fashion, through
asset prices, liquidity constraints and the pricing of risk—remain largely
unexplained" (Papademos and Stark 2010, 55). If these relationships
remain inexplicable, why make them a fundamental preoccupation of the
ECB? I doggedly asked this question during my research in Frankfurt.

The standard answer, one that I found persuasive though incomplete,
was that the careful and sustained analysis of changes in money and credit
can "deepen" an understanding of the behavior of prices over the medium and the long term. To "deepen" was code for analytical modalities
that address very particular institutional and constitutional issues. Central bankers—for the moment, lets say German central bankers—believe
that they can employ monetary analysis to detect not just the misbehav-
ior of prices but also disruptions of values that can threaten the integrity
of the social order.[5] They believe that this kind of analysis enables them
to interpret what are fully constitutional matters: how the regulation (or
misregulation) of money and credit establish the underlying facts or principles governing a polity, whether it is the Bundesrepublik or the European Union. Monetary analysis thus serves as a means to draw an institutional sociology within the analytical and interpretative purview of a
central bank. This variant of monetarism is based on the conviction that
proper management of money and credit can sustain a social order—that
is, it can generate a sustainable configuration of relations between and
among groups within a negotiated system of social justice. Deep engagements with money touch on the dialectic governing social life, not merely
the interests of finance and capital (Boyer 2005; Ho 2009).

By adopting the twin pillars, particularly the second pillar, the ECB
policy regime sought to maintain fidelity with this deeper set of consti-

tutional issues—with a system of values—linking European citizens to a shared economic fate. But this does not have to be read as some curious predilection of German and/or Austrian economics, but rather as something that was fully acknowledged by the most famous figure of the Scottish Enlightenment.

Andrea Muehlebach has looked carefully at the creative interplay between two famous texts by Adam Smith: *An Inquiry into the Nature and Causes of Wealth of Nations* and *The Theory of Moral Sentiments* (Muehlebach 2012). Crudely, the "invisible hand" can be viewed as governing the economic pillar, while the monetary pillar is informed by moral sentiments or, as I have indicated above, by ethical imperatives that contour a social order. When the crisis began to take hold in continental Europe, monetary policy was caught between the divergent values of financial markets and of national sovereignty revealing dissonant elements of the still incomplete political economy of Europe. The potential for discord is alluded to tangentially in the final section of Trichet's statement.

Afterthoughts

Two small asides, almost afterthoughts, to Trichet's statement that few people took seriously in mid-2006, became absolutely critical to the making (and perhaps unmaking) of the euro as a public currency, and, ultimately, for the constitutional integrity of the EU[6]:

> With regard to fiscal policies, the forecasts published recently by the Commission point to a broadly unchanged situation in the euro area in 2006 and 2007; deficit ratios are expected to remain at around the 2005 level of 2.4%, while debt ratios, after declining only marginally, are forecast at levels still above 70% of GDP. This is disappointing against the background of the economic outlook. Most countries with an excessive deficit have not corrected their position in a timely manner. Furthermore, there is a risk of consolidation delays in other countries. It is crucial to avoid the mistakes of the past, when many countries failed to consolidate sufficiently in good times. The Governing Council considers that more determined progress is required towards sound public finances in a number of countries, that concrete and credible measures should be implemented swiftly as part of a medium-term-oriented strategy, and that it is vital to consolidate confidence in the revised Stability and Growth Pact by ensuring the sustainability of public finances in the euro area.

In terms of structural reforms, the Governing Council reiterates its call for the implementation of firm measures to ensure open, competitive and well-functioning product and labour markets, so as to foster an attractive environment for investment and innovation and to promote flexibility in wages and prices. There is a broad and firm consensus that such reforms are beneficial in promoting growth and employment and in enhancing the resilience of the euro area economy to external shocks. At the same time, these reforms would further facilitate intra-euro area adjustments by reducing rigidities that contribute, in some economies, to wage developments that lead to high and persistent unit labour cost growth, higher inflationary pressure and losses in competitiveness. Examples of such rigidities are low productivity growth due to a lack of competition in some sectors and an explicit or de facto indexation of nominal wages to prices. All in all, a comprehensive set of reforms is essential to strengthen the foundations for sustained growth in output and employment across the euro area, to underpin the ongoing economic recovery and to further smoothen the functioning of adjustment mechanisms in the euro area, thereby facilitating the conduct of the single monetary policy. (ECB 2006)

Trichet's statement was less an anticipation of fundamental elements of the crisis to come than a recapitulation of what were already understood to be abiding weaknesses in the European political economy from the moment it was created, attributed to a flaw, widely acknowledged at the time, in the text of the Maastricht Treaty, and thus in the design of the euro (Connolly 1995; Mundell 1961).

The defect was striking: monetary policy in the proposed currency zone was to be conducted for an economic area in which national governments retained significant sovereignty, and thus control, over their own fiscal policy, while ceding monetary policy to the new central bank (Scheller 2004, 28). For many economists, most outspokenly perhaps, Martin Feldstein (1997), this arrangement was a formula for disaster.

The contradiction was in theory to be managed, if not resolved, by the now infamous "growth and stability pact" (SPG) that committed national governments to budgetary positions "close to balance or in surplus" with a deficit-to-GDP ratio not to exceed 3 percent and a debt-to-GDP ratio not to exceed 60 percent (Morris, Ongena, and Schuknech 2006; Scheller 2004, 33). These complex covenants were in tatters as early as 2002, largely because of the violations of their budgetary provisions, most notably by the German and French national governments, that for three years in a row, from 2001 to 2004, faced budgetary strains as they pursued stabilization policies to address the global recession of 2001–2. Though other euro member states were in a similar budgetary position, the situation was particularly ironic for the German government, and for the officials of the Bundesbank, because they were fully aware of these shortcomings in the design of the euro and they had been resolute in insisting on the pact as a means to control fiscal policies across the currency zone, as a key condition of monetary union (see Parker and Larsen 2005).

Trichet drew attention, in the final section of his prepared remarks, to the need for structural reforms. He did so in the rather upbeat terms of strengthening the prospect of sustainable growth and smoothing the operation of a eurozone monetary policy. In mid-2006 he was underplaying what he knew to be the unsettling reality. Restructuring just about every aspect of the entire public sector, along with aggressive liberalization and market reforms of the private sector, would be necessary to begin to redress the stark imbalances developing within the eurozone between core and what we now refer to as "peripheral" states. Ultimately, without a restoration of productivity in the peripheral states, their fiscal deficits would continue to grow. Differentials in productivity between, say, Greece and Germany were, to put it simply, at the root of the deficit issues, with the single currency exacerbating imbalances.

The architects of European integration embraced monetary union as a *political* agenda that fulfilled their dream of a federal Europe in which a common currency would further the aims of unification. Integration of a polity was to be achieved by means of supranational markets and a common currency. The issue of fiscal harmonization, however, could not be resolved in the intergovernmental conference that drafted the Maastricht Treaty. Member states could not agree on constitutional provisions necessary for the transfer of power over fiscal and budgetary matters from their national parliaments to Brussels, to the institutional authority of the EU. A resolution to relinquish national sovereignty over this range of governmental competencies proved to be unattainable in the early 1990s (Connelly 1995; Moravcsik 1998).

The incomplete nature of the monetary union thus implicitly incorporated a crisis, a future impasse the basic outlines of which were fully known to the architects of the treaty. They understood—in close approximation of the "neofunctionalism" of David Mitrany (1965) and Ernest Haas (1958)—that the crisis would likely be resolved by means of further political integration advancing the agenda of European unification over fiscal matters. The scale and staggering cost of the sovereign debt crisis that ensued in early 2010 would have dismayed but not surprised them.

CHAPTER EIGHT

Inflationary Tempest

Representations are social facts. — Paul Rabinow, *Writing Culture: The Poetic and Politics of Representation*

In September 2007 I was in Wellington, in the recently opened museum of the Reserve Bank of New Zealand (RBNZ). One exhibit caught my attention. I was drawn to a hydraulic contraption—the MONIAC ("Monetary National Income Analogue Computer")—a machine constructed by the New Zealand economist A. William Phillips (1914–75). It is arguably the "world's first macro-economic computer," built in the late-1940s to simulate the dynamic operations of the British economy:

> The MONIAC used water to model flows of money in a macro-economy. The linkages were based on Keynesian and classical economic principles, with various tanks representing household, business, government, exporting and importing sectors of the economy. Water pumped around the system could be measured as income, spending and GDP. The system was programmable, and the experiments with fiscal policy, monetary policy and exchange rates could be carried out. (RBNZ, n.d., "A. W. H. [Bill] Phillips, [MBE] and the MONIAC")

The display of Phillips's wonderful machine symbolized for me the abiding cultural enigma of how to represent the economy mathematically, linguistically, or, in this case, hydraulically—how to abstract this human creation about which we have a more-or-less dim understanding and over which none of us have much more than tenuous control.[1]

Accompanying the display was a short video clip produced many years ago (perhaps the 1970s or 1980s) illustrating the workings of the machine, with an economist in lab coat tending the hydraulic device with Chaplinesque flare. The figure in the video was, at the time of my visit, the governor of the bank, Alan Bollard (2002–12), who is, as it happens, an intellectual devotee of Phillips.

William Phillips is better known for the Phillips curve, which famously traced an inverse relationship between the rate of unemployment and the rate of inflation (Borio 2011; I. Fisher 1973; Phillips 1958; Samuelson and Solow 1960). The nature of this relationship, as Phillips described it, provoked some of the most important and influential debates in economic theory during the second half of the twentieth century, and it has continuing analytical relevance for monetary policy (M. Friedman 1968; Phelps 1968). Paul Samuelson, a key figure in these debates, has emphasized the historical contingencies that shaped and reshaped the authority of the Phillips curve as an instrument for relating "statistically the level of growth rate of wages or of the general price level to changes in the percentage degree of unemployment" (Samuelson 2008).[2]

During 2007 and the first half of 2008, the problem of addressing inflationary expectations was an overriding preoccupation of the personnel of the RBNZ as well as policymakers in all the major central banks of the world. I returned to Wellington for the purposes of further exploring the insights I had developed in Frankfurt—that is, viewing inflation as a function of language as manifest in the shifting articulation of the monetary policy story. Specifically, I wanted to follow the serialization of the governor's periodic monetary policy assessments as a means for managing an inflationary tempest that was swirling at the time. Telling the monetary story to the public during this period of resurgent inflation was increasingly difficult, the message far from salutary. Taming inflationary expectations risked a serious economic slowdown, if not a full-blown recession.

I expected this episode of research to follow a fairly predictable course in which I would observe the gradual process by which the RBNZ brought inflationary expectations in New Zealand under control and, incidentally, how Phillips's insights from half a century earlier could help in navigating the predicaments the bank was facing. I was fully aware of an impending monetary drama, but not of its staggering scale, complexity, or destructive force. What I imagined would be a concluding episode of research became a transitional chapter that opened the way for a more explicit examination of the exigencies underwriting a public currency. While in Wellington during this period, I began to see how the protocols of inflation targeting were begetting something else: a new monetary regime.

So, in this brief chapter I review the status of my project at the onset of the crisis. The major elements of the research came together rather suddenly during this period. Five ideas merged and/or were foregrounded. First, I further developed how the processes of research in central banks were aligned with the articulation of the monetary policy story. Second, I recognized the significance of the network of individuals working and managing various enterprises across key sectors of the economy, who continually provided the bank with acute interpretative insights gleaned, as it were, from within the beast. Third, as I scrutinized the communicative and pedagogic agendas employed by these central banks, my thinking about performativity was recontextualized and or supplanted by the notion of an economy of words. And fourth, I began to recognize the interpellation of the public as protagonists fully implicated in the monetary drama. These ideas and insights were all broached earlier, but it was only in late-2007 that they came together as a more or less unified perspective. That said, there were still gaps in my thinking, but at the time I wanted and needed a very concise intellectual toolkit that could serve the purposes of my own research as the issues I was studying were undergoing a quantum leap in complexity.

I also in this chapter make a brief detour to a conference that took place in Chatham, Massachusetts, sponsored by the Federal Reserve Bank of Boston, one dedicated to a retrospective assessment of the work of William Phillips. The speakers addressed the relevance of Phillips's work for issues facing central banks at that particular moment, but, more importantly for our purposes, they introduced to the scene reflexive actors capable of learning and reflection, and thus susceptible to persuasion. They rearticulated the Phillips curve across a dynamic communicative field within, as suggested above, a broader economy of words.

In what follows I examine a series of short documents and excerpts of documents that illustrate how policy was crafted to speak to the shifting predicaments of the New Zealand public over the course of a fraught twenty months.

Policy Assessment

I begin with one of the periodic communications, the "Policy Assessment," issued every six weeks by the RBNZ in support of its decision on interest rates. It is broadly analogous to the monthly statement presented by President Trichet in the last chapter, announcing the ECB's policy decision, though much more concise. In this particular case, the explanation of the bank's interest rate decision—the RBNZ's Official Cash Rate (OCR)—was made as the financial turmoil that commenced in August 2007 was gaining visibility and assuming urgency. Notably, the central bank decided *not* to alter interest rates; crucially, however, the language that the bank employed to model the economic situation was beginning to shift in anticipation of new sources of risk and uncertainty. The authors of the statement were searching for narrative forms and descriptive conventions that could begin to address and explain the nature of what we know now was an impending debacle (Bollard 2010):

Monetary Policy Statement, September 2007—Policy Assessment

The Official Cash Rate (OCR) will remain unchanged at 8.25 percent.

The outlook for economic activity and inflation has become more uncertain since we reviewed the OCR in July. Credit concerns and heightened risk aversion have led to significant turbulence in global financial markets. This development increases the likelihood of a weaker economic outlook for the United States and New Zealand's other key trading partners than in recent forecasts.

The consequences of this financial market turmoil for New Zealand remain unclear at this stage. However, we continue to expect a significant boost to the economy over the next two years from the sharp rise in world prices for dairy products and some other commodities that has occurred over the past year. A sharp decline in the New Zealand dollar since July, if sustained, will act to reinforce the effects of higher world prices on export sector revenues.

Recent inflation outcomes have highlighted widespread inflation pressures but indicators in recent weeks suggest that previous increases in the OCR are starting to dampen domestic spending, which will help to reduce those pressures. In particular, household borrowing growth is beginning to slow and turnover in the housing market continues to fall.

We expect the effects of stronger export revenues on activity and inflation to be broadly offset by a further braking effect from the interest rate increases undertaken earlier this year. However, in the short-term, CPI inflation is likely to rise due to the effects of a lower exchange rate and higher food prices. It is important that this temporary increase in inflation does not affect price or wage setting behaviour in the medium term.

The recent collapse of a number of finance companies and reduced liquidity within the non-bank lending institution sector generally could further act to dampen activity in some areas of the economy, such as property development or consumer financing. However, we currently expect those negative effects to be relatively contained.

At this point, we believe that the current level of the OCR is consistent with future inflation outcomes of 1 to 3 percent on average over the medium term. However, given greater than usual uncertainty at present, we will be watching to see how the upside and downside risks to the outlook are developing. (RBNZ 2007b)

In these 375 words the governor of the Reserve Bank of New Zealand captures the remarkably complex pricing phenomena he is charged with managing. At the outset, the central bank's intention is established—that is, to conduct "open-market operations" in a manner that will keep a key short-term interest rate, the Official Cash Rate (OCR), at a specific level (8.25%). In September 2007, this level for the central bank policy rate was one of the highest in the world. The body of Governor Bollard's text explains with concision the monetary policy stance in relation to prevailing conditions in New Zealand and globally during an unusually tumultuous period for financial markets.

Implicit in the statement is an underlying commitment to the open communication of the bank's policy, to clarity in explaining the analysis upon which the policy stance is based, and to candor in assessing the elements of uncertainty and risk in the assessment (Blinder 2004; Blinder et al. 2001; Blinder et al. 2008). The statement reiterates the specific inflation target that the RBNZ is committed to achieving and thus makes explicit the benchmark for assessing the bank's performance and, as we saw in chapter 6, establishing explicit measures of accountability for its governor. The Governors' Policy Assessment prefaces a longer document, the *Monetary Policy Statement*, that, again, under the sway of transparency, describes in considerable detail the economic analyses and projections that inform the current assessment and that are likely to influence future policy developments. As I had done in Frankfurt, I examined the sources of the Reserve Bank's monetary policy story as it gained intelligibility and suasive force in the processes of research and policy discussions.

Examining the communicative practices operating within another central bank, the Bank of Canada, Graham Smart demonstrated how these kinds of narratives performed a decisive and uncanny heuristic purpose (Smart 1999, 2006). His superb account was particularly relevant because the RBNZ employed at the time a modified version of the same Quarterly Projection Model (QPM) developed by and for the Bank of

Canada. Smart provides a basic account of the process of creating these scenarios:

> The *monetary-policy story* is constructed in three stages, over time and across a set of written genres, with each successive version offering a broader knowledge claim in the form of a more comprehensive account of the state of the Canadian economy. The narrative appears in the first stage as a cluster of what I refer to as *sector stories*, specialists' analysis of developments in different sectors of the economy; in the second stage, as a more encompassing, although still somewhat circumscribed, narrative about the Canadian economy as a whole, produced by a team of economists during a quarterly activity known as the Projection Exercise and inscribed in a document called the *White Book*; and then in the final state, as a fully elaborated institutional story, constructed by executives from the White Book and other sources of information. (Smart 1999, 257)

The storytelling exercise yields, as one Canadian executive put it, "an essential framework for thinking about the economy and about policy" (quoted in Smart 1999, 263), and the meetings associated with this exercise "provide regular occasions for negotiating competing interpretations of empirical phenomena and statistical data" (265). Yet, in its final manifestation a monetary policy story "is nowhere completely articulated in written form in any internal document; rather, it resides in the executives' discourse, surfacing in meetings and informal conversation, in whole or in part, and underlying certain assumptions and lines of argument in the texts they produce" (266). These actors freely acknowledge storytelling as implicit in negotiating various levels of formal empirical analysis, notably in reference to the bank's econometric model of the Canadian economy, the QPM. This ecology of discourses fostered the assimilation of "feelings," "intuition," "discretion," and "judgment," reaching into the reserves of "experience" within these institutions, and sustaining the "intersubjectivity—the grounds of shared understandings—that make possible the intellectual collaboration of bank's economists" (256).

A very similar, if not identical, "storytelling" unfolds in relation to the RBNZ model, the Forecasting and Policy System (SPS), yielding a narrative or narratives open to constant revision and modification as new data and new interpretative insights become available. In the first instance, what the discussions achieve is the translation of essentially historical data series and their rearticulation in the future tense as a representation of the evolution of economic activity, notably, of paths of economic output, employment, prices, interest rates, and exchange rates. These analytical practices yield a relatively stable baseline scenario of the New Zealand economy—its "central projections"—around which alternative simulations can be run and a series of alternative policy actions tested and evaluated. Feedback relations can be explored within this framework, and second-round effects revealed. The model serves as a vehicle for heuristic conversations.

There was another series of conversations that informed Governor Bollard's thinking—another means by which he engaged the economy in vivo, capturing sentiments and expectation that were driving it contemporaneously and prospectively. Like his colleagues at the Bank of England, Governor Bollard was in the "field" each month, traveling with one or two aides across the North and South Islands on visits to a selection of five hundred or so businesses that provide strategic perspectives on the New Zealand economy.[3]

The governor and his staff communicate central bank policy during these visits, but they also actively solicit stories—anecdotal data—from the employees, managers, and owners of these enterprises. They talk numbers, they talk trends, and they talk outlooks. They glean in these interchanges not only contemporaneous reports on the New Zealand economy, they also garner from these interlocutors the details and the contradictions typically lost or suppressed by economic statistics. In these exchanges, they put words not only to the ephemera of local expectations and sentiments, but to the rapidly changing competitive pressures unfolding in global markets, particularly among New Zealand's key trading partners. This network of interlocutors provides technical representations of the New Zealand economy, imparting (or restoring) social mediation and social context to economic analysis (Holmes and Marcus 2005, 2006, 2008, 2012).

These situated actors can narrate how shifts in exchange rates, the prices of agricultural commodities, or the price of oil impact the operation of a particular business. These accounts translate the abstractions of price into countless examples of situated social action and experience. Dairy and wool processors, vintners, tour operators, appliance manufactures, software engineers, real estate brokers, bank officers, trade union representatives, managers of construction firms and retail outlets, provide social contextualization of economic facts for the governor and his or her staff. The future continually encroaches on these narratives as projections of income and expenditures and, most significantly, in the articulation of plans for employment and investment by these enterprises. The RBNZ listed over fifty companies and organizations consulted during a recent quarterly "projection round," while noting that "contact was also made with other companies and organizations for feedback on business conditions and particular issues relevant to our policy deliberations" (RBNZ 2007b, 36). These interlocutors were simultaneously the source of bank intelligence and the primary audience for bank communication.

The analytical scenarios that emerged from within and outside the bank underwent a twofold interpretative process. First, as indicated in the last chapter, they were recast as essentially an argument or arguments for a specific policy stance. A small group of senior officials, members of the Monetary Policy Committee (MPC) and the smaller Official Cash Rate Decision Group, interpret econometric projections and other data and information, refining them for the purposes of advising the governor on the setting of the bank's policy rate, the OCR. Second, these data are rearticulated as a public statement, composed for the purposes of shaping and anchoring expectations on the evolution of prices. An even smaller group of advisors assisted Governor Bollard in drafting these public communications, among them the Monetary Policy Assessment reproduced above. These individuals craft and edit these statements, and, more generally, oversee the rhetorical expertise of a central bank (Smart 2006; Bollard 2010).

There are, however, particularly important junctures, like those that ensued in 2008, when the governor has drafted the document entirely on his own and this in turn highlights a distinctive aspect of the New Zealand inflation-targeting regime. Again, as we saw in chapter 6, under the terms of Reserve Bank of New Zealand Act of 1989 that established the current monetary framework, the governor is vested with an unusual degree of operational independence, and personal accountability. Put bluntly, a single individual was made *personally* accountable for the futurity of prices within an economy at large. Not only does this framework endow the economy with a reflexive voice, it *personifies* that voice in the person of the Reserve Bank governor.

Like President Trichet, Governor Bollard is not merely expressing an interpretative account or commentary when he delivers a policy assessment; he is making a communicative field within which the economy can be represented as a series of unfolding empirical facts. As I have suggested above, the "New Zealand economy" was thus being configured and reconfigured, in part through the communicative practices of the governor and other senior officials of the RBNZ as they sought to shape thinking and expectations. The governor's periodic policy assessment that accompanied the setting of the OCR yielded a metanarrative that could align heuristically countless perspectives and contexts by which firms, government agencies, households, and individuals can engage a financial future, thus marshaling the key contingencies that influence, if not regulate, the futurity of prices. The unusual power of the concise assessment was and is its "intertextual" capacity to frame and contextualize countless circumstances and thus to orient and align the ecology of discourses that constitute the economy of words (Brenneis 1999; Gal 2007; McCloskey 1994; Silverstein and Urban 1996).

Ecology of Discourses

In the following statement, a policy assessment of a mere 233 words, Governor Bollard's analysis shifts markedly as consumer prices in June 2008 were projected to significantly exceed the inflation targets as established in the Policy Target Agreement. The bank's policy rate was maintained at the 8.25 percent level, as it had been for almost a year. But, yet again, the econometric drama was rescripted, and the ecology of discourses that the RBNZ employed to model the situation linguistically and anchor expectations acquired new rhetorical urgency:

Monetary Policy Statement, June 2008—Policy Assessment

The Official Cash Rate (OCR) remains unchanged at 8.25 percent.

The global economy is currently experiencing significant increases in oil and food prices. These price increases are occurring at the same time as activity is weakening in many economies in response to the global credit crisis and slowing housing markets. In New Zealand, this confluence of factors is producing a challenging environment of weak activity and high inflation.

We project annual CPI inflation to peak at 4.7 percent in the September quarter of this year. Although much of this reflects higher food and energy prices, underlying inflation pressure also remains persistent. Nevertheless, we do still expect inflation to return comfortably inside the target band over the medium term. This is based on the expectation that commodity prices stop rising, inflation expectations remain anchored, and weakening economic activity contributes to an easing in non-tradable inflation.

The outlook for economic activity is now weaker than in our previous Statement. We project little GDP growth over 2008, and only a modest recovery thereafter, largely reflecting a weaker household sector. Government spending and personal tax cuts will provide some offset to this lower growth but will also add to medium-term inflation pressure.

Consistent with the Policy Targets Agreement, the Bank's focus will remain on medium-term inflation. Provided the economy evolves in line with our projection, we are now likely to be in a position to lower the OCR later this year, which is sooner than previously envisaged. (RBNZ 2008a)

GDP growth was projected to be minimal, the exchange rate of the New Zealand dollar was expected to depreciate, housing prices appeared to be falling, and the labor market was understood to be weakening. This appraisal of economic conditions allowed the Reserve Bank to "look through" the first-round price effects of inflationary shocks—projected to spike to 4.7 percent in the following quarter—and project that the rate of consumer price inflation would return to the target band of from 1 to 3 percent in the medium term of the Bank's three-year projection period. The bank's tight monetary policy was pushing the economy to the brink of recession. The spirit of William Phillips's curve imbued the analysis. The grim sequelae of economic shocks—the credit crunch, the deflating of the housing bubble, and the rising prices of commodities—were projected by the Bank to resolve the inflation situation by virtue of an economic slow-down, if not recession, in New Zealand and globally.

The econometric rescripting required, however, an agile articulation of the bank's intentions vis-à-vis the evolution of expectations. The bank is explicit in the statement appended to the Governor's Policy Assessment regarding its intention to *shape* pricing behavior, as follows:

> In these instances, a key to ensuring that medium-term inflation remains an-chored at low levels is that those wage and price setters do not alter their pric-ing behaviours in response to these near-term cost shocks. However, if firms and workers start negotiating prices and wages on the expectation that infla-tion at or above the 3 percent is the norm, then the Bank would have to re-spond with higher interest rates than assumed here. Leaving such behavior unchecked indefinitely would encourage many of the inefficiencies that persis-tently high inflation brings with it, such as distorting price signals and disadvan-taging low or fixed-income household. (RBNZ 2008b, 5)

The Bank thus communicates it intentions unambiguously. But why should the story be believed? Why is it credible?

In a highlighted section of the statement, with the heading "The Policy Target Agreement, and Maintaining Price Stability in Trying Times," the RBNZ reaffirms the intellectual premise of its monetary regime. At the moment when it is anticipated that the CPI target will be violated, a pedagogic opportunity arises, allowing the bank to model explicitly and transparently the rationale guiding policies and the practices of its personnel:

> It is at times like the present, faced with significant cost shocks, that the PTA is particularly valuable. By specifying an agreed medium-term inflation-target, which firms and household can count on being achieved in the medium term, it also provides the scope for us to accommodate temporary deviations from the target—even quite large ones at times. Without the medium-term target, firms and households would have little basis for knowing where future inflation would settle. (RBNZ 2008b, 7)

Monetary policy must in this view appeal to reflexive subjects inhabiting farms, firms, and households, recruiting them to participate in the anchoring of expectations. This entails subtle messages about the nature of time, the structure of motive, and the ability of the bank to influence prices in the medium term:

> The PTA also explicitly notes that there are a range of events, whose impact on the inflation rate would normally be temporary, that could cause actual CPI inflation to deviate from medium-term trend inflation. The implicit directive of the PTA is to "look through" such events and focus on medium-term trend inflation, or what is sometimes called core inflation. The implication of the PTA is that when inflation is outside the target range it is important to have a credible plan to return to target over a long-enough horizon such that the economy does not suffer from unnecessary instability. (RBNZ 2008b,7)

This lesson can be agonizing. New Zealanders were being asked to restrain their expectations—foregoing, notably, demands for higher wages—at a time when many of them were being squeezed, if not overwhelmed, by pricing pressures (Blanchard and Galí 2007). They, the public, were being asked to trust in the efficacy of monetary policy and contingencies of monetary theory to moderate inflation in the future:

> We will generally look through the first-round effects of relative price movements on CPI inflation (such as the effects of the oil price rise on domestic petrol prices). This is the case even if these movements are persistent and evolve

over a number of years. However, we will respond to any impact of relative price movement on inflation expectations and demand pressure. This follows the general principle that monetary policy cannot prevent relative price movements in the economy—because these are real phenomena—but monetary policy should focus on the underlying rate of inflation. (RBNZ 2008b, 7)

Thus, at the time when the quantitative target was breached the econometric allegory became the means for negotiating the complex rhetorical challenge of reshaping expectations pedagogically. The intellectual and institutional credibility of the bank was brought to bear on behavior in an effort to persuade New Zealanders to remain steadfast in their role as central bankers unto themselves.

Curve

At the same time (June 9–11, 2008) that the RBNZ and its governor were contemplating their policy assessment, a conference was taking place in Chatham, Massachusetts, sponsored by the Federal Reserve Bank of Boston, entitled, "Understanding Inflation and the Implications for Monetary Policy: A Phillips Curve Retrospective." The conference was held to commemorate the 50th anniversary of the publication of the New Zealand economist's 1958 article that outlined his famous and contentious framework, introduced at the outset of this chapter. But this was more than a retrospective; Phillips's model was projected onto a field modified by the conventions of inflation targeting, upon which the public had become protagonists, actively making the economy as a nuanced communicative phenomena.

In his opening remarks for the conference, which he hosted, Eric S. Rosengren, the president and chief executive officer of the Federal Reserve Bank of Boston, outlined concisely the historical significance and contemporary relevance of the Phillips curve:

A key element of the Phillips Curve framework is the assumption that significant excess capacity in the economy should exert downward pressure on inflation. While this key link in the Phillips framework provokes considerable skepticism in some quarters, it nonetheless serves as the underpinning of the inflation forecast for many private forecasters, much of Wall Street, and indeed many of the models utilized within the Federal Reserve System.

This widespread use reflects the fact that forecasts of inflation do seem to improve when measures of excess capacity are incorporated. These models derive their success from the simple empirical observation that during recessionary periods, the inflation rate tends to fall. Over the past 50 years, the rate of total CPI inflation has tended to be lower after a recession than before; and the proxies for excess capacity capture this business cycle regularity. The intuition behind this empirical regularity is that, with widespread current and expected excess capacity, firms have greater difficulty increasing prices, workers' expectations of inflation decline, and they thus demand smaller wage increases. As a result, during a recession wage and price inflation slow, and the economy returns to full employment with a lower equilibrium inflation rate.

Despite the heavy reliance on a Phillips Curve empirical framework in many models, the extent and reliability of the short-run tradeoff between excess capacity and the inflation rate remain matters of much debate. In addition, how inflation expectations are set remains an issue that economists are only beginning to understand, and an area of considerable disagreement. (Rosengren 2008, 4–5)

The dynamic framework that Phillips posited traces the inflationary path of the business cycle, emphasizing how recessionary dynamics—the creation of excess capacity—will reduce the utilization of labor and capital, dampening demand across households and industries and thereby restraining or undercutting increases in prices. This is precisely the kind of economic harm the inflation-targeting framework is intended to moderate or to avoid entirely. The magnitude and trajectory of the economic difficulties that coalesced in mid-2008 seemed to prefigure a storm that would inevitably follow the proximate path of the Phillips curve.

In his speech delivered at the conference, "Outstanding Issues in the Analysis of Inflation," Chairman Ben Bernanke reviewed modeling assumptions that addressed the then current pricing drama, but also, as suggested above, he went considerably further. After speaking to the general issues of measuring and forecasting inflation, he turned to the dynamics of learning, invoking implicitly the Keynesian pedagogic habitus:

In a traditional model with rational expectations, a fixed economic structure, and stable policy objectives, there is no role for learning by the public. In such a model, there is generally a unique long-run equilibrium inflation rate which is fully anticipated; in particular, the public makes no inferences based on central bankers' words or deeds. . . . Allowing for the possibility of learning by the public is more realistic and tends to generate more reasonable conclusions about how inflation expectations change and, in particular, about how they can be influenced by monetary policy actions and communications. (Bernanke 2008)

"Learning" in this formulation presupposes reflexive subjects participating fully in unfolding econometric dramas. These subjects have the capacity to continually evaluate the evolution of economic conditions. They are attentive, with every transaction of goods and services, to how information is created, communicated, and contextualized. In the face of shrewd appraisals, blatant hype, and apocalyptic scenarios, these actors model an economy that speaks to their circumstances. Recognition of this simple possibility—that actors can think and learn—reveals the communicative imperative that has formed the premise of this text. It presumes subjects who are themselves actively modeling the economy, anticipating its operation for their own purposes. These insights on the nature of knowledge production and the circulation of economic ideas altered fundamentally my thinking about the operation of performativity. I responded by recontextualizing performativity within the far broader and more far-reaching notion of an economy of words, the representational enterprise creating the economy as a communicative field and empirical fact (Callon 2007; MacKenzie 2003, 2006; Miyazaki 2013).

Models proliferate. Some of them are attuned to the financial press that reports on those monetary scenarios that emanate from central banks; others are aligned with the analyses of government and private-sector economists. Expectations can be informed by astute political commentaries that evaluate alternative econometric scenarios. They can be further informed by the "deep articulations" in which networks of interlocutors continually create metaphors and exchange interpretative stories.

These protagonists learn from employers and employees, from union representatives and managers, from coworkers, friends, and acquaintances. They pursue their modeling of economic conditions in dark corners of local pubs and in meeting halls of dairy cooperatives. They can learn from suppliers, from clients, from sales representatives. Above all, they experience pricing firsthand in their grocery bills, in their mortgages, in their budgeting of income and expenditures for households and firms. They assimilate "folk variants" of the Phillips curve that speak with metaphorical, if not mathematical, precision to their economic circumstances and their existential struggles. They create models in real time drawn from experience allowing them to make inferences about the future—their future—

and it is by virtue of this learning and this modeling that they participate in the alignment of expectations and the evolution of consumer prices (Granovetter 1985; Riles 2001, 2004).

Crunch

I returned to New Zealand on September 16, 2008, and as I walked through the airport, I saw the news flash that Lehman Brothers had collapsed. I knew that the crisis was changing and intensifying, and that the predicament for central banks had shifted decisively. A few days earlier, the RBNZ had reduced the ORC to 7.5 percent, acknowledging that the economy was experiencing a "marked slowdown." By the end of the year, the OCR was further reduced to 5 percent.

In Washington, and in particular, at the New York District Branch of the Federal Reserve System, an unparalleled episode of experimentation in modern economic history was under way. Within a matter of days, fundamental elements of the global financial system were simultaneously dismantled and remade in ways that would have been unthinkable a few weeks, or even days, earlier.

The major commercial banks in New Zealand were under overseas ownership, sparing the nation from the turmoil and expense of directly propping up the banking system, but the curtailment of credit and the ensuing collapse of demand for the nation's exports loomed in late September. What the RBNZ faced was how to anticipate and address the particular aspects of the global crisis in terms of their impacts on various sectors of the New Zealand economy. The inflation-targeting regime provided the principles for addressing the challenge of a new metaphorical and metaphysical predicament: a credit crunch.

The issue in the final quarter of 2008 was to manage a situation in which credit was curtailed and growth was faltering. What had to be modeled communicatively was confidence: the construction of econometric allegories—open to continuous updating and revision—that would convey confidence in the financial system and the central bank (RBNZ 2008b). This had to be achieved as stories proliferated of mounting financial distress, if not panic, and as the data available to central banks became outdated or rendered superfluous as events intervened with astonishing speed. Compounding these communicative challenges were the temporal lags by which disruptions in the financial system affected the real economy, as well as the lags associated with monetary and fiscal policy interventions. Measurable outcomes of policy interventions were inevitably belated (Bollard 2010).

The possibility that infelicitous communications could themselves undermine financial stability and policy outcomes was felt acutely. In response to an earlier draft of this text, here is how a senior economist at the RBNZ, Tim Ng, framed the conundrum posed for central bankers seeking to shape expectations and stabilize, if not restore, confidence:

> There are areas of central banking other than inflation targeting and monetary policy where our words constitute actions intended to change behaviour, and thus the economy. I'm thinking of central banks' behaviour in making calming statements and statements that financial institutions are sound (numerous examples) through the current crisis. In part these are intended to keep financial institutions sound. If we feel there is a risk that depositors might have doubt about that and start a bank run, then the risk is that this doubt will become self-fulfilling. Hence we issue various calming statements to reassure them that we don't know something nasty that we are keeping from the public. So there is a more general phenomenon of central banks trying to influence behaviour by what they say, and steering the economy towards what they believe is a superior outcome. This would only work if central banks are widely believed by the public to be more knowledgeable about the economy and its current state and path than the public itself. Otherwise, we will be revealed to be confidence tricksters. Hence, central banks now spend a lot of time and resources maintaining research departments (typically central banks employ more economists, even in absolute terms, in a single institution than anyone else) and publishing research, in an effort to demonstrate that what they say about the economy and financial system should be believed. As your text argues, we now aspire not to be oracles, but scientists. (Tim Ng, personal communication)

The personnel of the RBNZ took exceptional care to promote precise communications during this tumultuous period. Every interaction with the press, the reporting of each new data series and policy action, was carefully contextualized and intermediated linguistically by bank personnel. As Mike Hannah, head of communications for the RBNZ, emphasized, it was not merely the increased contacts with the press, but the two-way nature of these communications that gained importance during this period. He sought both to anticipate journalists' responses to new information and to preempt misunderstandings and misinterpretations. But he also sought to glean journalists' responses and draw on their expertise to assess the nature of the public's reactions to the details of the unfolding crisis.

At the close of 2008 there was another allegory that began to enter into discussion, albeit tentatively. The RBNZ framed in its December 2008 policy assessment a scenario that with restraint and circumspection began to tell a story of economic recovery. It was a foundational analysis that recapitulated the basic facts of where New Zealand stood in the global economy in the early twenty-first century and the internal dynamics of the economy that would allow, in the medium term, recovery from the crisis. Centrally, this story anticipated improvements in terms of trade fostered primarily by the decline of the Kiwi dollar, and how these circumstances could over time establish the basis of an export-led recovery as global demand reasserted itself at some unspecified time in the future (RBNZ 2008c, 7–14).

The trade story also reveals the deeper shifts that the crisis confirmed, notably that New Zealand was now fully integrated in the economic geography of Australasia and the Asia-Pacific region. Growth in New Zealand, and in its main trading partner, Australia, was increasingly contingent on trade in commodities with China. China, as the crisis demonstrates, was dependent on consumption of its manufactured goods in North America and Europe.

These very basic facts inform the communicative modeling that began the conceptual labor of and for economic recovery. Expectations of a plausible future, and faith in that future, would underwrite economic recovery in New Zealand and globally. The accretion of information and experience over time would further refine and endorse these sentiments. Networks of interlocutors would communicatively mediate changes by which expectations would become intentions and intentions become tangible plans that could materialize in action for consumers and business people. The unforeseen will continually intervene, modifying or recasting these sentiments prospectively. Surprise is inherent in the modeling pursued by individuals and firms as they negotiate the contingencies of economic recovery and learn to act in relationship to inchoate circumstances. Recovery is thus enlivened by "structures of feeling" that can impel growth, but these sentiments operate in the wild and are, as we know, inherently fugitive (Williams 1981). Despite outlines of a plausible recovery at some point in the future, the economic situation in New Zealand at the opening of 2009 continued to deteriorate.

Within the inflation-targeting framework there is always the possibility of errors of analysis and judgment, infelicitous timing and imprecise communications that can yield a range of "suboptimal" outcomes, if not overt failures (Orphanides 2002). Moreover, there is always the possibility that expectations can arise that are resistant to this method of anchoring of prices, or, more broadly, that the evolution of the global economy will introduce new challenges that are refractory from the standpoint of current economic theory and recalcitrant in the face of conventional monetary interventions for managing rational or, for that matter, irrational expectations. In other words, it is precisely the possibility that this framework can "fail" that underwrites the experimental ethos (Miyazaki and Riles 2005).

I made two quick visits to the Reserve Bank Museum to examine the MONIAC more carefully. In late September 2008, in the midst of the credit crunch, I found the refurbished contraption relocated off to the right of the museum's entrance. The director of the museum came over and offered to turn the apparatus on. Water began cascading down from the top of the display along transparent channels and through calibrated valves that regulated the flow of liquid into various chambers that represented different sectors of the macroeconomy. I was not prepared for the simultaneous affect of the apparatus as a computational machine and as a kinetic sculpture. It was a pleasure to view the interplay of art, science, and craftsmanship in Phillips's brilliant model. I was, however, disturbed by one distracting aspect of the refurbishment: the annoying clicking sound of the little motor that recirculated water through the system. It reverberated like some cheap, underpowered child's toy. What were the conservators and refurbishers thinking? I knew that Phillips in the 1940s had used a sturdy hydraulic pump cannibalized from a Lancaster bomber in the original; the replacement sounded limp and pathetic.

My fears were confirmed in January 2009 when I returned again to the display to see if I could use the MONIAC to think through a simple representational problem. Even before I reached the contraption, my colleague in the museum stopped me and confided that the apparatus was inoperable; the motor had failed, water could not circulate, and the velocity of money and credit was zero. Keynesian ideas that Phillips modeled hydraulically had been neglected for decades, and to refurbish them in a matter of days or weeks was, as the malfunctioning machine portended, a difficult task that would yield uncertain outcomes.

At the end of January 2009, the bank had reduced the OCR to 3.5 percent, a record low, and indicated a willingness to go lower still. The gover-

nor noted in his statement the obvious: "The global economy is now in recession and the outlook for international growth has been marked down
considerably since our December Monetary Policy Statement. Globally,
there has been considerable policy stimulus put in place and we expect
this to help bring about a recovery in growth over time. However, there
remains huge uncertainty about the timing and strength of a recovery"
(RBNZ 2009a). Governor Bollard broached, however, one certainty: "Inflation pressures are abating. We have confidence that annual inflation
will be comfortably inside the target band of 1 to 3 percent over the medium term" (RBNZ 2009a).

One final hydraulic detail: New Zealand was the first economy to slip
into recession at the onset of the global financial crisis, but the proximate cause of the downturn was, in fact, unrelated to the crisis. A drought
in New Zealand had depleted the country's reservoirs, reducing hydro-
electric production and thus contributing to a contraction in measures
of GDP.

CHAPTER NINE

Liquidity-Trap Economics

If the interest rate is zero, bonds and money become in effect equivalent assets; so conventional monetary policy, in which money is swapped for bonds via an open-market operation, changes nothing. — Paul Krugman

In late spring 2009 the financial crisis was taking a decisive turn. The banking crisis had stabilized, although the leadership of the Riksbank was still apprehensive about the banking system in the Baltic states that posed particular problems for the major Swedish banks. Governor Stefan Ingves summarized the situation:

> Since the previous meeting there had been a widespread downward revision to forecasts of economic activity abroad. The Riksbank is now expecting to see the weakest economic activity during peacetime since the Great Depression of the 1930s. The crisis was triggered by a turnaround in the credit cycle after a period of growing financial and global imbalances. What was initially described as an essentially financial crisis has now developed into a general, global, macroeconomic crisis but with remaining severe problems in the financial markets. (Sveriges Riksbank 2009b)

Anders Vredin, director of monetary policy, noted:

> The gloomy international developments together with the surprisingly weak GDP outcome for the fourth quarter of 2008 mean that growth in Sweden this year has been revised down by 2.9 percentage points, to minus 4.5 per cent. Growth is also expected to be low in 2010 and unemployment is expected to rise to 11 per cent towards the end of 2010. In total, this development means that resource utilisation will be low throughout the entire forecast period. (Sveriges Riksbank 2009b)

As in the Great Depression, the global threat was the collapse of the aggregate demand sustaining the real economy. With great speed in the fall of 2008, the major economic powers, notably China and the United States, enacted massive stimulus programs, in the spirit of Keynes, to stem the decline in consumption and trade and thus stabilize the real economy.

Another profound concern arose during this period regarding the efficacy of monetary policy in a situation where the major central banks of the world had policy rates approaching zero. "In December last year [2008], the Federal Reserve, for example, cut its policy rate to an interval between 0–0.25 per cent, while in Japan the policy rate is 0.1 per cent and in Switzerland 0.5 per cent" (Svensson 2009, 2). These low policy rates also recalled a stark impasse that Keynes alludes to in *The General Theory of Employment, Interest, and Money* (1936). Keynes diagnosed the monetary anomaly concisely: "There is the possibility ... that, after the rate of interest has fallen to a certain level, liquidity-preference may become virtually absolute in the sense that almost everyone prefers cash to holding a debt which yields so low a rate of interest. In this event the monetary authority would have lost effective control over the rate of interest" (Keynes [1936] 2007, 207).

Controversy over whether or not Keynes was fully convinced of the plausibility of this kind of predicament, known as a "liquidity trap," persists, but the significance of the insight is unmistakable: there are conditions when *conventional* monetary interventions will have little or no impact (Leijonhufvud 1968). Looming for policymakers was the possibility that at precisely the moment when their monetary interventions were most needed, they could be rendered ineffectual by the curious problem posed by the inability to push central bank policy rates below zero.

Central banks, facing a situation in which conventional policy measures for increasing the liquidity available to the financial system had lost their full stimulative effect, embarked on a remarkable series of experiments with new instruments and communicative strategies to address the monetary predicaments posed as interest rates approached what is known as the "zero lower bound." Crucially, the inflation-targeting regime provided the framework for much of this experimentation. It framed a pragmatic series of policies and practices for escaping a liquidity trap by addressing the predicament of the zero lower bound, but it served also as a device for engaging analytically the nature of monetary phenomena and the metaphysics of policy. The framework was thus put at the service of *supporting* prices, preventing them from succumbing to entrenched defla-

tionary expectations. Along with his colleagues Ben Bernanke, Paul Krugman, Chris Sims, and Michael Woodford, Lars Svensson (2001b, 2003,
2006) had thought long and hard about these issues in the late 1990s in his
role as professor of economics at Princeton, as they then sought to solve
the predicaments of the contemporary Japanese economy over depart-
mental lunches. They crafted, along with Adam Posen, Kenneth Kuttner,
Olivier Blanchard, Bennett McCallum and others, a series of radical solutions in the spirit of Keynes's monetary policy *à outrance*.

In early 2009, however, Svensson was deputy governor of the Riksbank and he faced a new challenge: he had to make these vexing issues
in monetary economics, and the unorthodox policies he and his academic
colleagues had developed to deal with them, coherent to his colleagues
on the executive board of the Riksbank and, by extension, to the Swedish
people. The solution that he proposed required the central bank to "credibly promise to be irresponsible," as Paul Krugman (1998) portrayed it
(i.e., to commit to creating inflation), in order to address the severe conditions that the Riksbank faced at the time, or might face if circumstances
worsened.

Less than Zero

When I spoke to Professor Lars E. O. Svensson in his office in the Riksbank, he was on leave from his position at Princeton University to serve as
the deputy governor of the bank. During our conversation, he recounted
for me the story he had been telling since early 2009, focusing on the central problem facing Sweden: that real interest rates, that is, the nominal
interest rate minus the rate of inflation, were too high. The bank's policy
rate—the repo rate—stood at 0.5 percent at the time of our meeting.

At one point during the discussion, I asked Professor Svensson what
the "Taylor rule," the rule of thumb for setting the central bank policy
rate, indicated for the repo rate at that time. With paper and pencil he performed the calculation for a simplified Taylor rule. The result was negative, indicating that the repo rate should be set below zero. This apparent
absurdity—incited by a severe output gap—was the basis for the strategy
he developed for addressing the extreme monetary conditions that prevailed at that time. He also traced out on paper the spreads between the
bank's repo rate and bond market futures. The difference between the
two paths represented the space of disbelief that the Riksbank sought to

narrow. In other words, the bank had to persuade the bond market that the bank's commitment to a very low interest rate was serious and would be enduring, in order to narrow the very large spreads and better align the market's expectations with the bank's intentions (Zaloom 2009).

Svensson sought to take up the challenge of inflation targeting in extremis to address the ominous problems of deflation—specifically, the conundrum of the zero lower bound, the gap between real and nominal interest rates, and the vexations of a liquidity trap. The challenge also required Svensson to adopt a pedagogical stance, taking bewildering ideas from academic economics and rendering them as a candid, public discourse by which the Swedish people could assimilate obscure elements of economic theory as something that mattered to them.

The predicaments that emerged in early 2009 tested not only the analytical assumptions but also the ethical foundations of inflation-targeting. The absurdity of an interest rate below zero challenged the integrity of the monetary regime, redefining its communicative imperatives, given that inflation targeting had become a critically important means for underwriting confidence. The efficacy of the monetary policy no longer merely depended on crafting a credible story about an inflation target per se, the narrative had to address a far more consequential configuration of expectations under extreme conditions.

Svensson's forceful amplification of the theoretical assumptions and practices of inflation targeting laid the groundwork for the emergence of a fully public currency. As we will see, his "foolproof" method for resolving the crisis had unusual analytical and decisive communicative features. In what follows, I engage in an extended examination of one of his speeches that, as is characteristic of his public statements, not only explained the policy issues at stake at the time, but also served as an instrument of pedagogy and persuasion that refined the collaborative relations that gave life to a new monetary regime. It is not merely that Svensson can tell this story better than I can, his account *is* the story.

This chapter thus recounts how the conventions of inflation targeting were transformed to address the unusual predicaments posed by a liquidity trap. His excursion through the "essential logic of liquidity-trap economics," reveals both the stubbornness and plasticity of economic categories (Krugman 1999). In an account that is both playful and deadly serious, Svensson examined the apparent absurdity of pushing interest rates below zero. His account encompasses a range of interventions—that together constituted what he describes as his "foolproof method" of escaping a liquidity trap—most of which were adopted explicitly or implicitly to address the vertiginous monetary conditions that materialized during the crisis. But even those interventions that he proposed that proved too radical or otherwise unacceptable for policymakers are of critical significance insofar as they exposed the theoretical contingencies and practical constraints prevailing during this period. In other words, what follows is a basic articulation of how the major central banks of the world conceptualized the monetary challenges that emerged in the wake of the collapse of Lehman Brothers in September 2008. Svensson and his colleagues—notably Paul Krugman and Ben Bernanke—had systematically analyzed essentially the same conceptual issues a decade earlier to address the financial crisis and the lost decades in Japan. Svensson modeled a monetary reality that in principle policymakers could act upon.

The categories of macroeconomics, the simple distinction between "real" and "nominal" interest rates, the dynamic role of exchange rates, and the intertemporal protocols of inflation targeting provided the conceptual tools to address the central monetary predicaments. But insofar as the solutions to these issues required a reshaping of expectations prospectively, the crisis demanded another form of technical intervention: one that modeled the conceptual solutions communicatively.

Svensson's method encompassed the remarkable analytical work he and his colleagues had developed a decade earlier to address the puzzling nature of the enduring Japanese economic stagnation, which he rearticulated, not as an academic exercise but for the purposes of reconfiguring prevailing propensities to action or inaction in the midst of the Swedish crisis. He translated arcane issues in monetary economics into idioms of policy, into a coherent and workable agenda for escaping the perils of deflation and the inertia of a liquidity trap. By means of these communications, he sought to recruit elite representatives of the Swedish public—and even his colleagues within the Riksbank—to the task of resolving the crisis by recasting their expectations, their belief, and their skepticism about the future.

Japanese Conundrum

In order to understand Svensson's efforts, we need to briefly examine elements of the Japanese conundrum. Why had the vibrant and robust expansion of the Japanese economy that marked most of the postwar era suddenly succumbed to the lurching slump that had plagued the Japanese economy into the new century? These "lost decades," as they are termed, posed questions for monetary economics and, indeed, they reopened classic issues about the etiology of the Great Depression:

> The short-term nominal interest rate in Japan collapsed to zero in the second half of the 1990s. Furthermore, the Bank of Japan (BoJ) more than doubled the monetary base through traditional and non-traditional measures to increase prices and stimulate demand. The BoJ policy of "quantitative easing" from 2001 to 2006, for example, increased the monetary base by over 70 per cent in that period. By most accounts, however, the effect on prices was sluggish at best. (As long as five years after the beginning of quantitative easing, the changes in the CPI and the GDP deflator were still only starting to approach positive territory)." (Eggertsson 2008)

In December 1999, prompted by the Japanese case, Paul Krugman began his analysis of the liquidity trap with a rhetorical statement that framed his remarkably prescient insights in relation to the challenge it posed for monetarism:

> We live in the Age of the Central Banker ... in which monetary policy is generally believed to be so effective that it cannot safely be left in the hands of politicians who might use it to their advantage. Through much of the world, quasi-independent central banks are now entrusted with the job of steering economies between the rocks of inflation and the whirlpool of deflation. Their judgment is often questioned, but their power is not.
>
> It is therefore ironic as well as unnerving that precisely at this moment, when we have all become sort-of monetarists, the long-scorned Keynesian challenge to monetary policy—the claim that it is ineffective at recession-fighting, because you can't push on a string—has reemerged as a real issue. So far only Japan has actually found itself in liquidity-trap conditions, but if it has happened once it can happen again, and if it can happen here it presumably can happen elsewhere. So even if Japan does eventually emerge from its slump, the question of how it became trapped and what to do about it remains a pressing one. (Krugman 1999)

Krugman proceeded to work out the "essential logic of liquidity-trap economics," and he then laid out a series of alternative monetary strategies to deal with the Japanese situation.

Krugman began his analysis candidly with his own initial skepticism about the plausibility of the liquidity trap—viewing it initially as an artifact of "intellectual corner-cutting" of the standard Keynesian/Hicksian IS-LM framework.[1] He then went on to delineate his approach, showing how a liquidity trap *can* happen and, more importantly, how it can be escaped:

> So the intertemporal approach led me to a different destination than I expected. I thought it would show that the liquidity trap was not a real issue, that without the inconsistencies of the IS-LM model it would become clear that it could not really happen. Instead it turns out that a liquidity trap can indeed happen; but that it is in a fundamental sense an expectational issue. Monetary expansion is irrelevant because the private sector does not expect it to be sustained, because they believe that given a chance the central bank will revert to type and stabilize prices. And in order to make monetary policy effective, at least in a simple model, the central bank must overcome a credibility problem that is the inverse of our usual one. In a liquidity trap monetary policy does not work because the markets expect the bank to revert as soon as possible to the normal practice of stabilizing prices; to make it effective, the central bank must credibly promise to be irresponsible, to maintain its expansion after the recession is past. (Krugman 1999)

Krugman then concludes:

> Let me say this perhaps more forcefully than I have in the past. Inflation targeting is not just a clever idea—a particular proposal that might work in fighting a liquidity trap. *It is the theoretically "correct" response*—that is, inflation targeting is the way to achieve in a sticky-price world the same result that would obtain if prices were perfectly flexible. Of course in policy the perfect is the enemy of the good, and I would not oppose trying a variety of tactics to fight Japan's stagnation. But it is inflation targeting that most nearly approaches the usual goal of modern stabilization policy, which is to provide adequate demand in a clean, unobtrusive way that does not distort the allocation of resources." (Krugman 1999, emphasis in original)

By early 2009, these circumstances, as Krugman had foreseen, were manifest globally, and the solution he outlined became the basis of the "unorthodox" monetary policy pursued by major central banks (Posen 2010; Tucker 2009).

Foolproof Method

There was an unmistakable urgency and impatience to Svensson's account in 2009. As he put it in a speech early that year: "Many observers criticised the Japanese central bank for having reacted far too slowly and for being too cautious about testing various methods to escape from their liquidity trap. I believe that we at the Riksbank should be prepared with analyses and measures at an early stage" (Svensson 2009, 2). But, more immediately, he made clear that over and above the challenge of crafting a story to shape the expectations of the Swedish public was the hurdle of overcoming opposition to his radical prescriptions from within the Riksbank's executive board.

The resistance had two key elements. As Svensson acknowledged openly, while inflation was declining rapidly, there was no evidence of serious deflationary problems at that time, nor was there a threat of a sustained period of falling prices on the immediate horizon. And, perhaps more importantly, the "foolproof" experiments he espoused threatened to disrupt the carefully crafted communicative understandings that the bank had sought to nurture by introducing new conceptual issues that the Swedish public did not fully comprehend and strategies that might break with the bank's emphatic commitment to candor. Professor Svensson understood that he was pushing the inflation-targeting experiment into uncertain realms, realms in which the regime would have to sustain far more complex, preemptive communications in order to raise inflationary expectations:

> With a zero lower bound for the interest rate the central bank's credibility and its possibilities to affect inflation expectations are even more important than usual. I myself am convinced that the central bank's credibility can best be served by an open and transparent discussion of all of the available alternatives. This discussion should be held in good time before any of these alternatives may be needed, but in the hope that none of them will be needed. With a broad understanding that forceful measures are available, and with a readiness by the central bank to resort to these methods if the situation should so require, the general public and the market need not fear that the central bank will lose control of the situation and of inflation expectations in a situation with a zero interest rate. (Svensson 2009, 14)

But this action posed an abiding question: Is the foolproof method a creative extension and modification of the inflation-targeting regime, or is it a breach of the communicative relationship that the regime had established between the bank and the Swedish people? Svensson's proposal, and the opposition to it, revealed how under severe conditions policymakers struggle analytically and ethically with the communicative imperatives of the contemporary monetary regime. Insofar as communications are critical, I cleave closely to Svensson's own words aimed at renovating monetary reality. Let me be clear, his argumentation was at the time technically very challenging and by no means intended for a general audience. He no doubt understood that key elements of his analysis needed to be told and retold and gradually refined to make them persuasive, not merely to business, financial, and academic elites, but to broader segments of the Swedish public. Members of the Riksbank's board undertook part of this role of retelling and critical reflection on Svensson's message, as we will see in the next chapter.

Real Interest Rate

To say that interest rates are too high sounds remarkably simple. But again, under conditions of the zero lower bound, the problem is perplexing. Put simply, if a central bank's policy rate, the Riksbank's repo rate, is already so low that there is no room for downward adjustments, since the rate cannot be set below zero, what can monetary authorities do?

> The real interest rate is the nominal interest rate minus expected inflation. When the Riksbank cuts the repo rate the real repo rate also normally falls as inflation expectations are normally sluggish. In a situation with very weak aggregate demand, a low level of resource utilisation and low inflation a low and perhaps even a negative real interest rate is required to stimulate the real economy and thus, as far as possible, stabilise inflation around the inflation target and resource utilisation around a normal level.
>
> The Riksbank cannot, however, cut the repo rate more than to zero. But even if the repo rate is set at zero, the real interest rate may be too high to have the desired stimulation effect on the real economy. In such a situation monetary policy faces a binding zero lower bound for the interest rate. The major question is then how monetary policy should be conducted, to avoid a binding zero lower bound and to escape from such a situation by using means other than lowering the interest rate. (Svensson 2009, 1)

Svensson outlined the general nature of the threat:

> Inflation throughout the world is also falling rapidly. It is possible that the level of inflation can become negative and that we will thus see deflation in some

countries. Deflation for a short period is not a major problem. We even had this in Sweden a few years ago. But if deflation is prolonged, and especially if inflation expectations fall and deflation expectations arise, the situation can become very problematic. The combination of very low policy rates, a weak real economy and the risk of deflation has thus revived the debate about how monetary policy can and should be conducted in the event of a zero interest rate bound.

For Sweden, a scenario with deflation and a zero interest rate is as yet not particularly likely. However, at the Riksbank we must of course be prepared for all eventualities and consider what measures would be possible and appropriate in such a situation. We must also think about how we can minimise the risk of ending up in such a situation. (Svensson 2009, 2)

He clarified what constitutes the real interest rate[2]:

I have already said that, in the case of a binding zero lower bound for the interest rate, the real interest rate is too high compared to the level appropriate to stabilise inflation around the inflation target and at the same time stabilise the real economy. To be precise, it is the real market rate, that is the market rate met by households and firms minus expected inflation, that is too high. The market rate exceeds the repo rate with a spread that is determined by various risk and liquidity premia. This spread is now unusually large due to the financial crisis. This means that the market rates are positive even if the repo rate is zero. (Svensson 2009, 3)

He turned to a means for intervening in the bond market to push down rates so that they were more closely aligned with the bank's policy rate:

Even if the repo rate is reduced to zero, the real market rate can be too high, because the spread is large and/or because the expected inflation is low. The real market interest rate can thus be lowered, if the spread can be reduced. The measures implemented by the central banks and other authorities in various countries to improve the functioning of the financial markets, what Ben Bernanke calls "credit easing," can reduce the spread and thus contribute to a lower market rate. However, even if the various spreads are still larger than normal, it is, quantitatively probably only a rather moderate reduction of the real market rate that is possible in this way. The really substantial effect on the real market rate can instead be achieved if inflation expectations can be raised. (Svensson 2009, 3)

He examined how the play of expectations might induce a policy nightmare:

It is particularly dangerous if ... expectations of deflation arise, that is expectations of negative inflation. The real interest rate may then become far too
high. A nightmare for central banks is a downward spiral, in which a too high
real interest rate slows down the economy and leads to increasing deflation
and expectations of decreasing inflation, which in turn lead to a still higher real
interest rate that slows down the real economy even more and leads to even
greater deflation. (Svensson 2009, 3)

Svensson outlined policies that the central bank *could* potentially employ in the event that the crisis worsened or remained unresolved. He
sought to reassure an elite Swedish public that there were other means of
intervention that the central bank had in its repertoire of policy tools—
albeit experimental tools—if conventional strategies of intervention lost
their efficacy. He also demonstrated how central bankers in these circumstances depended heavily on words to perform the labor of monetary policy. Modeling the economy linguistically and communicatively
was an overriding concern; averting disastrous outcomes depended fundamentally on shaping public expectations preemptively with persuasive
communications.

Svensson, as a senior official of the bank, was thus carefully negotiating the problem of the bank's "reputational risk" and, again, the dynamics
of confidence in extremis. He not only had to explain unorthodox experiments in monetary policy, he had to recruit the Swedish public and the
markets to participate in the achievement of specific policy ends broadly,
as we have seen above, to sustain the level of prices in the face of deflationary pressures. The reputational issue for central banks was simple: Do
they have the tools to underwrite confidence and thus resolve the crisis?

Three Steps

Svensson outlined in the speech delivered in Stockholm, a speech that
closely tracks his academic writings, the stark economic challenges taking shape in February 2009 at the height of the crisis. Here again is the
challenge:

With a zero lower bound it is therefore important for the central banks to affect and raise inflation expectations in some way. How this should be done is
the real problem with a zero lower bound for the interest rate and a liquidity
trap. It may even be necessary to raise inflation expectations above the inflation

target for a while in order to achieve a sufficiently low real interest rate. This means that the central bank must get people to believe that it will knowingly and deliberately strive to exceed the inflation target. How can a central bank that normally strives to create low inflation expectations and meet the inflation target promise, with any credibility, that it will exceed the inflation target in the future? When we discuss and evaluate various policy alternatives for monetary policy in a liquidity trap, we should thus start from the most important criteria for assessing their effectiveness—how effective alternatives will be in affecting inflation expectations. (Svensson 2009, 3–4)

Svensson then enumerated his heretical three steps, encompassing his "foolproof way," as he termed it, for escaping from a liquidity trap for a small, open economy. He focused first on endowing the inflation target with a "memory," and second, on tethering the exchange rate to a price-level target. The former is an elegant and well-known approach that is in fact part of the official policy framework of the Reserve Bank of Australia, the objective of which is to achieve an inflation rate of 2–3 percent, *on average*, over the medium term.

Svensson elaborated on the curious assertion that an inflation target can be endowed with a memory, imparting a compensatory means to correct for under- or overshooting the target:

> In a case where there is a risk that inflation will be too low, or even negative, for a couple of years it may be appropriate, in order to avoid the disadvantage with a standard inflation target ... to tighten the inflation target and temporarily interpret it as a target of 2 per cent for average inflation over the next five years, for example. This would mean that the central bank would then compensate for low inflation during the first years with higher inflation in the subsequent years so that the five-year average is on target.... If the central bank by means of convincing analyses and forecasts can gain credibility for such a temporary price level target—a temporary average inflation target—the price level target's inherent stabilisation of the real economy could then be used. (Svensson 2009, 5)

Manipulating the exchange rate was far more radical, reintroducing into monetary policy what some monetary authorities find distasteful. More than distasteful, this second element of Svensson's proposal augured competitive and potentially self-defeating devaluations of the world's currencies, which would amount to a "currency war." Understanding his second strategy required a brief aside on monetary theory; its aims were, however, rather simple: "An exchange rate target that is consistent with the price level target is announced and the exchange rate is pegged to this exchange rate target until the price level target is attained. If, for example, the price level is to be raised by 10 per cent, the exchange rate target is set so that the currency depreciates by 10 per cent" (Svensson 2009, 7). This kind of intervention turns on the key observation that the exchange rate—unlike the policy rate—has no lower or upper bound.[3] Bank interventions are focused on the currency markets: "The currency is depreciated and the exchange rate held at a temporary exchange rate target until the price level target has been attained" (11).

This second strategy required a bit more clarification, to explain how the exchange rate can serve as a tool to influence the price level in the future. Starting with the "interest rate parity rule," Svensson demonstrated the analytical link between the current exchange rate and the expected future price level, and then noted the following key point for policy interventions[4]:

> The direct link between the current exchange rate and the expected future price level first leads ... to the insight that the current exchange rate depends on the expected future price level and can be used as an indicator of the latter. But the link also leads to the idea that cause and effect can be reversed. Instead of the expected future price level determining the current exchange rate, the current exchange rate can determine the expected future price level. To be more precise, the exchange rate can be used as a policy instrument when it is no longer possible to lower the interest rate because it is already zero. Unlike the policy rate, the exchange rate has no upper or lower limit, as Bennett McCallum pointed out early in the discussion of Japan's liquidity trap. (Svensson 2009, 6–7)

Ben Bernanke pointed to the most far-reaching historical example of this strategy: "A striking example from U.S. history is Franklin Roosevelt's 40 percent devaluation of the dollar against gold in 1933–34, enforced by a program of gold purchases and domestic money creation. The devaluation and the rapid increase in money supply it permitted ended the U.S. deflation remarkably quickly. Indeed, consumer price inflation in the United States, year on year, went from −10.3 percent in 1932 to −5.1 percent in 1933 to 3.4 percent in 1934" (Bernanke 2002a). Svensson's strategy thus had historical precedent both in Sweden and the US; a depreciation of the currency was engineered by holding to a temporary exchange-rate target until the price level target had been attained. The method had proved effective in creating expectations of a higher future price level, and thereby simultaneously providing stimulation to the real economy (Svensson 2009, 11).

Svensson's policy of last resort amounted to a strategy to achieve a monetary expansion by means other than by changing the policy rate:

> This method is a very drastic action. It shows that the central bank really means business and lends credibility to the price level target. It may therefore affect expectations of the future price level much more than any other measure. The method is verifiable as it consists of action and not just talk, and its logic is very clear. Raised inflation expectations would reduce the real interest rate, stimulate the real economy and increase inflation, and the price level would move upwards towards the price level target. The real economy would also be stimulated directly by the fact that exporting and import-competing sectors would be affected positively by the short-term real depreciation that would arise due to the short-term sluggishness of the price level. (Svensson 2009, 7–8)

Svensson emphatically discounted criticisms that this method would amount to untoward currency manipulation[5]

> Every measure that managed to increase expectations of the future price level would in fact also automatically lead to a weakening of the currency. Using the exchange rate as a policy instrument should therefore not be seen as more controversial than using any other method that leads to expectations of a higher future price level. (Svensson 2009, 8)

The third element of the strategy is initiated when the price level target is achieved: "The currency is allowed to float and monetary policy returns to normal, either with the old inflation target or with the continued use of a price level target if this is deemed to be advantageous in the longer term" (Svensson 2009, 7).

In the next chapter, I delve more deeply into the problem of translating monetary economics into a public discourse. Specifically, I will examine the deliberations within the Riksbank's executive board's monetary policy meeting of April 20, 2009, and, among other things, how Professor Svensson's views operated within this discursive space.

When Professor Svensson entered the boardroom of the Riksbank to discuss policy matters, his analytical work in monetary economics took on a different significance, his confidence in his "foolproof" method notwithstanding. When he introduced his academic insights to the discussions with other members of the bank's board, engaging their perspectives, a different means and method for modeling the Swedish economy unfolded. The deliberations of the Riksbank's executive board represent not merely a simulation of abstract economic conditions, but the articulation of what I believe is the ethical foundations of the inflation-targeting regime. Technical matters became acute social concerns, as the members of the board confronted an audience, the Swedish public—an immanent public—whose members had to be persuaded by their insights and their commentary. The constitution of the public, as we will see, was increasingly important in the refinements of the inflation-targeting experiment for the purposes of imparting confidence.

They, the six members of the board, had to arrive at a policy stance that was not merely correct from the standpoint of monetary economics, but a stance that could sustain the bank's persuasive authority. Svensson's interventions during the April meeting of the board went to the heart of these issues, and seemed to challenge the carefully crafted relationship the bank had refined for years with the people of Sweden.

CHAPTER TEN

The Overheard Conversation

We also put a great deal of pedagogic effort to it all. — Lars Heikensten, Governor of the Riksbank (2003–05)

When I visited the Riksbank in 2009, the prevailing challenge for the bank, and for virtually all central banks globally, was the restoration of confidence, as I indicated in the prior chapter. Inflation targeting was refunctioned for this purpose. Its communicative conventions—and specifically the status of the monetary policy story—assumed an overriding importance as the exigencies of monetary policy and financial stability converged. Rather than merely anchoring expectations about a price target, the communicative protocols were realigned to address the spectrum of sentiments and expectations that can underwrite or undercut public confidence. Controlling the parameters of the monetary policy story and communicating them with care and circumspection served as the vehicle for imparting confidence at a time of considerable uncertainty.

As Graham Smart (2006) has argued, the monetary policy story is perpetually updated and continually interpreted and reinterpreted. It is, however, routinely stabilized textually during the Riksbank's bimonthly executive board meetings, albeit fleetingly. The story is embodied in two textual forms: first, as the Monetary Policy Update (initially presented to the board as a draft); and second, as the minutes of the board's deliberations published two weeks after each meeting. The Monetary Policy Update is the outcome of institutional discussions, primarily on the part of the research personnel of the bank. The minutes of the meeting represent responses to and elaborations on the Update, primarily on the part of board members. The minutes thus record how the monetary policy narrative—developed in conversation—was spoken by policymakers who

carefully parsed the story, conferring on it emphasis, coherence, verisimili-
tude, and thus, persuasive power. Here again, we have access to how the
economy is modeled linguistically for emphatic, performative purposes.

Anders Vredin, as director of monetary policy, was responsible for the
regular drafting of the Monetary Policy Update, a report that ran about
eight pages with a few additional pages of appendices and charts, etc. The
text, completed just prior to the Riksbank board meeting, provided the
immediate point of departure for the conversations. Like the reports of
the Reserve Bank of New Zealand, which we examined in chapters 6
and 7, the monetary policy story in Sweden unfolded in response to the
particular circumstance facing the Swedish and global economies in early
2009, while simultaneously having continuity with prior reports and anticipating future revisions and updates.

Vredin had participated in the development and refinement of the
inflation-targeting regime in the Riksbank, and he was acutely aware of
how details of economic and monetary analysis assume a communicative
dynamic as part of what is an unfolding policy conversation. He also fully
understood that over and above robust programs of economic and monetary research, a communicative relationship that the bank had carefully
cultivated with the Swedish public was, and will continue to be, at the
heart of the inflation-targeting regime, and perhaps its most valuable feature. He understood too that the efficacy of monetary policy engendered
collaboration with various segments and strata of Swedish society. By virtue of the attentively crafted relationship that the bank had refined over
decades with its various constituencies, the public learned to entrust their
expectations to the bank's communicative agenda (Heikensten and Vredin 2002; Jansson and Vredin 2004).

The conversation among the members of the committee was unusually
expressive at the April meeting. No particular data series, no particular
variables, were decisive in their deliberations. Rather, members carefully
contextualized the overall economic situation as a framework for modeling, and thus animating, faith and credit. But, of course, they themselves
were performing this intellectual labor from within one of the key institutions charged with managing economic and financial affairs; hence their
representational labor, their conversation, was itself the material shaping
a dynamic contextual and situational field (Latour 2005; Westbrook 2008).

The more-or-less contemporaneous publication of the board's meeting
minutes was not merely an adjunctive element to the inflation-targeting
regime; rather, it was an instrument that had a profound function in its

own right. The dynamic monetary story presented in the minutes was an instrument for simulating and imparting confidence.

Conversation

The deliberations of the executive board are by no means bereft of spontaneity or surprise, but the positions articulated are typically well rehearsed. They have been discussed among participants prior to each of their six annual meetings, and they are aligned with the draft monetary policy statement that, among other things, projects a three-year path for the repo rate—the bank's long-range public projection, a distinctive feature of the Swedish experiment in inflation targeting—with specific recommendations for setting the policy rate. There is a strong serial character to these interventions, as each board member's position develops from meeting to meeting. In this way, their particular orientations become well known, if not entirely predictable, over time. Their positions were also, as we saw in the case of Svensson, communicated through rounds of public speeches and news conferences, particularly the one immediately following the meeting. The most direct access to the meeting is via the published minutes, a draft of which is made available soon after the board's meeting, allowing participants to make emendations and clarifications of their respective positions prior to publication. The minutes do not, however, succumb to predictable set pieces; rather, they encompass an active engagement between and among members of the board as they seek to fully explain their positions and their motives and thus model the economy communicatively (Abolafia 2004, 2005).

Centrally, the meetings assume an audience. The six members of the board outline positions, which serve as vehicles for addressing concerns of specific target groups: "There are several target groups for the Riksbank's communication and they include members of the Riksdag [the Swedish parliament], companies, households, banks and other participants in the financial markets, government agencies, organisations, media and employees of the Riksbank" (Sveriges Riksbank 2009a, 1–2). Their conversation yields a multilayered story about the then present conditions, while outlining a range of scenarios anticipating future economic and monetary circumstances. Members bring to the meeting their own technical expertise, their own network of contacts, and their own particular engagement with official and unofficial data, imparting diverse perspectives on the deliberation. Perhaps most importantly, the minutes begin to clarify, albeit implicitly, who constitutes the audience for monetary policy or, more figuratively, who is listening in on the board's deliberations. In my conversations at the Riksbank, particularly with Anders Vredin and his staff, and in subsequent conversations at the Bank of England, an immanent, as opposed to an abstracted, public came into view. Although I had acknowledged this possibility earlier, as we saw in chapter 3, it was in the following conversation among members of the Riksbank executive board that the proximity of the public emerged fully and consequentially.

The meeting in April 2009 was unusually important for this research for two other, interrelated reasons. First, insofar as the meeting unfolded when quantitative data were particularly difficult to read analytically, interpretation assumed a decisive role. Through their discussions, the members of the board carefully constructed the contemporary context of economic action, a communicative field infused with subtle and not-so-subtle configurations of feelings, sentiments, and expectations that, insofar as it conveyed interpretive coherence, could lend support to confidence—an active confidence that could be read from countless perspectives by the citizens of Sweden.

Second, in the situation the board faced in early 2009, members drew on experience, judgment, and moral suasion to control the parameters of the monetary policy story, and thus the public perception, understanding, and experience of the crisis. Confidence under these conditions required board members to orchestrate by means of a persuasive conversation what amounts to leaps of faith. The board members had to devise a basis for action motivated not merely or necessarily by rationality or reason.

I have emphasized the importance of the monetary policy story, and below I reproduce extended excerpts from the minutes of the Riksbank's executive board monetary policy meeting of April 20, 2009 (Sveriges Riksbank 2009b), in order to illustrate the process by which the story emerges and is elaborated. The members of the board speak directly to issues that have been the central preoccupations of this text, at an unusually important juncture. With great skill they model the financial and economic conditions linguistically and communicatively.

Communicative Field

The meeting opened with a brief, technical overview of "economic developments," with financial and monetary conditions presented by Mattias

Persson, the head of the Financial Stability Department, and by Anders Vredin, the head of the Monetary Policy Department. The draft Monetary Policy Update, as we saw in the last chapter, recommended an immediate cut of the repo rate, which stood at 1 percent at the time, to 0.5 percent. GDP growth was forecast at minus 4.5 percent for 2009, with CPI inflation running slightly negative for the year, and with unemployment expected to rise to 11 percent by the end of 2010. The Update further noted the obvious: conventional monetary policy was reaching its lower limit.[1] The discussion of the board focused on the background to and consequences of this recommendation.

Lars Svensson set the tone at the outset of the conversation with his review of "economic developments abroad," as summarized in the minutes:

> Svensson opened the discussion. He noted that the picture of developments abroad is very gloomy. Mr Svensson agreed with the view of international developments presented in the draft Monetary Policy Update. The forecasts for the real economy and inflation abroad have been revised down since the previous monetary policy meeting in February. Mr Svensson considered that many indicators of global economic developments were now showing a similar course to that at the beginning of the Great Depression, which gave cause for concern.

Economic forecasts were being revised downward and a precise assessment of the global economy was, at best, difficult. Each member of the committee sought nonetheless to give a tentative narrative structure to the economic predicaments facing the global economy. The commentary was restrained and matter of fact, and yet an unmistakable drama lurks in each intervention, as participants searched for a means to articulate a coherent and a responsible narrative.

Lars Nyberg's survey of conditions followed the appraisal outlined in the Monetary Policy Update:

> Deputy Governor Lars Nyberg essentially shared the gloomy view of international developments. World trade has continued to fall. . . . Capital inflows to most emerging economies have largely ceased. Unemployment has reached all-time highs in many countries and is expected to increase further. No positive signs can be seen in Europe.

Nyberg described a general scenario by which financial markets could be reanimated, if and when the appetite for risk returned:

When Lehman Brothers filed for bankruptcy in September last year, risk propensity among investors in credit instruments declined dramatically. There is
now substantial liquidity in many funds, hedge funds and insurance companies. This liquidity is waiting to be invested. At the same time there are companies with essentially sound conditions that will survive the crisis, and these
need funding. This applies to both financial and non-financial companies. When
investors are willing to begin taking slightly more risk again and companies
realise that they will have to pay slightly higher interest rates, the market will
slowly rise back on its feet.

Nyberg added that these positive circumstances would in all likelihood begin to surface even as the economic downturn continued to
worsen:

> It is therefore not unreasonable that the credit markets should come to life at
> the same time as the credit losses in the banks are growing and the economic
> downturn is continuing. . . . Companies with good credit ratings are now able to
> borrow. Other markets where activity has been almost non-existent since Sep-
> tember last year have also begun to slowly come back to life.

Deputy Governor Karolina Ekholm reiterated the nature of the challenges for Swedish trade and the degree to which the fate of Sweden was
tethered to economic conditions in Europe and the US:

> Ekholm shared the gloomy view and did not in principle envisage any rays of
> light. . . . Experiences from the 1930s show that a deep recession can involve
> temporary upturns. In addition, the real economic downturn in the United
> States is continuing, with falling employment and increased unemployment.
>
> Developments in Europe appear to be following the same patterns as in
> the United States, though with some time lag. A recovery in the United States
> is to be expected before a recovery in Europe. The problems in the German
> economy are troublesome for Sweden, which is strongly dependent on trade
> with Germany. Sweden risks facing a long period of weak demand for export
> goods.

Svante Öberg, who holds the position of first deputy governor, endorsed the analysis presented in the draft Monetary Policy Update, while
asserting that the risks to the forecasts were for further downward revisions. He further elaborated on the synchronized nature of the global

downturn and referred to an IMF report on how these events have historically played out:

> According to the IMF, the current financial crisis will probably result in an unusually long and deep recession as a result of the financial and global nature of the crisis. The IMF bases its analysis on earlier recessions in 21 developed countries since 1960. Its conclusion is that recessions associated with financial crises tend to be more serious and that the recoveries tend to be slower than normal. If the recessions are moreover globally synchronised, they tend to be even longer and to be followed by even weaker recoveries....
>
> Expectations are largely in line with the average of the five large financial crises in the industrial world during the post-war period ("the big five") and moreover in line with the average for recessions associated with financial crises and synchronised recessions, according to the IMF.

Governor Ingves drew attention to the coordination among monetary authorities globally:

> The authorities in different countries have taken a large number of conventional and non-conventional policy measures. One important question is whether this can reduce pessimism and infuse new confidence in the future. With all of the measures that have now been taken, the world economy is not facing a financial meltdown. The financial system is functioning tolerably, but only as the result of massive public sector support measures.

He then emphasized the problems of contagion globally and the risk of a very slow and uneven recovery from the crisis:

> But the risks remain in international terms with regard to self-reinforcing contagion effects between weak real economies and under-capitalised financial systems. In addition, the collapse in world trade is continuing. When trade credits are frozen, this disturbs the global supply chain of input goods needed before a product is ready for sale. In addition to declining demand, world trade is also therefore hit by supply shocks related to funding problems. Moreover, previous experiences show that the process of adjustment risks becoming long drawn-out, particularly in countries where saving has been low for a long time before the adjustment begins. Countries have different capacities and willingness to resolve problems in the financial sector; countries have also been hit by greater or smaller declines in export demand. This should mean

that when economic activity improves, it will not be in an entirely synchronised manner.

Deputy governor Barbro Wickman-Parak returned to the draft Monetary Policy Statement, agreeing with the modestly positive forecast of recovery it projected; she also allowed for the possibility of a more positive economic outcome and a more rapid restoration of confidence:

> The further ahead one looks, the more uncertain the forecasts are, of course. This is always the case, but the uncertainty is particularly great on this occasion for several reasons. The effects of the expansionary fiscal policy are uncertain and it is extremely difficult to assess when the normalisation of the financial markets will begin and confidence will be restored.
>
> Although Ms Wickman-Parak supported the forecast in the main scenario in the February Report, she considered then that there was reason to pay attention to the alternative scenario based on a more rapid recovery abroad and she also wished to highlight this possibility today. The motive for this is, as in February, that the financial system is undergoing a massive confidence crisis that has made a lasting impression on the real economy. Once confidence is restored, an upturn may be stronger than expected.

Finally, Wickman-Parak reiterated how confidence would reassert itself over time as the outlines of a discernable future became visible and plausible in people's daily lives. The global efforts to address the crisis and the cooperation among global central banks created the field upon which these kinds of scenarios could be built.

The board's deliberations turned to the issues of "economic developments in Sweden and the monetary policy decision." Mr. Öberg reviewed the weak economy and its influence on the key measure of consumer price inflation and the value of the krona. His account is very much in line with the Update:

> Öberg began the discussion by pointing out that in the draft Monetary Policy Update it is clearly shown that Sweden is in a severe recession. The Riksbank is now assuming that GDP will fall by 4.5 per cent this year and that the recovery will thereafter be fairly slow. Mr Öberg considered this reasonable as a main scenario, but as with international developments his assessment was that the risks of an even worse scenario weighed heavier. . . .
>
> He explained that he therefore considers that the Riksbank should cut the

repo rate to 0.5 per cent. Moreover, economic developments over the coming years look to be so weak that it is appropriate to keep the repo rate at a very low level for a long period of time.

At every point in their discussion of these technical issues, board members were sensitive to the Riksbank's credibility. Indeed, the management of credibility was an overriding concern of the participants.

Turning Things on Their Head

As the meeting proceeded, Lars Svensson introduced his proposal for unconventional monetary interventions. By now, his colleagues were all familiar with his positions and his inclination to turn things on their head and to argue against the grain. The position he staked out at the meeting recapitulated many of the points he had made earlier, but also opened some new issues. Again, he was emphatic about the urgent need to develop instruments of monetary policy to provide economic stimulus. He sought to explain to the members of the board and the public what he believed were the urgent circumstances that faced the Swedish and global economies:

> With a zero interest rate the major risk is that monetary policy will be too contractionary.... The danger with a zero interest rate is thus if spreads increase, if inflation expectations fall or if the krona appreciates. This makes monetary policy more contractionary and causes resource utilisation to fall and unemployment to rise.
>
> This shows how things are turned upside down with the zero interest rate bound, and how important it is not to become entrenched in traditional ways of thinking. It is often excessively high inflation expectations that have earlier been a problem in monetary policy. Now it is excessively low inflation expectations that are the problem. Previously, an excessively weak currency has often been a problem in monetary policy. Now it is an overly strong currency that is a problem and can make monetary policy too contractionary, while a weak currency helps to make monetary policy more expansionary and better-balanced. These circumstances entail a formidable intellectual and educational challenge.

The nature of the task was, as he understood it, to alter ways of thinking about money and monetary policy:

According to Mr Svensson, the intellectual challenge for the Riksbank is to get used to thinking along these new lines, to realise that high inflation expectations and a weak krona are good news now and make it easier for the Riksbank to stabilise the real economy. . . .

The educational challenge is to explain this new way of thinking and this new role for inflation expectations and the exchange rate to the general public and to market participants.

More precisely, the task entailed recasting the sensibilities of the public and market participants, altering the fundamental structure of their expectations about inflation. The radical nature of Mr. Svensson's recommendations was packaged in the language of "balance" and justified in terms of the limitation of conventional monetary strategies. He turned again to his technical analysis of the peculiar circumstances in which inflationary expectations are falling, pushing up real interest rates:

Inflation expectations in January this year were 1.1 and 1.5 per cent for the first and second years respectively. The average for the two first years was thus 1.3 per cent. Now in April they have fallen so they are 0.9 and 1.5 per cent for the first and second years respectively. The average for the first two years has thus fallen from 1.3 to 1.2 per cent, not very much but moving in the wrong direction. . . . This therefore means that inflation expectations are much lower than they should be according to historical patterns. All in all, inflation expectations are thus low and falling slightly. They thus give rise to a higher real interest rate and a more contractionary monetary policy. This is a cause for concern and must be monitored in the future.

He grounded the analysis in a less abstract and more compelling way by reframing it in terms of employment and the exchange rate:

Whether monetary policy is expansionary or contractionary is also affected very much by the exchange rate when the repo rate is close to zero and cannot be adjusted. According to an alternative scenario similar to that published in Monetary Policy Report 2008:3, the exchange rate has a very large effect on resource utilisation, employment and unemployment. A weakening of the krona by 5 per cent over the coming years compared with the Riksbank's forecast could now in round figures raise employment by 1 per cent and thereby could save approximately 50,000 jobs.

Correspondingly, a strengthening of the krona by 5 per cent compared with the forecast could lead to 50,000 jobs being lost. The way the exchange rate develops in future thus has great significance for resource utilisation and unemployment when the interest rate is close to zero. As mentioned earlier, the danger here is if the krona becomes too strong, not if it becomes too weak.

He concluded his discussion by advocating a more significant cut in the repo rate, beyond what was recommended in the Monetary Policy Update, to address the acute crisis of resource utilization and employment:

> Mr Svensson advocated cutting the repo rate to 0.25 per cent and to have a repo rate path where the repo rate is held at this low level for a long period of time, some quarters into 2011. Such a repo rate path entails a better balanced monetary policy, compared with the draft Monetary Policy Update, with higher resource utilisation and lower unemployment without inflation deviating too far from the target.

Svensson further dismissed any concern about such a low interest rate impairing the functioning of the financial system:

> Mr Svensson did not see any problems for banks and financial markets in cutting the repo rate to 0.25 per cent instead of 0.50 per cent. If there were any such problems they would in any case have minor significance in relation to the positive effects on the real economy, resource utilisation and unemployment.

The technical authority of Svensson's analysis was not in question. His intervention, however, raised other issues that went to the heart of the role of the central banker, and it is to these issues that we now turn.

Circumspection

Deputy Governor Ekholm's comments followed Svensson's, and represented a restrained response to his proposals:

> It is reasonable to expect that resource utilisation will be so weak that a well-balanced monetary policy, which takes into account attaining the inflation target and resource utilisation, should actually involve a lower repo rate than 0.5 per cent. The real economic developments actually motivate cutting the repo rate to as close to zero as is possible.

She hesitated from endorsing the more significant cut of the repo rate because of wariness about the zero lower bound and how it might impair the
functioning of financial markets:

> When the repo rate is very close to zero it is possible that problems may arise. For
> one thing the banks' margins could shrink, for another such a low repo rate may
> affect the liquidity in the private repo market where there is some trade in interest
> rates that are currently a couple of decimals below the repo rate. Ms Ekholm
> considered that it would be unfortunate if the monetary policy decision were to
> lead to the financial markets shrinking or to impair their functioning.

Ekholm recommended:

> The repo rate should therefore not be cut lower than to 0.5 per cent. However,
> this repo rate should be maintained for a relatively long period of time, even
> if it means that inflation excluding mortgage rates is expected to slightly over-
> shoot the target towards the end of the forecast period. The aim of maintain-
> ing a low repo rate over a relatively long period of time is to have a downward
> influence on interest rates at longer maturities.

But then Ms. Ekholm subtly endorsed Svensson's strategy as the next
line of intervention as the bank gained experience operating with the
repo rate near zero:

> Ms Ekholm also thought that one should keep the way open for a further cut
> of the repo rate to 0.25 per cent in the future if it appears that this can be done
> without having a detrimental effect on the functioning of the markets. One
> should moreover consider supplementing the repo rate cut further ahead with
> unconventional or extraordinary measures. The measures that would seem most
> appropriate are purchasing government bonds and housing bonds. This would
> also be with the aim of pushing down interest rates with longer maturities.

Ms. Wickman-Parak supported the proposal in the draft Monetary Policy
Update to cut the repo rate by 50 basis points to 0.50 percent. She also
was chary about the management of monetary policy in the vicinity of the
zero lower bound, where the bank had limited operational experience:

> Given the strained economic situation one might wonder why the Riksbank
> was not cutting the repo rate to 0.25 per cent or perhaps even lower. There is no

experience of how an interest rate close to zero functions so there are no safe answers to this question.

Wickman-Parak also reemphasized the possibility that "the international economy may recover more quickly and more strongly than expected when the situation in the financial markets normalises and confidence is restored." She then posited a scenario for recovery, a forecast that we know now turned out to be generally correct:

> The rapid fall in Sweden's exports could then [with restoration of confidence] come to a halt sooner and the recovery could be stronger. Production would be positively affected and after a time lag, so would employment. This would have an impact in the form of rising share prices and household wealth would recover. This would in turn also contribute to increased consumption in that households would reduce their high saving sooner and by more than is currently expected. A more rapid upturn in the economy could also reduce the risks of credit losses for the banks. This sequence of events would in this case occur during 2010–2011 and then one should consider the interest rate path, which shows the repo rate held unchanged until the beginning of 2011.

The recovery would then create other, more normal concerns:

> Although inflationary pressures are not a problem at present, things may look different then. For instance, commodity prices may have begun to increase more than expected. It may be so that the expansionary policy now conducted abroad may push up international inflation with a risk of increased imported inflation. The krona may not strengthen at the pace that is expected and even if it strengthens the earlier weakening may mean that cost pressures have built up which may be expressed in rising prices when economic activity rebounds.

Broadly, Wickman-Parak communicated simply and eloquently that the Riksbank would respond to changing circumstances and it was this flexibility that provided the most important strategic stance for addressing uncertainty. The public could have confidence in the board's willingness to act with care, judgment, and, above all, circumspection.

Governor Ingves acknowledged that undershooting the inflation target was a risk:

> Inflation expectations have fallen and are below two per cent two years ahead. The repo rate and the repo rate path need to be lower to counteract the weak

resource utilisation and inflationary pressures. It is therefore appropriate to cut the repo rate to 0.5 per cent and to present a repo rate path with a low interest rate during a relatively long period of time.

He was also concerned about how the low interest rates would impede the operation of financial markets and, notably, disrupt the monetary transmission mechanism. The purchase of government bonds was the likely course for the Riksbank to take if reduction of the repo rate did not sufficiently reduce long-term interest rates:

> If the repo rate were to become too low the transmission mechanism might become less effective. This is because some interest rates are lower than the repo rate. When the repo rate approaches zero, these interest rates would no longer be able to follow. A too low repo rate could also create costs in the financial sector as the result of, for instance, a reduction in the banks' margins. Purchasing government bonds can be regarded as the most natural extension of conventional monetary policy. Such purchases can reduce the long-term rate.

Ingves, like Svensson, was concerned that real interest rates needed to remain low, but he emphasized that the bank's ability to influence expectation could achieve that end. Reiterating his faith in the inflation-targeting regime served as the decisive rejoinder to his colleague:

> The Riksbank can stimulate the economy further, without cutting the repo rate to zero, if this should prove necessary. The most important measures concern ensuring that the real interest rate is sufficiently low. This can be done by influencing inflation expectations, which is made easier as the Riksbank has a numerical inflation target and publishes an interest rate path. The Riksbank can, for instance, announce that a low interest rate will be maintained for a longer period of time and demonstrate how the inflation path then approaches two per cent quicker than it would have done otherwise. This should contribute to counteracting expectations of excessively low inflation.

Ingves also mentioned specific intervention in the bond market available to the bank, if needed, to further influence expectations:

> A further possibility would be for the Riksbank to contribute to pushing down the rate on government bonds, housing bonds or commercial paper by purchases in the markets. There is also a portfolio balance effect if other market participants' demand for corporate bonds, for instance, were to rise as a result

of the Riksbank's purchase of government bonds. However, there is reason to await a more detailed analysis of needs and possibilities and legal issues before doing so. It will probably not arise until the Riksbank has done everything that can be done to facilitate the supply of credit with the aid of changes in terms for lending and deposits at the Riksbank.

Ingves rejected consideration of a more aggressive series of unconventional policy moves at the time of the meeting:

> What the Riksbank must consider further ahead is whether economic developments require further interest rate cuts and whether the current monetary policy then needs to be supported by more unconventional methods. It is always necessary to be prepared to be able to implement an alternative monetary policy if developments should require this, but such measures do not need to be implemented from today.

He explained his willingness to wait and see how the massive stimulative policies that had already been introduced by the Riksbank influenced economic conditions before considering unconventional measures. Like Ms. Wickman-Parak, Mr. Ingves expressed the need for caution, the need for the board to acknowledge the lags between policy actions and their measurable impacts on consumer prices. In other words, the board needed to anticipate how their policy actions might be already gathering force to create an inflationary impulse:

> Before taking more measures there is thus reason to evaluate the effects of the measures taken so far, in the light of the information received in the near future. Mr Ingves noted in conclusion that the discussion was currently dominated by the topic of how the Riksbank should manage monetary policy in the prevailing recession. As monetary policy is forward-looking, it is at the same time important not to overlook the potential inflationary impulses now being built in for the future. Price impulses from a weak krona and from high unit labour costs are two such factors.

Lars Nyberg asserted: "Export-dependent economies are hit hard when international economic activity falls as drastically as now. The repo rate must be cut as far as possible." He went on to make a general appraisal of the recuperative dynamics of the Swedish economy and its relative strengths versus other countries:

The Swedish economy is being relatively strongly stimulated compared with many other countries. Firstly, the weakening of the Swedish krona contributes to increasing the demand for Swedish export goods. This is no insignificant stimulation given how much the krona has depreciated. Secondly, a large share of housing finance in Sweden is at a short fixed interest period. This means that the interest rate cuts have a rapid impact on households' incomes and can contribute to holding up demand. One can see this now not least in the housing market. Thirdly, companies in Sweden are finding it easier to borrow than companies in other countries. The credit crunch has despite the problems been relatively limited. The banking system in Sweden is essentially sound, although credit losses will increase during the coming phase of the economic cycle. Fourthly, fiscal policy is expansionary, compared with other OECD countries.

He too is wary about the problems of the zero lower bound in the short-term credit market:

> Mr Nyberg took up the question of how the financial system may be affected by a repo rate level of 0.25 per cent. Is there even a risk that the functioning of the system will seriously deteriorate with such a low interest rate? This is difficult to assess, but the functioning will evidently deteriorate as the interest rate approaches zero. As it is of great importance that trading in the short-term market is maintained, it may be wise to keep at a safe distance. . . .
>
> Mr Nyberg considered that it would be appropriate to settle for a cut of 0.50 per cent. To reduce uncertainty over the future as far as possible, however, it is important to communicate that the repo rate will remain at this level for a long period of time, unless developments turn out much better than expected.

He also agreed about additional quantitative measures, if circumstances demanded, as well as the articulation of monetary policy and financial stability:

> The Riksbank can take further measures in addition to cutting the repo rate. That which immediately comes to mind is as several members have already mentioned, to buy government bonds or housing bonds, but it is not the time to take a decision on that today. . . . The most important thing the Riksbank can do to reduce the effects of the recession, now that the repo rate approaches bottom, is probably to contribute to the banks being able to lend money at rea-

sonable interest rates. Here the monetary policy objective coincides with the
objective of promoting financial stability.

Mr Öberg addressed the Svensson proposal directly:

> One could consider, as Mr Svensson advocates, cutting the repo rate further by
> one or more tenths of a per cent. There is great unity in the Executive Board
> that the repo rate should be cut as much as possible. But one must take into
> account the fact that the problems that can arise in the various markets when
> the repo rate comes down so low may be substantial and that it is then neces-
> sary to weigh the advantages of going further against the disadvantages. This
> is a question that must be studied further prior to the next monetary policy
> decision.

He addressed the issue of confidence in the bank's economic projections:

> What is important is that the Riksbank points out that the repo rate will be
> low for a long period of time and this is what today's decision is doing. It is of
> course difficult to determine how long the repo rate should remain low. And
> the further away in time, the more uncertain the assessment is. At present it is
> very difficult to say what the repo rate will be in 2011. This will depend on what
> one then expects to happen in 2012 and 2013. It is also a question of how much
> confidence people have in the Riksbank's interest rate forecasts. If the fore-
> casts are not considered credible, they will not have the effects that one obtains
> in the economic models.

He also emphasized the limits of policy:

> There are limits as to what economic policy can achieve with regard to allevi-
> ating the consequences for the Swedish economy of such a severe and global
> economic recession as the current one. For fiscal policy the limits are set by
> what is considered compatible with a long-term sustainable development in
> public sector finances. For traditional monetary policy the limits are set by the
> fact that there is a floor under which the repo rate cannot be cut. It is not pos-
> sible to avoid an economic downturn, but it is possible to prevent it from being
> too profound.

The key point made by Mr Öberg was that over and above a worsening of conditions, new analysis and a new consensus was needed before

a systematic application of a more aggressive range of extraordinary measures.

Ms. Wickman-Parak commented on the limits of policy:

> One should not exaggerate the opportunity to influence expectations of the future repo rate through the repo rate path. She also agreed with Mr Öberg that monetary policy has limitations. It cannot prevent a profound and rapid economic downturn in the world around us from hitting Sweden, but it can alleviate the effects. If the international downturn is long drawn-out, monetary policy's possibilities eventually become exhausted. Everything cannot depend on monetary policy.

She spoke directly to a professional audience seeking to fathom the executive board's thinking:

> With regard to carrying out unconventional measures, many market participants and analysts are wondering what the Riksbank will do now that the repo rate is approaching zero. Ms Wickman-Parak wished to underline in this context that the Riksbank is already taking extensive measures by providing the bank system with liquidity. These measures will continue as long as is necessary. Slightly further ahead it may be necessary to implement other measures if this is necessary.

In addition, Ms. Wickman-Parak made the case for refining analysis to address the specific situation in Sweden, and for the importance of thinking carefully about policy within the Swedish context.

Mr. Svensson restated the educational imperative, to explain to the public how and why overshooting the bank's inflation target was necessary and why it should not be seen as particularly worrying:

> If the general public and other economic agents believe in the repo rate path this will improve the ability to influence the economy through changes in the repo rate path. Using existing methods to estimate interest rate expectations with the aid of forward rates and with the new RIBA contract (Riksbank repo rate futures) one can obtain good information on whether or not the markets believe in the repo rate path.
>
> What can one do to create credibility for a repo rate path with a low interest rate over an extended period of time? One wants to create credibility for a more expansionary monetary policy further ahead. How can one do this?

Well, the Riksbank needs to commit itself to conducting a policy further ahead that will lead to higher inflation, overshooting the target, and to convince the general public and the market that the Riksbank will really tolerate inflation overshooting the target. This is part of the educational challenge mentioned earlier.

Ms. Ekholm asserted that credibility regarding the repo rate path was "a communications issue," and she was alert to the possibility that conditions might change in a favorable direction. She also noted that fiscal policy in Sweden was playing a constructive role:

> In connection with the question of monetary policy's possible limitations, she emphasised that fiscal policy also provides stimulation to the economy and therefore provides assistance to monetary policy. Ms Ekholm agreed with Mr Nyberg that fiscal policy is more expansionary in Sweden than in many other countries thanks to larger automatic stabilisers and pointed out that a better initial public finance situation could also contribute to fiscal policy having a greater effect. She considered that it was not the right time now to decide on alternative monetary policy measures, but that it is of course important to be prepared to do so in the future if the situation so requires.

Ms. Wickman-Parak made another key rejoinder to the Svensson proposal, invoking the issue of reputational risk:

> If one assumes that inflation expectations are a good way above the target over a couple of years and that inflation also overshoots the target, is it so certain that inflation expectations would after this be once again anchored around 2 per cent? There would be a risk that much of the confidence in the inflation target that was laboriously established in the 1990s would be undermined.

Governor Ingves made another decisive comment at the close of the meeting, emphasizing that decisions that were being made at the time of the meeting would inevitably shape the characteristics of the financial system that emerged after the crisis:

> The discussion on alternative measures reflects the fact that financial stability and monetary policy appear to have merged during the financial crisis. It is not always up to the Riksbank to manage the alternative measures that improve the functioning of the financial markets. It is important in this situation to think

through the financial structure in Sweden and how one wishes this to look in the future. The measures will to some extent govern the structure of the financial sector when Sweden comes out of the crisis. Mr Ingves shared Mr Öberg's view that one should carefully consider who does what in the public sector and that it is not self-evident that the Riksbank should take on all tasks related to the supply of credit. Finally, Mr Ingves' assessment was that measures to try to affect the exchange rate, over and above normal monetary policy, are not appropriate at present as Sweden has a floating exchange rate.

Two alternative proposals were voted on—"to cut the repo rate [which stood at 1%] by 0.50 percentage points and a proposal to cut the repo rate by 0.75 percentage points"—that would take the rate to Svensson's recommended level. The board approved the former proposal; unsurprisingly, one member entered a formal reservation:

> Lars E.O. Svensson entered a reservation against the decision and advocated cutting the repo rate to 0.25 per cent and having a repo rate path where the repo rate is held at this low level for a long period of time, some quarters into 2011. Such a repo rate path entails a better balanced monetary policy, with higher resource utilisation and lower unemployment without inflation deviating too far from the target.

Svensson's proposal had a marked and, perhaps, unanticipated consequence on the conversation. His strategies focused, as we saw in the last chapter, on economic theory and a reworking of the protocols of inflation targeting to address the particular challenges of the crisis. When I first read his proposal, it occurred to me that it rested on what might appear to be a sleight of hand—namely, the shift from an inflation target to an exchange-rate target, and then, when that target is reached, back to an inflation or price target. However transparently it might be executed, this seemed infelicitous insofar as it threatened to compromise faith in the Riksbank's communications. The sequence of protocols for anchoring and reanchoring expectations could be construed as a "trick," which, as Svensson noted, the Japanese public had not fallen for.

Svensson's proposals can, on the one hand, be viewed as an effort to further refine the regime by introducing new dynamics to the targeting framework, or, on the other hand (as suggested above), they can be viewed as a strategy that disrupted the calculus of expectations, thus diminishing its efficacy. He was, no doubt, fully aware of both possibilities. The response of the committee members suggests, however, another possibility. In the midst of the crisis, when data were uncertain and when confidence was the overriding concern, it was not merely the repo rate itself that mattered, but the integrity of the monetary policy story and the communicative relationships it sustained with the public.

Leap of Faith

Within the microcosm of the boardroom of the Riksbank, the macrocosms of the Swedish and global economy emerged with discernable features via a carefully orchestrated conversation. Belief and disbelief were simulated as participants evaluated monetary predicaments for themselves and, vicariously, for a diverse audience. The members of the Riksbank's board were acutely aware that with each statement—with what was spoken and what was left unspoken—they were engaged in a public deliberative process that itself served a profound purpose.

The members of the board listened carefully to each other and crafted their interventions in a manner that allowed for conflicting perspectives, differing emphases, and alternative interpretations, in which uncertainty and indeterminacy were essential and inevitable conditions. They were fully aware of the media, of various levels of public- and private-sector managers, of political officials, of market participants, and of the public in general. Not insignificantly, they were also aware that employees of the bank itself would overhear, as it were, their conversations. They sought to anticipate the questions of these target groups in order to speak to their motives and their expectations.

Central bank credibility was not conveyed by a technocratic officialdom whose knowledge, expertise, and judgment were, a priori, "superior," and hence worthy of trust; rather, authority emerged from complex narratives by which policymakers crafted statements that addressed coherently the concerns of diverse and dynamic public interests. These narratives simulated the substantive experience of the bank's target groups. The story, as we have seen in this case, was far from salutary or uplifting; rather, its purpose, its persuasive aim, was to provide the analytical material with which the shifting challenges of the present situation could be addressed by firms and households. The task demanded the amplification of communicative protocols of the inflation-targeting regime, by foregrounding the monetary policy story and the conversations that generated and sustained it.

A key task of this storytelling was to stabilize sentiments and expectations and not fully or necessarily eradicate fear. Fear and uncertainty were entirely appropriate elements of the story at that time. But what was needed was a story within which a broad range of more-nuanced sentiment and expectation could be evoked and brought to bear on the particular circumstances that prevailed in early 2009. The experience and judgment of board members was key to providing interpretative insights on the available data—data that were unusually difficult to read at the time. Significantly, board members recapitulated the history of similar crises and the means and manner by which they were resolved. Casting the monetary policy story prospectively was decisive. In their efforts to tease out how the circumstances of the moment could be read in multiple ways consistent with information, judgment, and experience, the issues at the heart of the crisis were rendered tractable. The board members' forward-looking appraisals were capable of orchestrating those leaps of faith by which investment, employment, and consumption plans by firms and households could become the basis of action in the face of uncertainty, when rational appraisals of risk and rewards were largely or entirely incalculable.

Four broad issues emerged from my work in Stockholm that became decisive in shaping my subsequent research. Each revealed the deeper and the broader communicative issues at stake in the management of a public currency:

1. In the midst of the crisis, the evolving monetary story became the means for shaping public perceptions of shared predicaments in a manner that made them recognizable and plausible. The storytelling was attuned to the diverse affective predispositions of the Swedish people.

2. By controlling the parameters of this narrative genre, the Riksbank board created an analytical account that could stabilize portrayals of the future with features that could be acted upon prospectively. Representations of the future were radically and explicitly performative. Members of the board sought to create expectations and structures of feeling and, thereby, modeled *affectively* the future as an empirical fact.

3. The bank's economic and monetary expertise, its research capabilities, are fully registered at every turn in the board's deliberation. What made the research persuasive was, ironically, the candid appraisal of the limitations of data and the acknowledgment of the uncertainties surrounding theory. The board demarked the threshold across which action was impelled largely by a leap of faith. The bank had more than mere information to offer, it had a relationship with the public, cultivated for de-

cades, that was decisive in summoning the ephemeral elements of confidence in the face of indeterminacy.

4. The basis of this communicative relationship was rooted in the creative field of economic action. Insofar as the members of the Riksbank's executive board were deeply engaged in conversations with networks of interlocutors, they sought to operate fully in concert with the public, fully wired into their communicative field, and fully aware of their unfolding dilemmas. The troubled economy and the dysfunctional financial system assumed the guise of shared predicaments, which the Riksbank's board understood were ultimately in the hands, the visible hands, of its target groups—the public—to creatively resolve.

The next two chapters recount the work I pursued at the Bank of England. The final insight that I developed in Stockholm became the key point of departure for the research I was to undertake in London: How did the Bank of England assimilate the creative capacities of its constituencies to achieve the ends of monetary policy and thereby further refine the communicative capacities of a public currency?

CHAPTER ELEVEN

Intelligence

What about the following? "To help pay for the war [World War II] would you rather (a) have higher prices (b) have higher taxes (c) have part of your wages saved for you till after the war?" The point one really wants to get at is this. Let us suppose that a given sum has to be got somehow out of wage earners which we might put at 5s [shillings] a week from a man earning £3 a week, 10s. [shillings] from a man earning £4 a week, 18s. [shillings] a week from a man earning £6 a week and so on. Obviously this is a pretty steep figure. Would it make a great deal of difference psychologically if, instead of being taxation, this was to take the form of deferred pay? In other words would the offer of deferred pay mitigate considerably the psychological blow, or would it make, as some people say, precious little difference? If you could, particularly in cases you interview yourself, try to elucidate this by means of some of your characteristic dialogues, one might get some faintly better indication of the views of gents who never meet any of those concerned. — Letter from John Maynard Keynes to Charles Madge, a founder of Mass Observation, November 1, 1940

The Bank of England has a small staff of regional agents that is continually assessing business conditions in the field. The bank has twelve agencies operating across the UK and reporting inferentially on the current state of economic conditions. The agencies pay particular attention to the distinctive characteristics of their respective regions, as well as to the relation of these regions to the UK economy as a whole. Agencies are designated for Central Southern England; the East Midlands; Greater London; the North East; the North West; Northern Ireland; Scotland; the South East & East Anglia; the South West, Wales; the West Midlands & Oxfordshire; and Yorkshire & the Humber.[1] They are each staffed by an agent, one or two deputy agents, and a small number of support personnel. Along with a coordinator based in London, the agents manage what is regarded as the most sophisticated network for gleaning contemporaneous information on the state of the economy of any central bank in the world.

Although the bank has had regional agents pursuing intelligence work since (at least) the early nineteenth century, when it operated a system of branch banks, the current structure dates from September 1997, when agents' assessments were introduced into the Monetary Policy Committee (MPC) process. This happened when inflation targeting was instituted as the official policy framework and shortly before the MPC was given full responsibility for determining monetary policy under the Bank of England Act (1998).

The agents and deputy agents are typically senior economists, often with extensive experience in other divisions of the bank, from financial stability to information technology; they understand the language of monetary policy and the analytical assumptions of macroeconomics. What they are called upon to do within this system is different; it demands that they adapt their training and experience for the purposes of an experimental field science.

The "network" is composed of approximately seven thousand contacts in the business community as well as in governmental and nongovernmental agencies, and seven hundred or so of these contacts are interviewed each month. The contact pool is selected "with a cross-section of companies in terms of sector, location and size, in order to get a reasonably balanced view of the latest economic developments. . . . The information has the advantage of being both timely and relevant to the current economic conjuncture. And because the Agents hold fairly lengthy discussions with their contacts, they can provide some real-world insight into recent developments. They also gather information on future prospects" (Ellis and Pike 2005, 424). There is of course an amplification effect that ramifies across this communicative field. Each of the seven thousand contacts, the moving parts of the apparatus, are continually in conversation with scores of their own contacts, creating an enormous epistemic network of secondary and tertiary actors that extends the field of intelligence-gathering far beyond the shores of the UK, yielding an apparatus for gleaning information with a global reach. The work of the agents is, then, to regulate the information that flows through this circuitry. The results of their confidential interviews are scored and summarized in monthly economic reports (MERs) and then encapsulated by the agencies coordinator in a concise briefing document, the "Agents' Summary of Business Conditions." The "Agents' Summary" is presented for discussion at the pre-Monetary Policy Committee meeting scheduled just prior to the committee's monthly deliberations on interest rates. The summary is subsequently published, along with the minutes of the MPC meeting. This is, of course, a more thoroughly formalized arrangement of just the

kind of intelligence gathering I described earlier in chapter 4 with respect
to the Federal Open Market Committee (FOMC) and the Fed's district
and branch boards.

What I will examine in this chapter is the operation of this intellectual apparatus—"the network"—that continually generates acute representations of economic conditions and the contexts within which those
conditions take shape. This remarkable performative network is embedded in the intellectual dynamics of the economy itself, and is inseparable from its operation. The system amasses the analytical work of individual contacts, realigning their intellectual practices—focused, in the first
instance, on maintaining the health and managing the viability of their
own businesses—and putting them at the service of the bank's Monetary
Policy Committee.

The agents are also the official representatives of the bank, and as
such, they communicate bank policy and bank insights on the state of the
economy to the business community by way of these direct conversations
with contacts. They also convey bank policy to the public through rounds
of speeches and presentations to business and other groups in their respective regions. Visits by senior bank officials also serve as occasions for
speeches and meetings that further the formal communicative and pedagogic function of the agencies and the bank as a whole. Hence, the agents
are deeply integrated in the continual exchange, refinement, and shift of
ideas that animates the British economy.

Typically, the agents visit their contacts alone or with a deputy agent or,
occasionally, with the agents' coordinator, and they also periodically have
a senior official of the bank in train. Each member of the MPC accompanies agents on an average of six times per year, and the Bank of England
governor, Mervyn King, also accompanies agents on six of these field
visits. Thus, the most senior officials of the bank periodically travel to various sites across the UK to participate actively in the interviews with contacts. Even in their absence, the agents feel the presence of the governor
and MPC members, who loom symbolically over all their interviews as the
primary audience for their acquired intelligence.

This "economics of walking about" (a phrase coined by David Blanchflower, a former MPC member) allows the representatives of the bank to
put aside the stochastic armor of an econometric pseudoworld of quantitative modeling in order to "do battle with evidence from the real one"
(Summers 1991, 146).[2] Policymakers find the information exchanged in
these meetings compelling, not merely as some kind of idiosyncratic, anecdotal material, but, as I have argued at length in this text, as informa-

tion that has a distinctive integrity in its own right. The process is crucial: policymakers participate both directly and vicariously with the network as an apparatus for learning. What does this mean?

The agents typically develop, via phone calls and e-mail exchanges, an agenda in advance of the meetings with a contact, whether it be a large manufacturer, a medium-size real estate developer, or any one of a variety of retailers. However, as agents were quick to point out to me, contacts are by no means restricted by these agenda, and they are often eager to direct the discussions about their businesses in directions that they feel are significant, if not urgent. Far from being perturbed by the initiative taken up by their contacts, the agents think that it is in precisely this manner that the generative and analytical potential of the network is cultivated. Indeed, it is the potential of contacts to portray their business predicaments on their own terms and in unforeseen ways that gives this information gathering arrangement its vitality. Contacts can expand the parameters of the economic discussions in a manner that can, and has, captured emergent conditions.

There are two major historical insights or discoveries that the network is credited with capturing. In the mid-1990s during a period of unanticipated price moderation, the agents were able to provide a compelling explanation. Their contacts were telling them that their costs were moderating because of China. This was at a time when there was little statistical evidence and a general skepticism among economists that Chinese suppliers could influence global prices, because of the then relatively small size of the Chinese economy. The consistent articulation of this fact on the part of a range of contacts was increasingly persuasive to the agents, and they in turn were able to convince members of the MPC of this reality long before it became a widely understood phenomenon.

Similarly, early in the last decade the unexpected moderation in wages across the UK was explained by contacts in terms of new patterns of immigration from Eastern and Central Europe. Immigration from the new accession countries of the EU expanded available labor, most notably in the booming construction industry, thus stemming constraints on the labor market that would otherwise have led to upward pressures on wages and prices. Again, what at the time remained an inchoate shift in the dynamics of the UK labor market was not fully evident from the standpoint of conventional statistical measures, and yet it was strongly expressed in the accounts of contacts in the field. In both instances, it was the contacts themselves who took some of the initiative of persuading the agents and the bank of decisive shifts in economic conditions that were, at best, dimly evident statistically or entirely invisible (Blanchflower, Saleheen, and Shadforth 2007).

These two historical calls raised the visibility and the credibility of the network, however, and as the financial crisis unfolded in late 2008 the agents' role and the value of the network was further enhanced. The requirement for up-to-date information to inform policy decisions, the need for refined appraisals of expectations and outlooks, the demand for information on credit conditions, on balance sheets of businesses, on wages, on prices and, crucially, on employment, could be accessed directly within a relatively short period of time via the operation of the network, generating an abundance of information and creating intricate representations of an economy in severe disequilibrium. But the network had another important dynamic: it could be employed to pursue specific questions in "real time"—which is to say, it could be used to systematically question businesspeople in the midst of the travails that marked the crisis.

Apparatus of Experience

Notably for this study, agents periodically meet among themselves for the purpose of discussing their substantive insights as well as their technical problems, but also for the purpose of improving their analytical methods. The agents are responsible for the design and continual refinement of this investigative apparatus. Faith in the apparatus's potential depends on its ability to wire into the research expertise of their contacts, whether for a chain of hair salons or a multinational aerospace corporation. Contacts have their own systems—their own methods and epistemologies—for pursuing an understanding of their situation, for research that is continually being crafted in the service of their own firm's economic interests within specific competitive markets and across particular social fields. It is this labor, at once analytical and creative, that the agents seek continually to assimilate and to report on.

Each month the agents rotate responsibility for drafting a list of "Hot Topics." The list, circulated among them internally, enumerates emerging issues that might be of interest to the Monetary Policy Committee in the near future. The document runs about a page in length and it gives insights on what the agents are beginning to pick up as potentially valuable intelligence on the state of the UK economy. Some of these questions are subtle, and some are obvious. An aside from the list compiled in July 2009, a period of painful disruptions, broached the paradigmatic question: "One theme of recent MA [Monetary Analysis] is that employment has not been cut as far as past experience might have suggested given the contraction in output seen so far. Does this fit with contacts' experience?" What does "experience" mean here? As we will see, experience licenses knowledge production in which the distinctive intellectual capacities and empirical perspectives of contacts are mobilized:

Hot Topics, July 2009

MER Topics

In addition to the regular monitoring, the following issues are of particular interest.

Rolling themes

Are contacts revising their sales targets/expectations? Are firms adapting strategy in the wake of any upside news (e.g. reviving capital expenditure, stepping back from plans for redundancies)?

One theme of the June MERs was that promotional activity had become less intense as retailers cleared excess stocks. Is this still the case?

Candidate conjunctural issues

Can we say anything about the pace of contraction of exports during Q2 relative to Q1? [One challenge for MA staff is to identify the expenditure analog of stabilizing output—exports are seen to be a strong candidate].

What have been the recent trends in spending on home improvement and maintenance? [Such expenditure accounts for around 15 percent of total investment]. One theme of recent MA analysis is that employment has not been cut as far as past experience might have suggested given the contraction in output seen so far. Does this fit with contacts' experience?

How widespread is evidence that corporate failures are impacting on supply chains (i.e. any sense that contacts are finding it hard to source key materials)? [The sense from previous MERs is that this sort of effect remains rare.]

Have retailers started to give any thought to how and how far they will pass on the forthcoming reversal of the VAT cut? How many have already reversed the cuts?

Credit conditions

Are non-bank contacts seeing any increase in bad debts?

How far have debtor days increased? Have they now reached historical highs? How much variation do you see across different firms?

Ronnie Driver, then coordinator of the agents, noted that the members of the MPC found visits with contacts compelling because they could "interrogate" business people, addressing questions directly to those actors engaged in the decision making in real time, decisions that would further shape economic conditions going forward. This coincides with the excitement that Tim Besley expressed earlier about his anthropological forays during his tenure on the MPC, when he could observe how business people were modeling the economic crisis from the standpoint of diverse micro-circumstances and situated predicaments. Interviews in the field provided a means to enter, as it were, the creative field of economic action, where the cognitive labor of the economy is performed. The interrogation process assimilates the experience, motivation, outlook, and analysis of contacts, imparting their intelligence to the members of the MPC. The network provides the circuitry to engage the decision-making dynamics that animate the economy in vivo—the reason and unreason that impels economic action. A simple interrogative stance defines this remarkable intellectual apparatus.

The dialogic is straightforward. Faced with a particular firm planning to lay off staff, an agent—or the MPC member accompanying the agent—can ask: Why? What are the specific contingencies that make layoffs necessary? How might conditions worsen or improve? Numbers and measures inform these dialogues, but they are continually modeled from specific contexts perceived from the particular perspectives of "situated actors" operating in particular businesses and under the sway of specific industrial conditions (Haraway 1988). What is the quarterly decline in sales? What are the monthly increases in prices? What are the costs that determine employment decisions? In the midst of the crisis, it was this kind of information, not fully or necessarily available in the standard statistical data series—accounts that captured the context and motivation of decision making—that was vital in the formulation of policy. Agents thus participate in this ongoing experiment in making the economy speak by way of an immersion in this communicative network, employing something that approximates a natural language as a dynamic analytical idiom. Put reciprocally, given that the economy depends on the continual, incessant generation of information for it's functioning, the network taps into this circuitry for the purpose of crafting policy.

More formally, the members of the MPC pose particular questions for the agents to pursue more or less on a monthly basis with their contacts, to help elucidate ambiguities in the quantitative data and/or to address particular pressing concerns (of the sort we saw in the letter from Keynes excerpted at the outset of the chapter, on the funding for the Second World War). In June 2010, the subject was "profit margins" and the agents drafted a questionnaire to be administered to contacts during their visits and reported the following month to the MPC.

I met with a group of agents who were gathering in Crewe, Cheshire, to discuss, among other things, the profit margins survey. Rosie Smith, Agent for the North East, had designed the survey; John Young, Agent for the North West, and Neil Ashbridge, Agent for Wales, described how the interview process worked.

The survey covered four broad questions. Most prominent was the direct question, "How would you describe your current gross profit margins?" with entries for "Well below 'normal,'" "A little below 'normal,'" "Around 'normal,'" "A little above 'normal,'" and "Well above 'normal.'" This questionnaire further elicited information on those factors influencing gross profit margins—changes in demand for the products or services of contacts; changes in competitive environment; change in the value of sterling; and changes in the cost and availability of credit. Two other questions asked how per-unit cost of sales, product prices, and gross profit margins had changed over the prior year and how they were expected to change in the ensuing year. Each question could be answered by merely checking a box, but the assumption was that contacts would have more to say and that the survey could accommodate this information. Agents knew that they would glean from contacts the connective tissue linking these issues together and that they would then be able to contextualize them in relation to the size of firms and circumstances of particular industries. With a survey covering barely a single sheet of paper, vital and extremely timely information was generated for the MPC. The results will be examined below.

Observational System

There is an important aspect to the agents' work that, at least superficially, appears to be aligned with conventional data collection following the representational orthodoxy of a spreadsheet.

Part of the aim of the agents' monthly survey is to quantify the information gleaned from contacts, to assign scores: "The individual judgments on what value to score are ultimately subjective ones, rather than being based on scientific models or methods. Instead, the scores are a simple way of translating the information from Agents' contacts into a quantitative assessment of the economy over time, as seen through the eyes of the Agents" (Ellis and Pike 2005, 425). Sixteen parameters are scored, with particular attention to changes in these variables; notably, some of these scores cover areas of the economy where there are no official statistics (Bank of England 2010a).

The scores are arrived at in this way: "[The score] for each economic indicator ranges from −5 to +5, with −5 typically denoting a rapidly falling level and +5 representing rapid growth. So a score of +5 for retail services prices would indicate rapid price inflation for those services. And a zero score for retail sales would indicate that the value of retail sales was thought to be broadly unchanged over the past three months compared with a year ago" (Ellis and Pike 2005, 425). The survey seeks to track the underlying trends, rather than more volatile shifts in the economy. Further, the scores are treated cumulatively, reflecting the information communicated in a series of interviews over a number of months rather than on the basis of one conversation with a single contact. "The regional scores are compiled along with Monthly Economic Reports (MERs) and sent to the coordinator who drafts a comprehensive national summary of all 12 agencies reviewing the economic conditions and the outlook for inflation. The Agencies send a total of 300 scores to the Bank's head office each month. The individual scores from each Agency are then weighted together to produce a set of aggregate scores for the UK economy" (Ellis and Pike 2005, 425). Again, the "Agents' Summary of Business Conditions" is presented to the MPC and published with the minutes of the MPC meeting. This is the summary of scores compiled between late May 2010 and late June 2010 and summarized with concision by Mr. Driver in early July:

- There had been some signs that *consumer spending* growth had slowed through Q2.
- Activity in the *housing market*, which had been rising gently for much of 2010, had also eased back.
- *Investment intentions* remained consistent with a gentle rise in spending, rather than a more robust recovery.
- *Export* volumes rose at a steady pace, with a growing number of contacts selling to new, fast-growing markets.

- *Services turnover* had continued to grow modestly, reflecting higher demand for professional services, as well as a small increase in distribution activity.
- *Manufacturing* output had risen further, on the back of stronger external demand and, to a lesser extent, domestic demand.
- *Construction* output had been little changed in recent months. But the level of activity remained lower than a year earlier, and contacts feared a further contraction over the next year or so.
- *Credit conditions* remained tight for many firms, although the Agents sensed that the availability of funding had improved a little during 2010.
- Contacts expected a small increase in private sector *employment* over the next six months, but public sector employment was expected to fall.
- *Pay* growth remained muted overall, although the upward creep in wage settlements noted in the past couple of months had continued.
- Businesses' *input costs* had risen further, reflecting increases in global demand as well as some supply shortages for certain components.
- Corporate *margins* had, on balance, been little changed over the past year . . . .
- *Consumer price inflation* remained elevated. Most contacts had expected a rise in VAT to be announced in the June 2010 *Budget*, but it remained too early to assess the degree to which the rise would be passed on to consumers. (Bank of England 2010a, 1; emphasis in original)

There have been efforts to compare the agents' scores with data generated by the British Office of National Statistics (ONS) to assess the former's accuracy. The latter information carries the full authority of the UK tradition of statistical measure and reporting, while the former, the informal scoring system, is persuasive in large measure due to the ethnographic engagements of the agents. Despite very different methods of data collection and scoring, and some mismatch of categories, interesting inferences can be drawn from a comparison.

Colin Ellis and Tim Pike (2005) undertook a preliminary study of the relationship between these analytical modalities for the bank; notably, they sought to investigate the degree to which the agents' scores anticipate the ONS measures of similar phenomena. They observed, "the highest correlation between ONS data on consumer services output and the Agents' score for consumer services turnover occurs between ONS data in the latest quarter and the Agents' score in the previous period: so on this basis the Agents' score 'leads' the official data by one quarter" (426).

But the relationship in other cases was far more uncertain. They note, for example, that while there is a "high correlation" between business investment intention and official measures of business investment, there are other cases in which the relationship is uncorrelated (e.g., construction output), and there are a few important areas—retail goods and retail services prices—which are "negatively correlated with the official estimates of inflation rates" (Ellis and Pike 2005, 428). The authors are unable to account for these misalignments, except to note that the variables are not entirely congruent and, of course, the methods of data collection are different.

Though it might be interesting to observe a temporal relationship whereby the agents' scoring anticipates subsequent ONS measures of similar phenomena, I argue below that this might misrepresent what is the distinctive analytical value of these two modalities, particularly how the former modality seeks to capture the dynamic nature of processes, while the latter seeks to affix a precise measure on phenomena.

Shifts in agents' scoring over time are important in and of themselves; however, the full report compiled by the Coordinator demonstrates that scores are not ends in themselves but only part of a more complex and meaningful arrangement for modeling economic conditions. When Ronnie Driver drafts the monthly summary, he is attempting to summarize the twelve agents' reports in reference to the analytical possibilities described above, to create a dynamic representation of the UK economy in the wild. He is not merely doing a computational summary of a spreadsheet. He is looking at the messy interrelationships between and among scores as they operate in something that approximates real time, rather than the abstraction and refinement of a formal empirical measure.

Descriptive Summaries

The descriptive summaries are, as we have seen repeatedly in similar official documents, restrained appraisals of an economy that was in mid-2010 facing serious challenges. Mr. Driver's skill is revealed in the manner in which he recast the accounts of the twelve agents, the MERs, into a comprehensive synopsis for policymakers. Evidence of the authority of the contacts is established in the first line of his summary: "Contacts report . . ."

The following extended excerpts are from the five-page descriptive analysis of the UK economy in the early summer of 2010. The categories and subcategories covered are Demand (including Consumption, the

Housing Market, Business Investment, Overseas Trade, and Inventories); Output (Services, Manufacturing, and Construction); Credit Conditions (Trade Credit and Bank Finance); Employment; Capacity Utilization; and Cost and Prices (Labor Costs, Non-Labor Costs, Output Prices, Consumer Prices). It is the agile navigation of different sectors and industries, moving among small-, medium-, and large-scale enterprises and linking them together in one comprehensive narrative that animates the monetary policy story. In these very concise summaries, diverse motives, experiences, and expectations are parsed in relation to shifting commercial challenges and predicaments. It is fully understood that closer scrutiny of the agents' intelligence will reveal ever-greater complexity and uncertainty. The level of detail provides the reader analytical purchase on how business people are interpreting and responding to unfolding conditions, as well as how their responses might themselves alter conditions going forward. Economic theory operates in the background of the accounts, informing the questions and linking implicitly the topics summarized, but engagement with theory is not the point of the story. Empirical insights, however well or imperfectly they conform to theory, are what matter.

There is an open design to the summary, inviting analytical scrutiny and elaboration on the part of policymakers and other readers. The economy is depicted in a manner that recognizes complex linkages—indeed, countless complex linkages among its moving parts. Credit conditions are a prime example; it is the interweaving of these credit conditions across sectors and industries and in relation to diverse commercial challenges that provides a framework for thinking through problems, generating insights on intricate financial predicaments in context, and representing them in relation to the motives and the creative responses of contacts.

Here is how the construction industry appeared from the perspective of the network:

> Following steep falls during much of the past two years, construction output had begun to stabilise in recent months. The recent stability had, however, masked divergent and offsetting trends in different subsectors. New residential construction had been recovering slowly for some months now, although the level of activity remained low, and developers continued to report concerns about future economic activity and difficulties in accessing bank finance. Offsetting the gentle recovery in residential construction, private commercial construction remained weak and the pipeline of projects had continued to dwindle, as existing work was completed but not replaced with new activity. And some public sector construction projects (eg road maintenance and social housing

projects) had already been put on hold or cancelled. The majority of contacts expected the further planned reductions in public spending to prompt a renewed fall in construction output over the coming year or so. (Bank of England 2010a, 3)

Credit conditions were similarly uncertain:

> Agents judged that the availability of bank credit had improved a little since the start of 2010. That said, conditions remained significantly tighter than those prevailing prior to the financial crisis, and individual businesses' experiences had remained extremely diverse. For example, small and medium-sized businesses, along with property developers and those with significant exposures to the construction sector continued to face particular difficulty accessing affordable finance. Demand for bank loans remained muted, with many businesses continuing to reduce their leverage by paying down bank debt. Bad debts had so far remained well contained, and insolvencies remained well below many contacts' expectations. But looking ahead, a number of contacts, particularly those in the property sector, expressed concerns about their ability to refinance loans. Some worried that these issues would lead to a rise in corporate failures over the coming year. (Bank of England 2010a, 3)

The summary refers to the impact of financial conditions across virtually all sectors of the economy, but particularly construction and real estate.

The report on employment conditions reveals how businesses and government organization are adapting to conditions, most notably how they are dealing with uncertainty:

> The Agents reported a modest improvement in private sector employment intentions. But the pickup in recruitment was expected to be limited: some companies would still be able to meet higher demand through increases in hours, including the reintroduction of overtime. And where companies were planning to recruit, they often planned to hire temporary staff, rather than increase permanent headcount, due to uncertainty about the economic outlook. Moreover, contacts felt that the news about public sector employment prospects had been less encouraging. Some public bodies had already begun reducing staff numbers, and the planned fiscal consolidation was expected to lead to further reductions in headcount. (Bank of England 2010a, 3)

The summary of capacity utilization, a key issue for the MPC, reveals the stresses and potential impasses facing businesses:

Overall, contacts reported that there remained an ample degree of spare capacity in the economy, although increases in demand had led to an incremental rise in capacity utilisation. Indeed there were sporadic concerns that stronger increases in demand would put pressure on some supply chains, especially
those where capacity had been cut or where operations had been consolidated.
And a few other companies, usually operating in the manufacturing sector, reported that they were working at or even above current capacity, following earlier reductions in their headcount. Most contacts reported little difficulty filling
vacancies, although recruitment of highly skilled individuals was proving more
difficult in some sectors. (Bank of England 2010a, 3)

Mr. Driver describes tentative developments in wage agreements and
how they are shaped by perceptions of inflation:

Overall, pay growth remained muted, although pay freezes had become less
common and the upward creep in wage settlements, noted over the past couple
of months, had become more widespread. Most contacts had agreed to small increases in pay to reward staff for a much improved trading performance, or in
some cases to retain staff in the face of an expected upturn in demand. Generally, contacts reported that pay negotiations had not been materially influenced
by recent inflation outturns, although some businesses had become more concerned about the impact that higher inflation might have on employees' future
wage demands. Total labour costs had been rising for a number of months, as
the restoration of hours and overtime, as well as small increases in bonuses and
commissions, had led to increases in employees' take-home pay. (Bank of England 2010a, 3–4)

The excerpt on non-labor costs is almost entirely preoccupied with
global markets for raw materials:

Most contacts reported further increases in materials costs in June. . . . In some
markets, such as those for fuel and timber, contacts thought that increased demand (particularly from emerging economies such as China) had been the
dominant factor pushing up prices. But in other markets—including freight,
paper, construction materials and electronics—supply shortages following reductions in global capacity during the recession had also played a significant
role. Imported goods prices had also continued to rise. Contacts attributed the
latest increase to a combination of rising Chinese inflation, and the recent fall
of sterling against the dollar (which had increased the prices of dollar-based

imports from the Far East). The rise in businesses' non-labour costs had not been universal, however. For example, energy costs had fallen for many contacts, who had renewed expiring contracts at lower rates. And many businesses had also benefited from lower rents or longer rent-free periods, reflecting the significant overhang of empty properties, and landlords' desire to retain tenants and prevent voids. (Bank of England 2010a, 4)

Output prices reveal, yet again, crosscutting influences:

Manufacturers' output prices had edged higher over the month, as the impact of spare capacity continued to be offset by pass-through of materials and fuel costs through escalator clauses and surcharges respectively. Some services prices had also begun to increase quarter on quarter, although the Agents judged that, on balance, prices remained below their levels a year earlier.... By contrast, output prices in the construction sector continued to decline, with many businesses bidding for work at, or even below cost, in an attempt to secure cash flow.

Despite only limited increases in output prices, the Agents reported that pre-tax profitability had been recovering during 2010, as increases in commodity and component prices had been offset by reductions in labour and operational costs made during 2009. As a result, businesses' margins had, on balance, been broadly unchanged over the past year. (Bank of England 2010a, 4)

The special survey on corporate margins yielded the following:

Contacts reported that weak demand and strong competition had contributed to downward pressure on their margins. Similarly, many reported that margins had been squeezed by increases in raw material costs, which few had been able to pass on in full. In aggregate, however, these influences had been broadly offset by reductions in labour costs and improvements to operational efficiency, most of which had happened during 2009.

Looking ahead, few contacts expected to be able to replicate the reductions in costs they had achieved over the past year. And, on balance, there was little evidence to suggest that firms believed they would be able to raise prices over the next twelve months. As a result, most contacts expected margins to remain steady over the next year. (Bank of England 2010a 5)

I claimed earlier, that the significance of the agents' summary extends beyond the details of the report itself. What do I mean? As I have maintained repeatedly in this text, the regular summation of business conditions month in and month out creates a dynamic context for the analysis of the shifting nature of the UK and the global economy. More significantly, it anchors decision-making to an evolving story that is in touch with the motives, expectations, and creative pursuits of businesspeople in every corner of the UK. This anchoring lends considerable analytical nuance to discussions, as well as imparting credibility to the communication of resulting policy decisions to the public. Policy decisions are credible, in large measure, because they can speak, as it were, to the kinds of dilemmas and predicaments business people experience and recognize.

Put simply, the agents' network closes the communicative circle. The shifting predicaments facing contacts and the creative responses pursued by them is acknowledged, if not fully integrated into the analytical agendas of the bank. And further, the agent's contacts represent the definitive audience for bank communications; they must be persuaded about the intentions and contingencies of policy action for them to have efficacy.

But there is one final and definitive aspect to the work performed by the agents and their contacts that is revealed, albeit implicitly, in the minutes of the MPC, and it may well be the most important aspect of the inflation-targeting regime: the subtle transformation of economic subjects in to creative actors. I noted earlier that the members of the MPC were a symbolic presence, even if they were not accompanying agents on their visits to contacts. Here, I suggest, reciprocally, that the agents and, most importantly, their contacts, were very much in the minds of the members of the MPC during the course of their monthly meetings.

Thirty-Six Steps

The minutes of the Monetary Policy Committee meeting held on July 7 and 8, 2010 (Bank of England 2010c), summarized in thirty-six concise sections, or steps, what transpired over the two days of deliberations. Motives are revealed and policy intentions are given analytical credence in reference to the systems of representation that have been the preoccupation of this text. The monumental amount of information—covering various official and private data series, financial market intelligence, and various models of monetary and economic conditions—that animates representations of the UK economy was distilled in prose interspersed with only the occasional numerical measure to update and refine the monetary policy story.

The bank's quarterly *Inflation Report,* with its fan charts, provides the projections that inform the monetary story, supplying "the collective judgment about the likely paths of inflation and output and the uncertainties surrounding those central projections" over the ensuing two years or so (Bank of England 2010b, 3). The report constitutes the fullest regular representation of the quantitative expertise of the bank along with rigorous critical scrutiny of the projections engendered by various models and statistical series (see Ashley et al. 2005).

The publication of the minutes is not merely, as noted at many points in this text, pursued in the interest of transparency, but rather because the public is implicated in the story and they are being recruited by virtue of these thirty-six statements to participate in the alignment of thought and action that monetary policy relies on. The minutes are thus a substantive basis of collaboration with various segments and strata of British society, with business people, with market participants, and with all manner of consumers and producers.

The members of the committee, like their colleagues in the Riksbank, have to persuade themselves about the appropriate course of action before they can persuade us, and they recounted, again with great succinctness, this process for our purposes and theirs. But unlike the minutes of the Riksbank's board, which recounted the conversation among identifiable members whose personal positions were articulated, the Bank of England's MPC minutes are summarized as a sequence of analytical insights that cumulatively simulated the committee's deliberative process. The members are identified only for the purpose of recording votes cast on the policy rate.

More than a year had passed since the publication of the Riksbank's minutes discussed in the last chapter, and yet many of the same basic issues confronted the Bank of England's MPC. For example, step 11 addresses the ambiguity of the global recovery:

> Against the background of continued regional divergences [among emerging, developing, and developed economies] in growth, during the month the available data and business surveys of global activity had softened. But the signal this provided about the underlying pace of the global recovery over the medium term was unclear. It was possible that they had reflected some impact from recent renewed financial market turbulence and heralded a more persistent reduction in business and consumer confidence. But it was also possible that they had reflected temporary factors. A slowing in manufacturing growth

might simply have pointed towards a waning of the temporary boost to growth
from the unwinding of the stock [inventory] cycle. (Bank of England 2010c, 3)

Step 16 addresses the broad conditions of the UK in the late spring of
2010, which were, as noted in regard to the fan chart in chapter 3, far from
clear. This particular excerpt from the minutes resembles many discussions I had over the last decade in various central banks in terms of its
candor:

> On balance, the available indicators from business surveys and reports from the
> Bank's Agents had softened during the past month. This accorded with the im-
> pression that a number of Committee members had gained from meetings with
> businesses around the United Kingdom. The manufacturing and services CIPS/
> Markit Purchasing Managers' Indices had fallen in June, although they had re-
> mained consistent with continued growth in output. More forward-looking in-
> dicators of business confidence and orders had fallen by rather more. The pic-
> ture was not straightforward to interpret, however, and some indicators, such
> as total car registrations, the BCC survey's domestic and external sales bal-
> ances, and the *CBI Distributive Trades Survey*'s retail sales balance, had picked
> up. Taken at face value, the business surveys had pointed towards a softening
> in growth between the second and third quarters. But the extent to which they
> had indicated more persistent weakness depended on the causes of their fall,
> which were far from clear. (Bank of England 2010c, 4)

Steps 22–26 addressed the issues of price. Step 22 looked at the ambiguities entailed in the measurement of inflation:

> There was a wide dispersion between the different measures of UK infla-
> tion. Prices of a range of goods had been increasing by more than they had on
> average during the past decade, whereas prices of a range of services had been
> increasing by less than their average rate. That was consistent with an effect on
> relative prices from the fall in the exchange rate. But there had also been signs
> of a pickup in services inflation in recent months and it was hard to gauge with
> any precision the scale or timing of the net effect of those changes in relative
> prices on the overall price level. (Bank of England 2010c, 5–6)

Step 23 examined the influence of spare capacity on prices:

> The recent downward trends in inflation, excluding energy and food, in the
> United States and euro area suggested that a substantial margin of spare ca-

pacity would cause inflation to fall back in the United Kingdom too, as the impact of temporary factors wore off. But the recent resilience of UK inflation had raised the possibility that the impact of spare capacity on inflation might be weaker or operating more slowly than in the past. (Bank of England 2010c, 6)

Step 24 looked at the issue of expectations:

The outlook for inflation over the medium term would depend upon the behaviour of households' and firms' inflation expectations. While most of the household surveys suggested that expectations for inflation one to two years ahead had risen over recent months, it was likely that they had been influenced by the recent outturns for inflation itself. There was less evidence of a material rise in measures of longer-term inflation expectations, which might matter more for underlying inflationary pressure. (Bank of England 2010c, 6)

Step 25 accounted for wages:

Private sector pay settlements had remained subdued, but current elevated levels of inflation and inflation expectations posed an upside risk to future wage settlements. The outlook for pay would also depend upon the behaviour of productivity as the economy recovered, and the extent to which public sector earnings and employment affected private sector wage bargaining. (Bank of England 2010c, 6)

Step 26 summarized employment:

Total employment had increased by 5,000 in the three months to April . . . with a particularly strong increase in part-time employment. The rate of unemployment was 7.9% in the three months to April, although the more timely claimant count measure had declined further in May, its fourth consecutive monthly fall. (Bank of England 2010c, 6)

Three steps encompass the decision on the policy rate and the continuing purchase of assets:

33. On balance, most members thought that it was appropriate to leave the stance of monetary policy unchanged. For them, the weight of evidence from both home and abroad continued to indicate that the margin of spare capacity was likely to bear down on inflation and bring it back to the target in the medium term once the impact of temporary factors had worn off. There remained

risks to this outcome to the downside, if the impact of the margin of spare capacity on inflation was greater than anticipated, and to the upside, if the private sector's expectations of inflation over the medium term rose. Against that background, the current level of Bank Rate and stock of asset purchases financed by the issuance of central bank reserves remained appropriate to meet the inflation target in the medium term. . . .

34. For one member, it was appropriate to start to withdraw some of the exceptional monetary stimulus provided by the easing in policy in late 2008 and 2009. Economic conditions had improved over the past twelve months and the inflation outlook had shifted sufficiently to justify beginning to raise interest rates gradually.

35. The Governor invited the Committee to vote on the proposition that:

Bank Rate should be maintained at 0.5%;

The Bank of England should maintain the stock of asset purchases financed by the issuance of central bank reserves at £200 billion. Seven members of the Committee (the Governor, Charles Bean, Paul Tucker, Spencer Dale, Paul Fisher, David Miles and Adam Posen) voted in favour of the proposition. Andrew Sentance voted against, preferring an increase in Bank Rate of 25 basis points. (Bank of England 2010c, 8–9)

Why should we be interested in these 3,348 words that yielded a decision not to change policy? Though the Bank of England minutes have different narrative conventions from those of the Riksbank, in both cases what matters is controlling the parameters of an analytical account that could stabilize portrayals of the future with features that could be acted upon prospectively. The evolving monetary story became the means for shaping public perceptions of shared predicaments in a manner that made them recognizable and plausible. Members of the MPC, like their counterparts in the Riksbank, sought to shape expectations and, thereby, modeled affectively the future as an empirical fact. That said, the Bank of England adds a decisive feature: a rhetorical feature that amounts to an acknowledgement by the MPC of the predicaments of the public. Though the agent's reports are referred to explicitly only once in the minutes, the summary document is in many respects a reflection of this microlevel modeling performed in the field.

The minutes, as we saw in the last chapter, operate as a heuristic device by which decisions are made plausible to the public, but the minutes also function instrumentally both to acknowledge and to foster the creative capacities of business people, market participants, and all manner of consumers and producers. Economic actors, members of the public, are implicitly acknowledged in the minutes as creative subjects, and it is they who face the predicaments outlined therein.

In July 2010 monetary policy, and particularly the extreme measures introduced at the height of the crisis, had achieved their main goal of engineering a recovery. Yet uncertainties proliferated and the MPC minutes are replete with questions that could not be answered with quantitative data or, for that matter, theory, at the time of the meeting. There was, however, a dynamic process unfolding largely beyond the reach of most conventional analytical modalities available to the Bank of England, that members of the MPC were, nonetheless, fully aware of.

The agents' contacts and the networks of subjects they represented were actively engaging each (and, undoubtedly, many, many more) of the uncertainties outlined in the minutes and finding creative ways to address, if not fully resolve them. These subjects were no doubt susceptible to all manner of self-interests and tragic misjudgments, but they who were the ones working out the challenges posed by the lingering crisis. It was their intellectual acumen that would sustain or subvert the recovery and, thereby, create the features of the monetary and economic landscape of the UK.

Closing the Circle

In a conference room of the bank on a hot late Friday afternoon in early July the agent for Greater London, Peter Andrews, gave a presentation to a dozen or so members of the Insurance Institute of London. It was a presentation that was strikingly similar to a performance I attended exactly a year earlier in which Anders Vredin addressed a group of hedge-fund mangers in Stockholm. Mr. Andrews carefully reviewed the performance of the UK economy since the onset of crisis. At that moment, the situation was particularly uncertain. Adam Posen, external member of the MPC, had described this ambiguity in a speech a few days earlier: "My interpretation here rests on the view that the UK economy is potentially switching between two states—a recovery, which we are now in, albeit perhaps an initially weak one for the many widely discussed reasons; and the renewal of a severe recession if not outright deflation" (Posen 2010b, 2). Mr. Andrews's talk recounted these circumstances with nuance and balance.

There was little, I suspect, that was entirely new in the review of the recent financial history from the standpoint of the audience. Mr. Andrews's account of the prior eighteen months was substantively very similar to the public accounts of senior personnel of the bank, notably those of Governor King and Deputy Governor Charlie Bean, that his audience would have no doubt been attentive to. There was, however, a key difference in Mr. Andrews's perspective.

Mr. Andrews's talk was delivered from the standpoint of the agent; which is to say, it was keenly aware of the predicaments of the business people he was addressing, sensitive to their diverse and continuing experiences of the crisis. While the charts and analyses were familiar, what was striking about the presentation was the rapport that Mr. Andrews had with his audience. Far from the distanced pronouncements one might expect from an official representing one of the world's major technocratic institutions, he spoke with a disarming candor, sensitivity, and acuity. It is precisely this kind of communicative relationship that this monetary regime depends on for its efficacy.

CHAPTER TWELVE

Representational Labor

It has been usual to think of the accumulated wealth of the world as having been painfully built out of that voluntary abstinence of individuals from the immediate enjoyment of consumption, which we call Thrift. But ... mere abstinence is not enough to build cities or drain fens.... It is Enterprise which builds and improves the world's possessions.... If Enterprise is afoot, wealth accumulates whatever may be happening to Thrift; and if Enterprise is asleep, wealth decays whatever Thrift may be doing. — John Maynard Keynes, *A Treatise on Money*

D avid Miles's talk was disconcerting. His style was energetic, if not upbeat, but his message was sobering. Miles was an external member of the Bank of England's MPC, and he was speaking to a group of students and educators representing the Education, Business and Enterprise Association (EBEA) who were attending a small, one-day conference at the bank entitled "The UK Economy—Made in Britain?" It was late June 2011; exactly a year had passed since I had sat in on Peter Andrews's presentation. Whereas Andrews's presentation navigated around the then consensus view of the bank, Miles's talk cleaved toward his *own* personal view of the economic challenges confronting the UK, a view that was not entirely congruent with the other members of the MPC. Drawing on his background as an academic economist and his experience as a managing director of a major commercial bank, he delivered a bleak view of the challenges facing the Bank of England. Like Andrews, his talk was marked by a disarming frankness. As he reviewed the basic trajectory of the UK economy since September 2008, the familiar account of the crisis increasingly sounded like a more extended saga, a tale he outlined in his sixteen PowerPoint slides.[1]

His presentation was arresting. Perhaps it was the starkness of his PowerPoint slides that lent drama to his account. For example, one slide traced the bank rate since 1694. It showed that over the course of its three-hundred-year history the Bank of England rates had never been near the 0.5 percent low prevailing at the time of the presentation. Another slide graphed the recovery in the level of output relative to pre-crisis trends for previous recessions: 1929, 1973, 1979, and 1990. The scale of decline in 2008 closely tracked the 1929 downturn. The rebound from the Great Depression was, however, to 97 percent after eight years, while the rebound in level of output for the then current decline was projected to be only 93 percent of pre-crisis levels over the same period. The 2008 recovery was expected to trail significantly all of the other four recessionary episodes.

"Mess" is not a term that central bankers use lightly. Mr. Miles used the term four or five times in his presentation as he worked through his slides. The recovery was lackluster, the health of the financial sector was in doubt, major commodity prices were on the rise, and the levels and trends of UK indebtedness—corporate, household, and financial debt as well as public debt—were worrisomely high. On the other hand, though the then current rate of inflation was far too high, the outlook for prices was encouraging, particularly as projected for early 2012 when year-on-year comparisons (after the impact of VAT increases in 2011) would look increasingly favorable. Mr. Miles alluded, with apparent ambivalence, to the austerity package introduced in 2010 by the coalition government of David Cameron that was reducing public-sector spending and consequently eliminating many public-sector jobs. He also alluded to the uncertainty posed by the work of the (John) Vickers's committee that was formulating, at the time, sweeping recommendations for the restructuring of the UK banking industry (Independent Commission on Banking 2011).

The two most emphatic points of Mr. Miles's presentation were that, retrospectively, monetary policy interventions were frustratingly inadequate and, prospectively, if the UK and global economies were subject to another major shock, the central bank had very limited scope for action—for meaningful and effective policy intervention. We were in the throws of a liquidity trap.

Later in the week, I had a chance to meet with a group of bank agents who I had spoken to a year earlier and who were in London to participate in the pre-Monetary Policy Committee meeting scheduled for the end of the week. In my discussion with Neil Ashbridge, Chris Piper, John Young, Peter Andrews, and Rosie Smith, I reviewed my prior conversations with them and invited their responses.

Chris Piper and Neil Ashbridge reviewed the situations in their respective districts of Central Southern England and Wales. I was impressed by their accounts, specifically by their reports of the complexity and dynamism of manufacturing in these two very different regions of the UK, and I bracketed off the question of what constituted manufacturing in contemporary Britain as a subject for future study. John Young drew my attention to the numerous construction cranes that were clearly visible from the window of the small conference room in which we were meeting. He was making the point, only partially in jest, that London was an "emerging economy," no longer fully, nor necessarily, tied to the fate of the rest of the UK but very much aligned with the vibrant economic conditions in the developing world. Rosie Smith described the methodological issues that the agents as a group were considering. I was struck by her aside that she and her colleagues were thinking about "what was left on the cutting room floor." Observations and insights, potentially relevant to the MPC, that were not fully or necessarily transmitted by means of current reporting procedures, were continually being brought to the attention of agents. How to make this intelligence instructive for the purposes of policy formulation was an abiding preoccupation.

More immediate was the prospect of additional reporting requirements for the newly created interim Financial Policy Committee (FPC) charged with overseeing financial stability in the UK. At the time of my visit it was unclear whether the bank would expand the operation of the current network to cover issues of financial stability or, alternatively, create an entirely separate surveillance system for the purpose.

Rehearsal

The following morning, July 1, 2011, I attended the pre-MPC meeting. These internal meetings at the Bank of England are typically scheduled for the Friday before the monthly MPC meeting when the staff representing various divisions of the bank provide briefings to the governor and eight other committee members on what they believe are the key issues relevant to the interest rate decision that will be made the following week. The meeting is held in the bank's Conference Center, a brightly lit and fully wired room with IT equipment and numerous flat screen displays. The nine members of the committee sit at a long desk in the front of the room and facing them sit the representatives from the various divisions of the bank participating in the presentations. Behind them are their colleagues who participated in drafting the eight presentations scheduled for

discussion. Tiered rows of seats behind the presenters are filled with perhaps fifty or so staff members, who serve as a very attentive audience. Per
that day's agenda, the presentations for the July 2011 pre-MPC meeting
covered the following:

Financial Markets *including "what do financial markets tell us about growth
prospects?"*
Money, Credit and Nominal Trends *including "bank funding costs"*
International Environment *including "international labour productivity"*
Demand and Output *including "prospects for consumption"*
Combined Supply, Costs and Prices
Agents' Special—"Prospects for employment"
Agents' Update
External Commentators

The reports were concise, running about fifteen minutes each, and were
followed by probing questions or comments from committee members.
The presentations were not simply reviews or updates of standard data
series; rather, they sought to address (often with ad hoc data) what staff
members believed were the key issues relevant to the current interest rate
decision as well as the broader and evolving analytical needs of the MPC.
The presentations and the discussions that ensued covered a candid engagement with the rough edges, ambiguities, and limitations of these analyses. Tightly argued, seamless analyses that fully resolved questions were
not necessarily the primary aim of the interchanges. Rather, participants
were groping for the threads of an analytical story upon which they could
build meaningful policy. That said, the bank's recently published "Inflation Report, May 2011" (Bank of England 2011a) served as a backdrop to
the discussion, constituting broadly the bank's baseline scenario.

Questions were raised on representational details of the PowerPoint
images that accompanied each presentation. Committee members, for example, made recommendations on refining graphic displays to achieve
clarity and coherence for subsequent presentations. There was an occasional call for an explanatory box to accompany a particular chart, notably by Adam Posen, an external member of the committee.

The collegial nature of the interchanges among bank staff and committee members during the three and a half hours of the meeting was
striking—not very formal, though by no means casual, discussions focused on a series of shared intellectual challenges. Respect for good ideas

and acute insights seemed to trump seniority, ratifying and reproducing the norms that govern the work of the bank. I was also impressed by the number of junior staff sitting in the back rows of the room, carefully observing the proceedings and assimilating the standards and responsibilities crucial for the management of a public currency. The meeting represented a small slice of an ongoing discursive process in which questions were continually refined, with new data and new analyses marshaled for the policy requirements of the committee. Research, reporting, and deliberation were serialized and continually in motion. Underpinning the bank's policy positions were wide-ranging discussions that often exceeded the breadth and scope of the debates unfolding outside the walls of the bank. The interplay of opinions inside and outside the bank was expressed in Gareth Ramsay's presentation at the end of the meeting. He wryly reported on what "external commentators," analysts in private firms as well as media commentators, were predicting regarding the decision that the MPC would arrive at on interest rates the following week, as well as the motives and analyses that they imagined were informing the committee members' votes.

The Meeting

David Miles was sitting on the left side of Governor King not far from where I was seated. He took an occasional note but was largely silent during the presentations, but I was reminded of something he had said in his earlier talk. He had, as noted above, stated emphatically that we were "*in a liquidity trap*"—banks were flush with money but reluctant to lend. Liquidity trap—as a metaphor—seemed to color just about everything that was discussed in the presentation. It was as if the term ceased to merely describe the circumstances of borrowers and lenders and now signified a wider, perhaps pervasive, predicament. Uncertainty trapped thought and action more broadly, further clarifying, inter alia, the meaning of the Japanese "lost decade." Lost were the firm grounds upon which to isolate and address policy issues with sustainable interventions. Relationships between variables were difficult to discern, analysis was unusually tentative, and forecasting had become increasingly perilous. Policy formulation was troubled, not least because there was doubt about what monetary policy could achieve under these circumstances. That condition, however, posed a wider predicament. Insofar as the Bank of England's capacity to project a persuasive story about the future had been degraded, planning and action were frustrated, if not foreclosed. Ideas were frozen.

Chris Piper delivered the penultimate presentation of the pre-MPC meeting on behalf of the agents. As he spoke, I was reminded of our conversation the day earlier, in which Mr. Piper had described the circumstances of a medium-sized electronics firm in his region. What crossed my mind will hardly surprise the reader. The majority of the issues presented in the meeting expressed the ongoing concerns of Mr. Piper's business contacts in central-southern England. The issues raised in the meeting as more-or-less discrete analytical matters had already been incorporated in the pragmatic work, the cognitive labor of these contacts by which they planned and managed the day-to-day operations of their diverse enterprises. The fate of Greek bonds may not yet have been a pressing concern, but many of the other macroeconomic and monetary issues—the conditions in domestic and international markets, shifts in taxation policy, movements in exchange rates, and the cost and availability of credit— were fully within the intellectual ambit of business people and consumers. Contacts, however, couched these issues in the routine measures by which they maintained the viability of their respective businesses. Purposeful intelligence was applied on the micro level to the basic issues (and many others) examined in the pre-MPC meeting and solutions were generated—some successfully, some not. However severe the challenges, some firms were doing well; indeed, some were doing phenomenally well. Micro-level action in the face of a liquidity trap, insofar as it succeeded in generating growth for particular firms in the face of numerous impediments, could have incremental effects potentially solving the issues of the macro-level recovery. But these solutions were, at the time, idiosyncratic; they did not yield a growth story.

It was not merely that the agents' contacts were positioned in ways that afforded them a closely textured purview on the situation they were operating in, a purview that might be relevant to the MPC; rather, it was that they—the network of contacts—were *crafting understanding of their situations in order to act in and upon them.* Contacts were continually engaged in developing strategic solutions to essentially the same situations confronting the committee. In their decisions to expand or curtail payrolls, to increase or decrease investment, to borrow or lend, to adjust wages or to modify prices, contacts were addressing the substantive issues of the UK economy in vivo, in real time. These economic actors were continually experimenting with representational strategies that bridged micro- and macroeconomic issues, endowing the future with strategic attributes, however tentative, that they could act upon in the face of the challenges and uncertainties posed by a persistent global slowdown. The circumstances of the recovery were being addressed and potentially resolved by means that were not fully or necessarily visible in the interplay of conventional aggregate data. In its ability to access the managerial strategies by which firms analyze information and deploy resources, the MPC process had within its reach a means to tap into the creative acumen of the network. The question was how to make these strategies, and the insights underpinning them, informative as a basis for policy.

An old genre shared by business and anthropology—the case study method—could, it seemed to me, begin to bridge this analytical divide. Case studies, updated on a monthly or quarterly basis, could provide multiple perspectives on the issues driving (or restraining) the economy. It is a method that recaptures the information left on the cutting-room floor, as Ms. Smith noted, and incorporates perspectives of firms that, as Mr. Young observed, may be domiciled in the UK but operate fully in relationship with the commercial realities unfolding overseas. Rather than merely providing new sources of data, case studies of bellwether firms could provide access to the evolving *strategies*, the commercial techniques, and the planning priorities that intersected with the policy exigencies of the MPC.

After the meeting, I was asked to fill out a questionnaire concerning my impressions of the pre-MPC process. My very brief response recommended the incorporation of a small number of short case studies that illustrated both the dilemmas facing contacts and the solutions they were developing to engage, if not resolve them. The purpose would be to further enhance what I believe are sophisticated ethnographic styles of analysis that are implicit in much of the MPC process, and to make them formally available to the committee. Foregrounding examples of how particular enterprises have developed a means to escape the inertia of a liquidity trap and, by so doing, resolve issues that might seem intractable from the standpoint of aggregate data would, I thought, enhance analyses of the present and near future. The case method could also further enhance the bank's investment in a particular relationship with the public, a relationship that, again, treats them as reflexive subjects, subjects who are continually learning, who are continually addressing unprecedented circumstances with new ideas and new conceptual frameworks that can impel or foreclose action. Giving these strategies expression can, it became apparent, serve distinctive public interests, as we will see below.

Upside/Downside

The MPC had its two-day meeting on July 6 and 7. The minutes of the meeting reflect the unusual impasse: "The risks to inflation in the medium term remained substantial in *both* directions" [emphasis added]. Strong arguments could be made that prices were poised to move in either direction. The minutes model the committee's decision as follows:

> The key risk to the downside was that demand growth would not be sufficiently strong to soak up the pool of spare capacity in the economy, leading inflation to fall materially below the target in the medium term. The latest indicators suggested that the pace of global activity had slowed, although it was not clear how persistent this would prove to be. Some of the slowing in global activity reflected the temporary impact of the continuing disruption to supply chains caused by the Japanese earthquake and tsunami in March, and the effects of the elevated price of oil. The risks posed by an intensification of the sovereign debt and banking problems within the euro area to the prospects for economic activity and the financial system at home had remained substantial. The funding costs faced by the major UK banks remained elevated, in part reflecting those risks emanating from within the euro area, and were likely to continue to affect the price and availability of credit to many households and businesses adversely. Indicators had pointed towards continued modest underlying UK GDP growth in the second quarter and, more tentatively, to some softening in the outlook for the third quarter. But the implications of weaker activity for inflation would depend on the factors that had caused it. Partly in response to the more downbeat news on the outlook for economic activity, investors had put back their central estimate of when official interest rates would begin to rise and the sterling effective exchange rate had fallen modestly. This was likely, in time, to provide some countervailing stimulus to economic activity.
>
> The key risk to the upside was that the period of elevated inflation would persist for longer than the Committee expected. Expectations of above-target inflation could become entrenched in price and wage-setting behaviour; employees might press harder for wage increases in response to recent declines in living standards; or there might be further upward pressure on prices arising from energy and other internationally traded goods prices. According to one survey-based measure, households' expectations of inflation in the medium term had increased markedly, to a little above their previous peak in 2008. But measures of inflation expectations derived from financial markets had been stable. There was no clear evidence that higher inflation expectations had

begun to feed through into wage-setting behaviour. Earnings growth had remained subdued. But earnings growth was affected by a range of factors, making it hard to infer clearly what impact inflation expectations might have had. It remained unclear how much comfort to draw from recent labour market developments, given the puzzling behaviour of productivity over the recent past. (Bank of England 2011b, 6–7)

The bank was poised in anticipation of the moment when risks would be "crystallized"; in the interim, the MPC's position on interest rates and asset purchases remained essentially the same as they were a year earlier:

> Overall, the balance between the upside and the downside risks to inflation in the medium term had not changed sufficiently over the month for Committee members to change their views of the appropriate setting for monetary policy. The risks to inflation in the medium term remained substantial in both directions. The Committee set monetary policy to balance those risks around the 2% inflation target. If it were to become clear that one of those risks had crystallised— and the medium-term outlook for inflation had deviated materially from the target in either one direction or the other—the Committee would respond by changing the stance of monetary policy. (Bank of England 2011b, 7–8)

Seven members of the committee voted in agreement with the governor's proposition to maintain the bank rate at 0.5 percent, two indicated a preference for an increase of the rate by 0.25 percent, in order to curb what they believed were inflationary risks. Regarding the proposition on maintaining the asset purchasing program—quantitative easing—at £200 billion, eight members voted in favor and one member, Adam Posen, voted against the proposition, preferring an additional £50 billion in stock purchases in order to further increase monetary stimulus.

My belief that largely undetected micro-level strategies might be resolving the then current economic challenges facing the UK was notional, but it intersected with a story that members of the MPC are inclined to embrace. Indeed, many members are ardently committed to it. These and other stories could be reframed in relation to the business cycle, which holds that over the medium and long term, market forces will gradually return the economy to trend levels of growth. Under this scenario, watchful waiting and patience could be invoked as the best policy. More aggressive strategies of intervention and experimentation, like those advocated impatiently by Adam Posen, could also be given narrative form and urgency if conditions were to worsen. During the course of a year when monetary policy barely changed, the micro- and macroeconomic allegories were redrafted to address what were significantly changed circumstances.

This brings us back to the key issue of the book: the raison d'être of a public currency. Continually articulating policy decisions in relationship to the challenges facing various categories of consumers and producers and narrating them back in a manner that can speak to the British people, whether, as we have seen, they be schoolchildren or insurance executives, distinguishes or defines this monetary regime. The public interest is thus framed and reframed within a persuasive monetary policy story that acknowledges the unfolding predicaments of firms, households, and individuals. Sterling is underwritten not by fiat, not reserves of precious metals, but by means of the bank's communicative apparatus that creates narratives fashioned from information/data/intelligence/experience that can orchestrate policy by means of a carefully crafted conversation.

And yet, in the summer of 2011, despite the bank's forecasts and policy interventions, enterprise remained somnolent. The British economy continued to slumber. Why?

The work of the Bank of England demonstrated, as I have argued in this and prior chapters, how the monetary policy story served as a nuanced relational framework. But during this period the interplay between the liquidity trap and the austerity program of the British government (in which the bank's governor was implicated) revealed something else (Giles 2012). I began to see how the conversations between the central bank and the various sectors of British society were about promises, promises that sustained a delicate public interest. The renegotiation and revision of those promises could render the future uncertain, if not opaque, entrapping thought and enterprise in caution.

Antinomies of Thrift

From my earliest encounters with central bankers, I have been impressed with their careful use of language. I ascribed this attention to language, as I have argued in the case of the leadership of the Bank of England, to their largely optimistic conviction that the continual refinement of a communicative relationship with the public will further enhance the management of monetary affairs. That view is unchanged, but I overheard much more.

The meeting in early July 2011 illuminated a central preoccupation of the text, notably the problem of uncertainty and its relationship to the representational nature of data. A year earlier in Stockholm I had begun to think of the conditions of a liquidity trap, the notion that ideas could be frozen as a function of uncertainty. And, relatedly, I began to wonder how "uncertainty is generated by the system itself" (Skidelsky 2009, 84). The Bank of England and other major central banks faced during this period a classic impasse in which the data were conflicting and confidence subdued or absent. The impasse had an "empirical" basis: banks were not lending to consumers, businesses were not borrowing, and growth was faltering. In the discussions of the pre-MPC meeting, participants were struggling with contextual and situational information, employing language to model the unstable nature of financial and economic facts in a manner that might render the future tractable.

In the previous chapter I noted that the bank's agents had made two remarkable historical calls that captured emergent shifts of the UK and global economies. They, the agents, had uncovered how the development of China was unexpectedly influencing global prices, and further, they had discovered how new patterns of immigration into the UK—the outcome of new EU policy on the cross-border movements of people—were altering the dynamics of wages. Both discoveries were, at best, dimly apparent in conventional data series, and yet they could be evoked by means of conversations with participants, protagonists who were modeling economic phenomena in real time and adapting their practices of production, distribution, and consumption accordingly. There was a suspicion, perhaps a certainty, broached in the work of the agents, that transformations were in train for which there was limited statistical coverage and virtually no analytical purchase. Changes were at any given time unfolding that were not susceptible to statistical measurement but could be elicited in the field by means of conversations between the agents and their contacts.

We are inclined to think of innovation, or enterprise more generally, as a technological issue. What I have been suggesting in this text is that it is also a representational phenomenon and hence a communicative phenomenon that central bankers seek to influence, if not master. We are inclined to focus on the new machines, the new gadgets, the new DNA sequences, new software code, even new financial products, as constituting the engines of growth and the fabric of innovation; we are less aware of the role of metaphor and language as decisive instruments of change and innovation (Fischer 2007). And, as we have seen in earlier chapters, the relentless modeling of the metaphorical intricacies of terms like "confidence" not only stabilize or destabilize macroeconomic outcomes, they are its narrative fabric.

Learning, impelled by the representational processes involved in the continuous updating of information, and, above all, the resulting revision of concepts and subtle modification of categories, simultaneously define what we know and constrain how we can act. Unprecedented phenomena can, on the one hand, be disguised by preexisting language conventions and terminologies, but they can, on the other, be evoked anew by means of interpretative processes pursued by human interlocutors who parse analytically economic and financial conditions by means of language. The redefinition of the composition of the UK labor force or alterations in the pricing dynamics of the global economy could be modeled linguistically long before they could be fully measured statistically. The agents' network is designed to capture precisely these dynamic economic phenomena.

A liquidity trap as an intellectual impasse can be disrupted, if not resolved, by representational labor that creates a viable "growth story." There is an obvious analog in the paradigmatic work of venture capitalists. Sunder Rajan (2006) has posed this as the classic challenge and opportunity, notably for venture capitalists working in genomic sciences, who must negotiate the predicaments of finance with a promissory vision of financial payoff (if not windfall)—an agile narrative designed to disrupt established metaphors and tropes and create new ones, often with little in the way of "solid empirical data." This kind of representational labor drives enterprise and innovation.

The participants in the pre-MPC meeting understood and/or hoped that representational enterprise was afoot by which an escape from a liquidity trap was potentially in the works, and they sought to capture its emergent motifs, to interpret its features, and to shape its future course. They knew too that there were sectors or subsectors of the UK economy where the liquidity trap was being eroded by means of a persuasive growth story, one that reendowed the future with features that could animate the leaps of faith that drive innovation. Conventions of economic thought and action were the subject of this kind of incessant representational labor.

Keynes provided the first half of the characterization of the representational economy: "In Keynes's economics, the invisible thread of convention took the place of Smith's invisible hand of the market in shaping systemic outcomes, setting deep parameters with which the intentional behaviour of rational human beings takes place" (Skidelsky 2009, 83). What I have been developing is the second half of this insight: that conventions are in flux, open to continuous revision and modification. Language sustains not merely the ideas that might animate a future, but the structures of feeling, the sentiments and expectations that make them real, as justifications for action and inaction. The unstable nature of these rules and understandings drives the representational economy, imparting to economic life a creative authority. To gain access to the "deep parameters shaping behavior" we must account for how conventions are being continually recrafted. Uncertainty is a function of the intellectual practices by which conventions are creatively made, subverted, and remade. Again, markets are a function of language.

What I overheard at the pre-MPC meeting had to do with the unfinished and or unacknowledged nature of a public currency provoked by a liquidity trap. What was entrapped was a growth story. Fiscal austerity—thrift—pursued by the British government was explicitly about the curtailment or withdrawal of a promissory vision in the name of budgetary responsibility and financial probity: values, as Keynes suggests, that do not in themselves contribute to the building of cities, draining fens, or, for that matter, writing software code. So what I began to understand during this period was that the monetary story was about promises, about negotiating and renegotiating an evolving social contract, a series of economic and monetary interests that can speak to the predicaments of the public. If austerity is allowed to usurp the representational labor underwriting growth stories, wealth will decay.

In the summer of 2012, representational enterprise was afoot across the English Channel that could model anew the euro as a public currency by means of a renewed promissory vision. Britain continued to lurch in and out of recession as enterprise slumbered.

CHAPTER THIRTEEN

Manifesto for a Public Currency

Commitment to monetary stability is not only grounded in its economic merits but is also a cornerstone of the social contract. — Benoît Cœuré, member of the executive board of the European Central Bank, March 2, 2013

In Frankfurt the new, translucent headquarters of the ECB was approaching completion in the summer of 2012. The two curved highrise towers were nearing their topping-out levels, with the South Tower at 43 stories and the North Tower at 46 stories. The bridging platforms that link the towers across a glass-shrouded atrium were also in place, and the renovation and refurbishment of the attached Grossmarkthalle was well underway. But confidence in monetary union, the irrevocable commitment made by euro member states to a common currency, appeared to be in tatters.

On July 26, 2012, Mario Draghi, the new president of the ECB, broached the notion of a "convertibility risk," that had heretofore been unspeakable by senior officials of the bank, the utterance of which could in itself provoke the unraveling of the eurozone. Why would he do such a thing?

The sovereign debt crisis that began with revelations about Greece's deficits in early 2010 had quickly expanded to a massive upheaval that threatened the financial stability of the entire euro area and, ultimately, the overall performance of the global economy. In the ensuing sixteen months, in what appeared to be an unending series of emergency meetings in Brussels, Frankfurt, Athens, Berlin, Paris, and Washington, senior officials designed and debated interventions to address the quickening emergency that seemed to continually outpace and thwart institutional solutions. Not since the Paris Peace Conference of 1919 had such intense, fractious, and brutal negotiations on the fate of Europe been pursued—deliberations marked by a similar degree of miscalculation, deception, and what many viewed as incandescent bad faith.

I indicated at the outset of this text that my purpose is not to recount the intricacies of this debacle but rather to examine what is emerging from this incredible "mess," as David Miles termed it with characteristic understatement. I address this issue by focusing on what appears to be a yet another prosaic account of a central banker. Yet this account was unusual, with new and far more significant ambitions. Specifically, I examine Mario Draghi's effort to redesign the communicative architecture of the euro in order to speak to the predicaments of the European public beset by uncertainty. Yet to do this meant approaching the precipice: acknowledging that the ECB had lost control of the management of monetary policy.

In this penultimate chapter, I focus on statements by Draghi delivered, not in Frankfurt, but first in Brussels on July 9, 2012, to the Economic and Monetary Affairs Committee (ECON) of the European Parliament as part of the regular "monetary dialogue" between the two institutions, and then at an investment conference in London on July 26. There are also a series of supplemental documents I examine—a report by the president of the European Council and a paragraph in an International Monetary Fund (IMF) report on Spain—all drafted at about the same time by members of a network of overlapping groups of technocrats drawn from the European Commission, the ECB, and the IMF, who had come to form the intellectual apparatus for addressing the crisis.

Draghi's presentations were delivered at a time when the political momentum for aggressive programs of austerity in the peripheral states of the euro area, that had been at the cornerstone of the EU's response to the sovereign debt and banking crisis, had slowed. Europe as a whole had entered an economic slowdown, and policies that pushed for relentless austerity, espoused most insistently by German Chancellor Angela Merkel and French President Nicolas Sarkozy, faced increasing popular resistance. There was also a growing recognition, among experts and lay observers too, that austerity was, in fact, worsening the sovereign debt and banking crisis. Sarkozy's defeat to François Hollande in the May 2012 presidential election marked a shift in the policy to one that, at least rhetorically, emphasized programs for economic growth. It was at about this time that Draghi cautiously assumed a leadership role in publicly defining and articulating the issues at stake in the crisis, employing a very particular form of representational labor.

Communicative Relationship

Issues of public debt, fiscal policy, financial stability, and economic restructuring, and their relationship to the euro, were exposed in 2010 and 2011, most excruciatingly in Greece, Ireland, Portugal, Spain, and Italy, and they became part of an expansive political debate across Europe. The technical workings of the euro were linked openly by commentators to the operation of public and private finance, which in turn became aligned with the predicaments—the personal predicaments—of European citizens (Herzfeld 2009; Razsa and Kurnik 2012). Assumptions regarding employment, social welfare, and taxation were disrupted, and the features of a discernable future came to be obscured, if not erased. The promises of welfare and dignity that underwrite the European social model were threatened by the crisis. The conduct of public finance by a number of member states and the oversight capabilities of EU institutions were discredited by these interrelated crises, threatening not merely a European financial order but a constitutional order (Åslund 2012; Buiter 2011; Issing 2011; Roubini 2011; Schäuble 2011).

Interventions to address these problems extended across debt and equity markets, parliaments and ministries of national governments, EU institutions and agencies (some created in the midst of the crisis), commercial banks, central banks, and intergovernmental regulators, notably the IMF—with all of these parties acting separately and in concert. Many of these interventions were contentious, inciting intense debate and disagreement among experts, politicians, and the public. The challenge facing Europe was to orchestrate what amounted to a constitutional convention in the midst of what threatened to become an economic and financial calamity. To gain purchase on how these entangled issues were attaining systematic articulation, I turned my attention to an institution that I had worked in two decades earlier, the European Parliament.

The parliament, while largely powerless to solve the substantive issues at stake in the crisis, nonetheless functioned as a single institutional setting in which the crisis of the euro was discussed (more or less) openly. The parliament is a deliberative body with overt public accountabilities, and thus a fundamental reason to create a European-wide explanation of the nature of the crisis and the character of the interventions employed to address them. Though the parliament was very much on the sidelines from the standpoint of crafting and implementing specific policy interventions, it had this other role of orchestrating and communicating the "facts" and circumstances of the crisis publicly.

Again, the Economic and Monetary Affairs Committee (ECON) of the parliament exercises an oversight role by means of a quarterly "dialogue" with the ECB, in which the president of the ECB provides an overview of economic and financial conditions in relation to the bank's policy positions as well as addressing specific questions posed in advance by members of the committee. Since early 2009, the committee has drawn heavily on panels of experts who, during quarterly meetings, spoke to the technical issues at stake in the crisis for the European financial system. By mid-2010, the conversation increasingly focused on the quandaries of sovereign debt and banking and the efforts to address their intricate features. The expert reports were concise, and crafted to address a broad parliamentary audience. Substantively, they provided information on the range of institutional responses to the crisis—including the role and functions of the newly established agencies of the EU, notably the European Financial Stability Facility (EFSF), the European Financial Stability Mechanism (EFSM), the Securities Market Program (SMP), and the Long Term Refinancing Operation (LTRO)—as well as appraisals of the technical remedies that were being proposed and implemented. The briefing papers were often critical, at times scathing. What the ECON hearings themselves provided was one of the few settings in which some of the most obscure issues of the crisis and the efforts to deal with them were given an ongoing narrative expression, wherein issues were being addressed as fully European concerns demanding European-wide solutions.

The inextricable problems of sovereignty and indebtedness ensnared institutional thought and action in Europe over and above the conditions of a liquidity trap. Plausible financial interventions were continually thwarted by what were constitutional constraints. The competencies of the EU institutions were continually challenged by the political impasses in member states and by powerful financial interests. Interventions to resolve sovereign debt issues further threatened the soundness of the European banking system. Austerity programs depressed growth, added to unemployment, and further exacerbated financial imbalances and indebtedness. Whatever solutions were arrived at had to survive the scrutiny of global financial markets continually pricing existing debt and dissecting the risk characteristics of any proposed financial interventions. In the background was the growing sense in the parliament that with each passing day the hardships for European citizens were intensifying. Further in the background, there was a growing sense that the potential for extreme political responses was gaining ground, generating a recognition of political vulnerability that had the effect of further limiting the latitude for action and scope of remedies available to engage the technical issues of the crisis. The ECON committee members were presented with largely unvarnished details by the panel of experts (Belke and Klose 2012; Gros, Alcidi, and Giovanni 2012; Sibert 2012; Wyplosz 2012).[1]

Change of Guard

An earlier ECON quarterly meeting on October 4, 2011, was devoted to an appraisal of Jean-Claude Trichet's tenure as president of the ECB, in anticipation of his imminent retirement. The briefing papers also addressed the astounding challenges facing Trichet's successor, Mario Draghi. Perhaps the meeting was scheduled long before the full significance of the sovereign debt crisis was understood. Perhaps it was initially imagined to be one of those occasions when the work of a great technocrat is lauded and the successes of a European institution are celebrated. In any event, the nine briefing papers were muted in their acknowledgment of Trichet's record of managing inflation, which matches or exceeds the record achieved by the Bundesbank. The reports, taken together, had one overriding message: that the crisis bequeathed to Mr. Draghi was intractable, with no obvious means of escape, unless the ECB and its new president dramatically altered their roles and by so doing forcefully redefined the fundamental nature of the crisis.

Trichet, as we have seen, fiercely, and at times fanatically, defended his control of the communicative dynamics of the euro. The sovereign debt crisis, however, subverted his narrative authority and compromised the consensus-based policy tradition that had guided ECB policies. By mid-2011 there were serious discussions in the media about the expulsion of the weaker members of the eurozone. Severe disagreements about the ECB's emergency policies—notably the direct purchase of bonds of member states—led to the resignation of senior German officials, notably Axel Weber and Jürgen Stark, from their executive positions at the Bundesbank and the ECB, respectively. The Maastricht Treaty, which explicitly forbade constitutionally one member state bailing out another, was for many officials an insurmountable obstacle to ECB intervention (Sinn 2011). There were reports of senior officials contemplating how the abandonment of the euro might be orchestrated. How serious these plans might have been is open to question, but the "unthinkable" had been broached: the breakup of the eurozone or the exit of a number of its members was open to discussion. Some of the resulting scenarios for a breakup were circulated, perhaps as part of the fractious negotiation over each tranche of the Greek emergency loans; some were no doubt the result of utter fatigue with the complexities of the problems of Greek political reform and economic restructuring. The Wolfson Foundation had even established a special prize, with a substantial monetary award (denominated in pounds sterling), for a reasonable and workable plan by which a member state could exit the euro area.

Ingrained assumptions regarding the virtues of savers and the less-than-admirable qualities of debtors played provocatively into political discussions. Why should "responsible" citizens of Germany, the Netherlands, or Finland, for example, be forced to pay, yet again, for the "profligacy" of their Mediterranean neighbors? Keynes, of course, was keenly aware of the "paradox" lurking in this parable, and its consequences ([1936] 2007, 84). He demonstrated that crises like this are, at their deepest level, about global imbalances, notably *under*-consumption and *excess* savings in creditor countries like Germany and *over*-consumption and *under*-savings in debtor countries like Greece. To tell this story authoritatively is excruciatingly difficult. Persuading the German public that it might be *their* savings rate and *their* under-consumption that was at the heart of the crisis was, at least from their perspective, an utter absurdity. They were far more inclined to reduce the micro-ethics of the crisis to the "unassailable" fact that a German worker must wait until she is 67 before receiving full pension benefits, while neighbors in Greece are eligible a decade earlier (T. Friedman 2012). The insult to the cognitive balance sheets of the German public opened the way for destructive and implacable political responses that challenged the deepest assumptions of European integration (Holmes 2000).

The corresponding allegories that emerged in the periphery—euro member states subjected to aggressive programs of austerity, fiscal, and market reforms—had a different character. They arose out of personal hardship, anguish, and injury to citizens, as well as a sense of growing national humiliation as the role of their elected representatives and democratic institutions were overridden or usurped by European Commission, ECB, and IMF officials, and, even more troubling, by global financial markets. Government spending was aggressively slashed, wages and benefits cut, taxes raised, and unemployment continued to rise. Each peripheral state was in the midst of economic contractions, with Greece in the midst of a full-fledged depression and regions of Spain edging closer to wide-spread economic slump. Caustic allegories were also articulated within member states, with animosities awakened or reawakened between and among regions, notably in Italy and Spain.

By the summer of 2012 there were apprehensions gaining expression that more than the rescue of the euro was at stake, that the spirit and historical rationale of the European project was imperiled. The possibility that technocrats and senior government officials had lost control of the integration story, leaving events open to wide-ranging populist and rancorous nationalist narratives loomed. And yet Draghi's address hinted to the contrary; he implied that something was changing, something might be transpiring that exceeded the details of crisis resolution, pointing toward a new—albeit a crude and incomplete—technocratic and communicative framework. Why this inkling of hope?

Draghi's statement to the parliamentary committee recounted his broad assessment of the upheaval and his anticipated role in its resolution. What he articulated would have been unthinkable a year earlier. What was achievable had changed. The deterioration of economic conditions across Europe was playing a role, perhaps a decisive role, in fostering a willingness to address the stark details of the crisis. Most notably, the ability of the ECB to conduct monetary policy had been compromised, its constitutional mandate impaired. This in itself served as an emphatic pretext for unprecedented action. Cautiously, and with little in the way of hype, Draghi crafted a story, an evolving institutional story, by which confidence could be reestablished and the issues of the moment addressed if not resolved. Deeper still, Draghi provided hints about how the entire project of European integration was being transformed and endowed with new communicative features.

Draghi, in contrast to his predecessor, was carefully disentangling the ECB from the thrall of the Bundesbank. At a time when a consensus about technical solutions to the crisis was gradually taking form among technocratic elites, what was needed was to establish the rationale for those solutions within a sustainable public discourse. The challenge Draghi faced was to model a communicative relationship by which the public was persuaded to collaborate in the restoration of faith and credit in an irrevocable monetary union. In the statement that follows, Draghi struggles to delineate this kind of story. As we will see, depending on one's perspective, the substance of what he spoke was either audacious or tragically misguided.

Ownership of the Future

Halfway through Draghi's statement of July 9 (which runs fewer than two thousand words), he turned to a question posed by the ECON committee on the role of the ECB in the "economic adjustment" programs and the bank's oversight and management roles, describing the simple formula that evolved to address the crisis and daringly speaking of "aftermath."

In what reads as technocratic deadpan, he delineates in the simplest terms possible the nature of ECB financial assistance, the reforms it is demanding as the conditionality of loans, and the mechanisms of surveillance that were in place to insure compliance. There is no strict invocation of the provisions of the Maastricht Treaty or some other austere constitutional principle; rather, the aims of the programs are expressed in pragmatic terms of restoring the creditworthiness of member states such that they can regain access to the credit markets and thus regain financial viability.

Draghi then turned to another more disquieting issue to support his rhetorical interventions. He acknowledged that to model a communicative relationship with a European public—to recruit them to a task of restoring features of a discernable future to their social lives and to underwrite that future with institutional faith and credit—required troubling acknowledgments about the past. An acceptance of responsibility was necessary to render the circumstances of the crisis tractable and to give the European public "ownership," as Draghi termed it, of their future:

> Today's economic environment obliges all countries to take a very critical look at their past—and it obliges all to take a very objective view of their future.
>
> It is only against the background of the past that the adjustment programmes currently underway in several euro area countries can be understood. It was past economic developments and policies that led to excessive imbalances in a number of countries. And it was those imbalances—fiscal, macroeconomic and external—that were neither healthy nor sustainable.
>
> Unsustainable imbalances provide the objective need for adjustment programmes—and the degree of the adjustment is directly related to the extent to which past policies were misguided.
>
> Policy adjustment in the euro area takes place under market pressures, but less so than for countries outside the euro area because being part of monetary union shelters countries against some pressures, notably on the exchange rate.

But this does not mean that the degree of policy adjustment can be lower. The schedule of regaining full market access within a few years applies here too. Therefore, perseverance in bold and necessary reforms is crucial.

A critical success factor is ownership of the programmes by governments, parliaments and ultimately the citizens of the countries concerned. An essential precondition for ownership is that policy-makers communicate clearly about the economic rationale for adjustment. As I have suggested, this means taking a critical view of the past and an objective view of the future.

This process has started. Increasingly, national policy-makers make the case for reform strongly. They point to past developments in explaining the background of adjustment and now highlight the many beneficial elements of reforms. Some of these reforms improve fairness by combating tax evasion or rent-seeking by vested interests, and they improve the efficiency of the public sector.

National policy-makers are now increasingly making a central part of their objective the overall aim of EMU: to sustain economic well-being in the absence of major imbalances, and to generate sustainable growth in a competitive environment. (Draghi 2012a)

When Georgios Papandreou early in 2010 revealed that Greece had been less then candid about its fiscal situation, thus precipitating the sovereign debt crisis, few in Europe were or should have been entirely surprised. Put bluntly, Greek political leaders had misled the European public, but their misrepresentations had been hidden in plain sight. The public deferred to their authority while harboring deep misgivings about the judgment and trustworthiness of political elites. Greeks, perhaps more than any other Europeans, cultivated scathing commentary in this regard, and, ironically, some had long hoped for political intervention by the EU to address what Greek politicians could not speak to. European officials too were fully aware of the defects of the euro, the misguided policies of euro member states, and the kinds of unsustainable imbalances that were looming, but these insights, as we saw at the end of chapter 7, were rarely brought to public attention. The spread of the crisis, as well as the catastrophic banking emergency that ensued, may have been hard to foresee, but what Draghi said was obvious: that preconditions for the crisis were set in place by misguided and/or unsustainable policies that must be acknowledged and redressed to sustain economic growth and well being. Programs of reform and restructuring had to be made coherent to the public in relation to the past history of political mismanagement.

Draghi's statement then veered to a positive appraisal of the results of the reform process, which itself served as the basis of and for confidence, despite at the time much evidence to the contrary:

> In my view, a great deal of progress is underway in this respect.
>
> For example, the Irish authorities have maintained a strong track record for maintaining reform momentum throughout their programme. They have also taken important steps towards restoring the stability of the financial system.
>
> In Portugal, programme implementation remains good and important progress has been made in such areas as the labour market, the housing market, the general competition framework, the judicial system and the transport sector. The Portuguese authorities remain fully committed to achieving this year's fiscal target.
>
> The Spanish authorities too have shown that they remain fully committed to accelerating the structural reform agenda and putting the financial sector on a sound footing. They are also committed to improving external competitiveness to lay the foundations for more sustainable prosperity.
>
> Even without programmes, many policy-makers are bold in reform. In Italy, for example, reforms to increase competition, reduce the administrative burden and increase labour market flexibility have been important measures. The country's spending review will help to achieve the fiscal targets.
>
> Virtually all other countries are undertaking measures to improve fiscal solidity and the basis for sustainable growth without excessive imbalances. So despite the current challenges, countries' progress is strong and the fundamentals of the euro area as a whole are sound.
>
> The euro area's fiscal deficit is declining towards 3% of GDP; price stability is ensured; and the external accounts have remained close to balance. All these are reasons to pursue reforms with a strong degree of confidence. (Draghi 2012a)

In the wake of the arduous and fraught efforts to deal with the Greek, Portuguese, Irish, Spanish, and Italian situations, after countless meetings and consultations, Draghi is suggesting that something fundamental had been accomplished over and above the explicit aims of the reform programs and emergency interventions. New understandings, new arrangements, and new working relationships among key institutions have been established by virtue of the crises. What was achievable and unachievable has shifted and new understandings are beginning to emerge among the institutional elites as to what is necessary to begin to fully achieve fiscal union. Restated, the processes and practices that had emerged to grapple with the issues of the crisis had changed the facts of the crisis. How did this work?

Stress Test

Broadly, what we know is that groups of experts had by the time of Draghi's presentation been struggling for over a year with the complex contingencies of the various crises, vetting them, often in excruciating detail, in endless rounds of meetings providing policy remedies—remedies typically amounting to limited short- and medium-term interventions. Senior and mid-level officials of the European Central Bank and the European Commission and their staffs, along with their counterparts in ministries of national governments, constituted the intellectual core of this apparatus. The epistemic network also drew in experts in public finance and constitutional law from academic institutions, think tanks, banking institutions, and, as the crisis intensified, the staff of the IMF. These people crunched and re-crunched numbers and thrashed out briefing documents, technical analyses, and formal agreements that were drafted, rewritten, amended, overwritten, further revised and then rejected, accepted, or forgotten. Crosscutting discussions of European law and, notably, the constitutional mandate of the ECB, were continually brought to bear on policy proposals and remedies. Supervisory and oversight procedures were crafted to monitor the efficacy of policy interventions. Senior political leaders positioned themselves in relation to these technical documents, interpreting them vis-à-vis their national constituencies and partisan interests. Negotiations over loans and austerity programs—between and among peripheral states, the ECB, the European Commission and the IMF—traced the limits of macroeconomic adjustments, political persuasion, and, above all, public forbearance.

Incidental to the arduous work of dealing with the particular issues of crisis management, these working groups had assimilated what was perhaps the most thorough and nuanced understanding of interrelated elements of the political economy of the euro area available. Over the course of little over a year, through trial and error, they had developed informal understandings and working relationships to address systematically the issues of the crisis. Put simply, they had learned from the Portuguese, Irish, Greek, Spanish, and Italian episodes what interventions and remedies worked, and what didn't. They learned about the striking historical and cultural differences defining configurations of finance and political economy of these nations. They learned too of the sensitivities and anxieties of diverse national constituencies, not only in the member states in need of assistance, but in those called upon to provide assistance. Not insignificantly, they also confronted the bastions of power, privilege, and immunity that characterized the "private" financial prerogatives of European elites.

Equally important was the reflexive dynamic of this learning process, amounting to a deep anthropology of EU institutions (Shore 2000). What these institutions could and couldn't do was constantly tested. With each phase of crisis management, the incomplete design of the EU in general, and the ECB in particular, was confronted. This incompleteness, however, also held out the possibility that working understandings and even creative interventions could be developed to address what were in many respects unforeseen and unprecedented challenges. Again, there was the full recognition that using the circumstance of the crisis to compel what were understood to be absolutely necessary reforms across the eurozone, addressing, most notably, competitiveness, budgetary discipline, and banking regulation, was, in their view, fortuitous. Engineering policy interventions around explicit constitutional constraints and limitations imposed by the Maastricht Treaty created some of the most vexing dilemmas for this coterie of technocrats. What had they learned?

The final section of Draghi's statement summarized a report that had been published a few days earlier, entitled "Toward a Genuine Economic and Monetary Union." Drafted under the leadership of the European Council president, Herman Van Rompuy, and coauthored by the president of the European Commission, José Manuel Barroso, and by Draghi himself, representing the Eurogroup and the ECB, the document demonstrated that a shared position on fiscal and monetary union—a collaborative vision—had emerged from the wrenching negotiations:

A longer-term vision for EMU

Why then do we still have tensions in a number of market segments? Let me first stress that a lot has been done at country as well as euro area level in terms of economic reforms and governance. But we need full implementation. We have to make clear that EMU is a union based on stability at national and aggregate levels.

Stability at national level means completing reforms to ensure sustainable growth without major imbalances. Stability at aggregate level means implementing the vision recently presented at the summit.

The central message of that vision is this: the euro is here to stay—and the euro area will take the necessary steps to ensure that.

In my view, the core of the report submitted by President Van Rompuy is the identification of four building blocks:

First, a financial market union *that elevates responsibility for supervision of banks to the euro area level.*

Second, a fiscal union *that reinforces oversight of budgetary policies at the euro area level and also provides some fiscal capacity to support the functioning of the currency area.*

Third, an economic union *with sufficient mechanisms to ensure that countries can achieve sustained prosperity without excessive imbalances.*

And finally a political union *that strengthens the legitimacy of EMU among euro area citizens and deepens its political foundations.*

These four building blocks are mutually consistent and coherent, and should be pursued in parallel. I am looking forward to the work on a roadmap that has started. In my view, three issues deserve particular attention:

First, we need to move towards a further sharing of sovereignty in the fiscal, financial and economic domains. There can be no shortcuts in establishing a sound and stable EMU.

Second, EMU is an integral part of the Treaty. This calls on all relevant bodies and actors to engage constructively on improving its functioning, not only at Union but also at national level. To call for an impeccable application of the Treaty and at the same time refuse closer union mentioned in Article 1 of the Treaty is inconsistent, to say the least.

Third, we need to accompany deeper euro area integration with significant progress on democratic legitimacy and accountability. There is no doubt that you and your colleagues — the members of the European Parliament, the directly elected representatives of the citizens of Europe — will continue to play a central role in the steps towards political union.

Thank you for your attention. (Draghi 2012a)

Separately, the IMF had officially sanctioned this program. A former IMF official, Gabriel Sterne, suggested that I look at an unusual section of an official report entitled "2012 Article IV Consultation with Spain Concluding Statement of IMF Mission," published a few days earlier on June 14, 2012. Paragraph 7 reads as follows:

Spain's prospects will also be helped by further progress at the European level.

There is an immediate need at the euro area level to ensure adequate bank funding and mitigate contagion. But a lasting resolution to the Euro area crisis will require a convincing and concerted move toward a complete and robust

EMU. This requires a roadmap toward a banking union and fiscal integration. A clear commitment in this direction, in particular on area-wide deposit insurance and a bank resolution framework with common backstops, is essential to chart a credible path ahead. (IMF 2012)

This statement is remarkable insofar as the IMF is not merely confirming participation in a particular series of interventions to aid a specific country, but rather it is ratifying prospectively an outline of a comprehensive program to begin to address the entire eurozone crisis.

Taboo

I indicated above that the constitutional challenges marked the most serious impediments to action by the ECB to address the crisis. The purchase directly of debt of member states—violating the "no bailout" clause of the treaty—provoked what appeared to be insurmountable constitutional obstacles for the officials of the Bundesbank and the political leadership of the German government. Without this kind of intervention, the cost—that is, the interest rates demanded by the market to fund ongoing Spanish and Italian financial needs—would be crushing. At the end of July, in a speech—in many respects it was more a series of informal comments—to the Global Investment Conference in London, Draghi hinted at an argument that trumped these constitutional inhibitions. His opening comments amounted to a manifesto of sorts for a public currency:

> The ... message I would like to send today, is that progress has been extraordinary in the last six months. If you compare today the euro area member states with six months ago, you will see that the world is entirely different today, and for the better.
>
> And this progress has taken different shapes. At national level, because of course, while I was saying, while I was glorifying the merits of the euro, you were thinking "but that's an average!," and "in fact countries diverge so much within the euro area, that averages are not representative any longer, when the variance is so big."
>
> But I would say that over the last six months, this average, well the variances tend to decrease and countries tend to converge much more than they have done in many years—both at national level, in countries like Portugal, Ireland and countries that are not in the programme, like Spain and Italy.

The progress in undertaking deficit control, structural reforms has been remarkable. And they will have to continue to do so. But the pace has been set and all the signals that we get is that they don't relent, stop reforming themselves. It's a complex process because for many years, very little was done—I will come to this in a moment.

But a lot of progress has been done at supranational level. That's why I always say that the last summit was a real success. The last summit was a real success because for the first time in many years, all the leaders of the 27 countries of Europe, including UK etc., said that the only way out of this present crisis is to have more Europe, not less Europe.

A Europe that is founded on four building blocks: a fiscal union, a financial union, an economic union and a political union. These blocks, in two words—we can continue discussing this later—mean that much more of what is national sovereignty is going to be exercised at supranational level, that common fiscal rules will bind government actions on the fiscal side.

Then in the banking union or financial markets union, we will have one supervisor for the whole euro area. And to show that there is full determination to move ahead and these are not just empty words, the European Commission will present a proposal for the supervisor in early September. So in a month. And I think I can say that works are quite advanced in this direction.

So more Europe, but also the various firewalls have been given attention and now they are ready to work much better than in the past.

The second message is that there is more progress than it has been acknowledged.

But the third point I want to make is in a sense more political.

When people talk about the fragility of the euro and the increasing fragility of the euro, and perhaps the crisis of the euro, very often non-euro area member states or leaders, underestimate the amount of political capital that is being invested in the euro.

And so we view this, and I do not think we are unbiased observers, we think the euro is irreversible. And it's not an empty word now, because I preceded saying exactly what actions have been made, are being made to make it irreversible.

But there is another message I want to tell you.

Within our mandate, the ECB is ready to do whatever it takes to preserve the euro. And believe me, it will be enough. (Draghi 2012b)

At the close of his remarks, Draghi made a rather offhanded comment that tested the limits of the speakable and the unspeakable:

> These premia [the inordinately high interest rates] ... have to do more and
> more with convertibility, with the risk of convertibility. Now to the extent that
> these premia do not have to do with factors inherent to my counterparty—they
> come into our [the ECB] mandate. They come within our remit.
>
> To the extent that the size of these sovereign premia hampers the func-
> tioning of the monetary policy transmission channel, they come within our
> mandate.
>
> So we have to cope with this financial fragmentation [by] addressing these
> issues. (Draghi 2012b)

Stating that there was a "convertibility risk" influencing the divergent pricing of debt among member states acknowledged what everyone knew—
that the market was pricing the possibility that the sovereign debt of some
member state or states would ultimately be paid off in reissued national
currencies, currencies which would in all likelihood be of diminished
value.[2] Crudely, the higher the interest premia demanded by the market,
the more onerous the burden on the member state and the more overt
the expectancy of its exit from the euro. But, of course, this was a self-
fulfilling proposition:

> By admitting that this "convertibility risk" now exists, the ECB president has
> implicitly acknowledged that the permanence of the single currency is not fully
> credible in the financial markets. The recognition of redenomination risk after
> a potential devaluation is one reason, he implies, why sovereign bond yields are
> now so high in Spain and Italy. He has said that this prevents the ECB from
> transmitting its intended monetary stance into those economies, which gives
> the ECB the right to take direct action to reduce these bond yields. (Davies
> 2012a)

Draghi averred that there was a paramount authority—the ECB's constitutional mandate to manage monetary policy across the eurozone—that
overruled restrictions on bond purchases as well as other unorthodox in-
interventions. Perceived convertibility risk, the interest premia, imposed by
the bond market was a clear and irrefutable challenge to the ECB's management of interest rates. To restore the ECB's authority demanded that
these differentials be eliminated, not merely to relieve the financial bur-
dens imposed on specific member states, but to restore the ECB's control
over the *transmission* of monetary policy, which would, thereby, reestab-
lish the credibility of the common currency.[3] The purchase of short-dated

bonds by the ECB under what came to be known as "Outright Monetary Transactions" (OMTs) was deemed by Draghi as the means to accomplish this constitutional gambit (ECB 2012; Zingales 2012).

The proposal was welcomed and supported by political leaders, notably even in Germany, though almost immediately it was subjected to restrictions and conditionalities aimed at continuing pressure on those member states petitioning for this kind of assistance, requiring them to cede further control and supervision over economic and financial matters to the so-called triumvirate (representatives of the European Commission, the IMF, and the ECB). There were many other potential obstacles; nevertheless, Draghi's interventions, however tentative, represented a means to begin to create a plausible, if not robust legal basis for new and unprecedented ECB initiatives. The ECB, in Draghi's view, had the right—indeed, the obligation—to undertake those initiatives necessary to retain its control over monetary policy, and this assertion of the bank's legal authority was translated into a mantra that began to be repeated by senior officials of the bank, that the ECB would "take whatever measures necessary" to preserve and protect the viability of the common currency.

Most of the journalistic attention at the time was focused, quite rightly, on the dramatic nature of the OMTs, the resulting restoration of ECB control of the transmission mechanism of monetary policy, and Draghi's new and emphatic refrain. I turn, in the last section of this chapter, to a different, perhaps far more important, aspect of the transformations that were gaining articulation in the summer of 2012. Finance and political economy were, I will argue, allied in a manner that spoke creatively to the predicaments of the public, extending the reach of a new monetary regime.

Promissory Vision

Over the course of eight weeks or so in the summer of 2012 Draghi had orchestrated a series of interventions that could meaningfully address the overall crisis. The elements of his proposal, though technically daunting, could be articulated in a simple fashion encompassing a handful of essential features. Above all, the program could be communicated—it could be made plausible to various strata and segments of the public. Indeed, its efficacy depended on a communicative dynamic that was future-oriented and designed specifically to shape or reshape expectations. The time horizons and the ends and purposes of policy interventions had shifted. The EU was no longer simply focused on pressing emergency measures to forestall some impending calamity or merely buying time to orchestrate the details of fiscal union; it now had a "longer-term vision," permitting a very different kind of intellectual labor and, perhaps, far more consequential outcomes. Again, the crisis served not only as the pretext for further programs of integration, but also, for the purposes of this text, the impetus for exploration and reevaluation of the imperatives defining a public currency.

The endless rounds of meetings, the never-ending scrutiny of conflicting proposals and remedies, the continual encounters with policy dead ends—this messy and uncertain process itself—far from signaling the unraveling of the European project, was in fact furthering, perhaps resolutely, the pragmatic design of the European project (Monnet 1976; Shore 2000).

In mid-2012, the technocratic challenge for the EU matched the scale and historical significance of the Cold War challenges confronted by the original architects of the European project. However, rather than pooling of national sovereignty by means of new supranational institutions—the classic agenda of European integration—the emerging challenge was to transform the nature of public finance in order to restore and strengthen the viability of the European social model. In other words, the crisis was provoking and then catalyzing a redesign of finance and political economy to underwrite the *other* great project of European integration, the project of *solidarity* (Holmes 2000; Rabinow 1989).

Draghi not only acknowledged the urgency of imparting a relational language to the monetary regime, but he asserted in his London remarks that enhancing "social cohesion" was the decisive feature of the EU's approach to the crisis. Significantly, the earlier monetary union of Germany in the 1990s was accomplished with the same language; the substantial funding of unifications has and continues to be paid for with a "solidarity tax." That said, the commitments to sustain social welfare and the promises to preserve human dignity were rarely acknowledged as overriding concerns in the midst of the crisis, but in the summer of 2012, Draghi saw fit to foreground them as such, as an essential feature of a "promissory vision" (Sunder Rajan 2006, 115).

Many inside and outside of Europe had good reason to be deeply skeptical of this claim of fidelity to the weighted terminology of social cohesion and solidarity, and they had every reason to dismiss it as a convenient, if not cynical rhetorical gesture. But the notion that to save the euro required a redesign of the basic imperatives of the financial system and opening them to public scrutiny was nonetheless theoretically plausible. In other words, not just a completion of the project of monetary union, but something more ambitious was needed, something that both ratified the original promissory vision of the European project and went beyond it. What might this transformation look like?

David Westbrook has outlined the fundamental criteria for refunctioning elements of the financial system aligned explicitly with the pragmatic ideals of social cohesion:

> In a global society in which social commitments have been capitalized and are held on a portfolio basis by highly leveraged and interdependent institutions, the traditional imagination of finance—how to intermediate scarce capital between savers and worthy entrepreneurs, while preventing fraud—should lose its dominance, to be replaced by a more custodial understanding of the vitality of stable capital to social order and humane understandings of institutions. The pension fund, the university endowment, or the sovereign debt portfolio, rather than the venture capitalist and the entrepreneur, should become the paradigmatic figures for contemporary thinking about capitalism and its regulation. Should the relevant elites take this conceptual turn, the aesthetics and social practices of securities regulation will be far different from those that have characterized the last several decades. (David Westbrook, personal communication)

Westbrook's agenda approximates what Draghi and his colleagues were contemplating, though they might demur that this transformation was already underway and, as suggested above, its principles of solidarity and social cohesion had become essential instruments for the resolution of the then current upheaval in Europe.

If the project of monetary union could be threatened by the utterance of "convertability risk," perhaps it could be saved by the classic terminology of "social cohesion." This is, of course, little more than facile shorthand for what is truly at stake here, the acknowledgment that the resolution of the challenges facing Europe required a language—a language capable of modeling societal commitments and promises; a language that could account for the circumstances, in some cases, the dire circumstances, of a diversely constituted European public.[4] Draghi's agenda for social cohesion and solidarity started, not insignificantly, with European-wide bank deposit insurance, a scheme that linked the private vulnerabilities of depositors to the construction of a banking union.[5] The task was to create a terminology for the technical working of public and private finance that could address human expectations in a manner that is sufficiently persuasive to re-endow the future with discernable features.

Draghi's most powerful and shrewd insight, as indicated above, was that there was now an audience, a vast audience across Europe that had not yet been constituted as recently as 2009, an audience increasingly anxious for the kind of message he and his colleagues were formulating. Despite the stirring of all manner of populist radicalism and intellectual discontent, there was an anxious public eager for the kind of program—simple, persuasive, and timely—outlined above. There was a broadly constituted European public increasingly eager for a common agenda cast in the familiar metaphors and tropes of European integration, a public that was increasingly impatient with technical objections, divisive political partisanship, and narrowly framed financial interests thwarting efforts at resolution. Here, too, Draghi interpellated an emerging public as protagonists with whom he could collaborate to alter the course of the crisis and shape its aftermath (Lippman [1927] 2002). The public—particularly the Europeans among us—were assuming a decisive role in crafting and articulating monetary stories modeling hopes and outcomes.

Despite this optimistic appraisal, there is no doubt Draghi's agenda may end in tears. Indeed, a small journalistic and academic industry has grown up around crafting catastrophic stories about the impending collapse of the euro (Sinn and Wollmershäuser 2012). What Draghi admitted was that the currency had, under pressure from the bond market, become untethered from narrative management of the technocratic officialdom of central banks. He further conceded that if central banks lose control of the monetary story, lose control of their communicative relationship with the public, there are alternative narratives available for stabilizing or destabilizing the link between money and the existential circumstances of the public. In late 2011 and early 2012 the communicative features of the euro were severely tested in just this fashion as the technocratic discourse of the ECB faltered and highly contentious monetary stories circulated revealing how a public currency can attain highly dissonant features.

Draghi and his colleagues radically recast the monetary allegory in the summer of 2012. What will result is uncertain. What we do know is that a remarkable monetary drama is unfolding in which monumental shifts of expectations are in play. Whatever the fate of the euro, the outcome in all likelihood will rest on the ability of central bankers to model the future with persuasive words that can sustain—enhance even—the operation of a public currency.

CHAPTER FOURTEEN

Totality of Promises

In a commercial age wealth is largely made up of promises. — Roscoe Pound, American legal scholar, 1946

Experiments that have been the subjects of this text are ongoing; they do not lend themselves to hard and fast conclusions. The monetary regime, the cumulative outcome of these experiments, is similarly in the making and its ultimate status and outcome remain uncertain. What can be said is that monetary phenomena have acquired a distinctive nature over the last three or four decades, and this text has presented a means to begin to conceptualize these dynamics.

I have examined at length in this book the protocols of inflation targeting, with particular attention to their communicative features. I have recounted how the ideas that guided the targeting innovations, notably the continual refinement of the monetary policy story, led ineluctably to the emergence of a public currency. By the onset of the financial crisis, a monetary regime was emerging that was predicated on but not simply reducible to the protocols of inflation targeting.

Central bankers have since at least the 1980s been engaged in a deep (though implicit) anthropological exploration, a search for new means by which monetary affairs could be anchored conceptually—not to gold or to regimes of fixed exchange rates, but by means of an evolving relationship with the public, a relationship in which our predicaments could serve as the fulcrum of policy. The public was recruited to participate in the staging of this drama by means of persuasive analytical stories intended to shape expectations and, thus, economic behavior prospectively. Research sustained and enlivened this evolving communicative relationship, research that, among other things, continually gleans the descriptive, explanatory, and interpretative labor of economic actors, incorporating their intelligence for the purposes of formulating policy. The challenge for central bankers, many of whom had a hand in designing this regime, is thus to navigate and manage the shifting grounds upon which members of the public became protagonists in the monetary drama and their predicaments the imperatives of and for policy. The rancorous struggles that emerged, notably in the midst of the European sovereign debt crisis, forced in 2012 a creative articulation by Mario Draghi of what is broadly at stake in the management of a public currency: the totality of promises that bind us together.

Ben Bernanke and his colleagues on the FOMC were also busy in 2012, addressing the discontents of the crisis with a new set of priorities by which they revised the relational and communicative dynamics of the monetary regime. In the restrained language of FOMC press releases, they too elaborated the manifesto for a public currency with an acute promissory vision.

As noted in chapter 3, in the FOMC statement released to the press on January 25 there was a belated commitment to an inflation-targeting regime, but the press release also broached the outline of an agenda that foreshadowed a radical departure from the orthodoxies of that regime, one that few noticed at the time (Davies 2012b; Harding 2012). The presaging came in a section addressing the nature of employment and unemployment:

> The maximum level of employment is largely determined by nonmonetary factors that affect the structure and dynamics of the labor market. These factors may change over time and may not be directly measurable. Consequently, it would not be appropriate to specify a fixed goal for employment; rather, the Committee's policy decisions must be informed by assessments of the maximum level of employment, recognizing that such assessments are necessarily uncertain and subject to revision. The Committee considers a wide range of indicators in making these assessments. Information about Committee participants' estimates of the longer-run normal rates of output growth and unemployment is published four times per year in the FOMC's Summary of Economic Projections. For example, in the most recent projections, FOMC participants' estimates of the longer-run normal rate of unemployment had a central tendency of 5.2 percent to 6.0 percent, roughly unchanged from last January but substantially higher than the corresponding interval several years earlier. (FRB 2012a)

This commentary remained largely unelaborated on during the course of the year, though there was a long paper, delivered in August by Michael Woodford at the Jackson Hole conference sponsored by the Kansas City Federal Reserve Bank, that provided critical academic background for what Bernanke and his colleagues were contemplating. Then, in the December 12 FOMC statement and in the lengthy news conference by the chairman that followed, the policy imperative was articulated

> In particular, the Committee decided to keep the target range for the federal funds rate at 0 to 1/4 percent and currently anticipates that this exceptionally low range for the federal funds rate will be appropriate at least as long as the unemployment rate remains above 6–1/2 percent, inflation between one and two years ahead is projected to be no more than a half percentage point above the Committee's 2 percent longer-run goal, and longer-term inflation expectations continue to be well anchored. (FRB 2012b)

With its famous concision, the committee was establishing the rate of unemployment as the targeting mechanism for its interest rate policies. It was casting its statutory obligation of "promoting maximum employment" as an overt priority for its future decisions. Put simply, it would publicly target an unemployment rate. But it was doing more; it was also providing us, the public, with its model, a simple conceptual formula by which we could anticipate future FOMC policy decisions. This "forward guidance" anticipated a time, which could not be precisely dated, when the exceptional monetary measures created to deal with the crisis would be curtailed and/or reversed. We would know when that time approached by observing the unemployment rate and adjusting our expectations accordingly (Woodford 2012).

An inflation rate speaks to the abstract behavior of prices; an unemployment rate speaks to the existential struggles of labor. Shifting from an emphasis on the former target to the latter thus has more than a technical significance foregrounding a different promissory vision, a different constellation of public interests. The members of the FOMC were certainly not seeking to endorse by means of this shift in policy anything like a vast European social model encompassing solidarity, guarantees of social welfare, and human dignity, but their commitment nonetheless spoke to something like an American articulation of the social contract.

One of the most curious features of central bank communications, as indicated at every turn in this book, is their propensity to disguise with a linguistic austerity, so to speak, their most profound and far-reaching features. In the FOMC statement from early 2012 there is an aside that is easy to overlook or to dismiss as mere boilerplate:

> The Committee seeks to explain its monetary policy decisions to the public as clearly as possible. Such clarity facilitates well-informed decisionmaking by households and businesses, reduces economic and financial uncertainty, increases the effectiveness of monetary policy, and enhances transparency and accountability, which are essential in a democratic society. (FRB 2012a)

But this prosaic declaration may well constitute the clearest statement of the social contract encompassed by a public currency. Rather than an explicit guarantee of any particular benefit, subvention, or ennobling prerogative, the commitment is to provide us with the intellectual material—data and analysis—by which we, the public, can make decisions, by which we as protagonists can sustain the totality of promises of a distinctive social order.

Notes

Chapter One

1. Mervyn King (2004) used the term "public currency" in passing with no elaboration, to my knowledge. I have developed the concept in this text in a number of different ways that may or may not be compatible with King's original intentions or subsequent reflections.

2. There is a rich anthropological literature on money, value, and exchange, extending from the classic works of Marcel Mauss and Branislaw Malinowski to the contemporary scholarship of Marilyn Strathern, Terrence Turner, Stephen Gudeman, Bill Maurer, Keith Hart, Chris Hann, and David Graber, to name but a few. In this book, however, I have sought to introduce a very different body of theory that anthropologists are typically unfamiliar with. Broadly, these theories cover the tradition of monetary theory with particular attention to the work of J. M. Keynes as well as the work of a range of contemporary monetary economists.

3. Again, viewing "markets as a function of language" was first proposed to me by Annelise Riles.

4. Central bankers can assess the impact of their policy decisions on interest rates in the relative pricing of assets in financial markets (see Zaloom 2009). They can also measure inflationary attitudes by means of surveys. The survey conducted regularly on behalf of the Bank of England clearly states the issues it wishes to pursue: "The nine questions asked in these quarterly surveys seek information on public knowledge, understanding and attitudes toward the MPC process, as well as expectations of interest rates and inflation and also look to measure satisfaction/dissatisfaction with the way the Bank of England is 'doing its job.' Five questions that are asked annually cover perceptions of the relationship between interest rates and inflation and knowledge of who sets rates" (Bank of England, n.d., "Bank of England/GfK NOP Inflation Attitudes Survey").

5. It will, no doubt, take considerable time before the failures of central banks are fully adjudicated. What can be said is that the personnel of central banks are

themselves reviewing these issues and assessing their own action and inaction, their own judgments and misjudgments, their own misguided faith in theories and methods during the last decade or two. Indeed, the scope of critical scrutiny generated from within central banks may equal or exceed the critical appraisals emanating from outside these institutions. To date, I have found the writings of Claudio Borio, deputy head of the Monetary and Economic Department and director of research and statistics at the Bank of International Settlements (BIS), most informative in setting out the basic issues pertaining to how inflation targeting, in particular, was implicated in the prehistory of the crisis.

6. Ann Stoler (2008) has acutely framed these uncertainties as "epistemic anxieties." These pervasive doubts arise from situations in which technocrats confront situations in which the analytical tools that constituted their specialized expertise prove inappropriate or inadequate for the tasks they are designed to regulate and manage, demanding, as we will see, creative action rather than the mere adherence to rules. Stoler examined what might appear to be a very different set of historical circumstances, the Dutch colonial administration in Indonesia. Yet she captures what is a fundamental challenge for virtually all forms of technocratic management. She demonstrates that epistemic anxieties were not merely incidental affective conditions of the Dutch colonial officials, but a central predicament confronting their administrative practices. These officials continually faced situations in which precisely the tools that constituted their specialized expertise were inappropriate for oversight and management of the world they were charged with administering. The conceptual categories, the administrative systems, and the protocols of accountability were inadequate to the task of representing the staggering complexities and dynamism of the colonial East Indies. Stoler's analysis allows us to see how management of the colonial system was, in many respects and by virtually all parties involved, improvised.

Chapter Two

1. The term "economy of words" hearkens back to the "verbal tradition," as Mary Morgan terms it, that predated the rise of "neoclassic" economics in the second half of the twentieth century; the verbal tradition was largely usurped by neoclassic economics with mathematical representations of economic processes. Morgan provides a superb account of the history of economic modeling, fully acknowledging the resilience of narrative as integral to modeling and to the styles of reasoning developed and practiced by economists (Morgan 2012, 217–55) See also note 2 below.

2. Donald MacKenzie elegantly describes the broader significance—the deep transformative grammar—of the contributions of Latour and his followers: "Detailed attention to the active, transformative processes by which scientific knowl-

edge is constructed breaks down the canonical view in which there is a 'world' entirely distinct from 'language' and thus undermines standard notions of reference in which 'words' have discrete, observable 'things' to which they refer" (2006, 22).

3. See also MacKenzie's delineation of "generic, effective, and Barnesian" performativity, which serve a different heuristic role (2006, 15–21).

4. The efficacy of inflation targeting is by no means a settled matter: "Laurence Ball and Niamh Sheridan (2005) look at a large sample of countries and show that adoption of inflation targeting does not help explain the recent move toward low, stable inflation. Monetary policy has improved both in those countries that have adopted inflation targets and in those that have not. This world-wide improvement in inflation outcomes could be because the world economy has not had to deal with supply shocks as adverse as those experienced in the 1970s or because central bankers have learned from the experience of the 1970s that high inflation should be assiduously avoided. But the evidence shows that inflation targeting is not a prerequisite for good monetary policy" (Mankiw 2006, 16). Again, see Borio's (2011) systematic appraisal of these shortcomings and their consequences.

5. In a subsequent brief conversation with me in 2010, Professor Besley noted that his early life and early research in East Africa had made him fully aware of the possibilities of ethnographic method and anthropological ideas.

6. Part of my initial interest in the work of Keynes derived from his insistence that "ordinary discourse" could capture the rich complexities and interdependences of economic phenomena: "It is a great fault of symbolic pseudo-mathematical methods of formalising a system of economic analysis . . . that they expressly assume strict independence between the factors involved and lose their cogency and authority if this hypothesis is disallowed; whereas, in ordinary discourse, where we are not blindly manipulating but know all the time what we are doing and what the words mean, we can keep 'at the back of our heads' the necessary reserves and qualifications and the adjustments which we shall have to make later on, in a way in which we cannot keep complicated partial differentials 'at the back' of several pages of algebra which assume they all vanish. Too large a proportion of recent 'mathematical' economics are merely concoctions, as imprecise as the initial assumptions they rest on, which allow the author to lose sight of the complexities and interdependencies of the real world in a maze of pretentious and unhelpful symbols (Keynes [1936] 2007, 297–98)." Early in my research I saw this turn toward linguistic modeling as compensatory, as a means for circumventing the limitations inherent in quantitative analysis. As the project developed, I became convinced that this kind of modeling of economic phenomena with words was far more significant, serving as a bridge to the performative dynamics operating naturalistically in the economy in vivo.

7. Dominic Boyer provides an account of Jürgen Habermas's notion of "communicative rationality" as follows: "Habermas argues, that communicative ratio-

nality cannot be predicated upon nonnormative or self-interested considerations in the long run, but rather only upon intersubjective coordination and normativity.... For Habermas, the blueprint for this more rational, coordinated mode of sociality has always lain dormant in the logical functions of rational communication. It is a linguistic potentiality inherent in propositional structure that has been 'unexploited' apparently for no other reason than the subjects do not full appreciate 'the potential of the binding ... force of good reason'" (Boyer 2005, 237). In general, I think this is precisely the kind of communicative action that central bankers aspire to and the linguistic potentials that they seek to exploit. What complicates matters is that in their efforts to manage expectations central bankers continually encounter human sentiments and motives that are indifferent to or entirely antagonistic to reason and rationality. Here the work of Kaushik Sunder Rajan (2006) is decisive. His analysis of the management of "hype" in biotech companies demonstrates how shaping expectations that are not fully or necessarily rational can impel or disrupt creative action (see Keynes [1936] 2007, 161–62).

Chapter Three

1. An archivist at the Bank of England was the first person to tell me this story, one that I heard retold by other officials of the bank.

2. The bank further elaborated on the representational labor performed by the fan chart as follows: "The MPC's projection for GDP growth is presented in the form of a fan chart rather than a single point forecast because the future is inherently uncertain. But the past is uncertain too. Official measures of past GDP growth are regularly revised as new information is received and methodological improvements are made. In forming its projection, the MPC makes allowances for 'data uncertainty.' ... But until recently neither the scale of these adjustments, nor the range of uncertainty around them, have been explicitly reported.... [Fan charts] therefore show the MPC's best collective judgment of the most likely path for the mature estimate of GDP growth, and the uncertainty around it, both over the past and into the future" (Bank of England 2007, 39).

3. Put reciprocally, the economy requires the continual generation of multiple and conflicting representations (often misrepresentations) by business, government, and the public in order to make it work. The incessant representation of economic conditions is pursued to address, if not always solve, creatively human predicaments in the wild.

4. In an influential article published two decades ago, a well-known and perhaps unlikely figure, Lawrence Summers, described how shifts in economic thinking might establish the precondition for the anthropological issues pursued in this study: "Good empirical evidence tells its story regardless of the precise way in

which it is analyzed. In large part it is its simplicity that makes it persuasive. Physicists do not compete to find more elaborate ways to observe falling apples. Instead they have made progress because theory has sought inspiration from a wide range of empirical phenomena. Macroeconomics could progress in the same way. But progress is unlikely as long as macroeconomists require the armor of a stochastic pseudoworld before doing battle with evidence from the real one" (Summers 1991, 146).

5. This is, in part, an anthropological polemic. There is much I can and have learned from Akerlof and Shiller, as well as behavioral finance more broadly.

6. The monetary economist Michael Woodford—echoing the observations of Robert Lucas Jr. (1986)—traces the arc of these innovative practices, framing essentially the anthropological question pursued herein: "Central banking is not like steering an oil tanker, or even guiding a spacecraft, which follows a trajectory that depends on constantly changing factors, but that does *not* depend on the vehicle's own expectation about where it is heading. Because the key decisionmakers in an economy are forward-looking, central banks affect the economy as much through their influence on *expectations* as through any direct, mechanical effects of central bank trading in the market for overnight cash. As a consequence there is good reason for a central bank to commit itself to a systematic approach to policy, that not only provides an explicit framework for decisionmaking within the bank, but that is also used to explain the bank's decisions to the public" (Woodford 2005, 2–3). Woodford is introducing into the field of monetary policy what anthropologists would call "reflexive subjects," that is, actors whose future-oriented sensibilities can influence the course and magnitude of economic activity. The communicative imperative of central banks is premised on the "appearance" of these reflexive agents within the field of economic action—agents endowed with capacities and capabilities that can be mobilized to achieve specific policy ends of central banks through a systematic exchange of information and ideas (Mervyn King 2005b; Lucas 1986). Woodford (2012) in his own sophisticated modeling work seeks to incorporate the decision-making capacities of central bankers and their responses to new information into his projections of prices and interest rates. George Soros (1994, 2008) has struggled long and hard to persuade economists of the key role played by reflexive subjects in the operation of financial markets.

Chapter Four

1. Unscheduled FOMC meetings are rare. They are typically called in the event of an unforeseen shock to the economy and the financial system or, as in this case, in the event of new data relevant to policy decisions becoming available to the committee between scheduled meetings.

2. For full job descriptions for the district and branch directors, see FRB, n.d.,

Role and Responsibilities of Federal Reserve Directors. Note, in particular, the recent restrictions on their roles, pursuant to the Dodd–Frank Act, regarding the election of the presidents and first vice presidents of the district branches, as well as directors' access to confidential supervisory information (41).

Chapter Five

1. "As early as October 31, 1972, before the first oil shock, the Council of Ministers of the European Community passed a resolution that called for the member states to: progressively reduce the growth rate of the [broad] money supply . . . until it equals that of the real [GNP], augmented by the normative price rise determined in accordance with overall economic aims and after taking account of the structural development of the relationship between money supply and national product. This target is to be reached not later than the end of 1974" (Posen 1997). In a section of the September 1973 Deutsche Bundesbank *Monthly Report* titled "Monetary Policy through Control of the Central Bank Money Supply," the Bundesbank stated that it "based its policy on the consideration that the banks' need for central bank money ultimately depends on the scale of the expansion in bank lending," and that it was prepared to make additional central bank money available "only in so far as such [provision] was consistent with its monetary policy target of reducing the inflation-induced excess money supply" (quoted in Posen 1997).

2. The Bretton Woods rules had allowed for very limited discretion in the exercise of monetary policy. "Monetary coordination in Bretton Woods system centered on the construction of a new fixed exchange rate regime. In consultation with the IMF, member states agreed to set the value of their currencies at predetermined rates and promised to keep their currencies trading in international markets with a band of 2 percent (thus plus or minus 1 percent of the predetermined central rate) at all times. In practice, their dislike of exchange-rate variability led the European countries to stay with a smaller margin of three-fourths of 1 percent (.75%) on either side of the dollar. Though not originally designed to do so, the Bretton Wood system soon evolved into a fixed exchange-rate system pegged to the dollar, which in turn pegged to gold at the fixed rate of $35 an ounce" (McNamara 1998, 74).

3. "In fact, the main reason why CBM was initially chosen as target aggregate was the Bundesbank's perception of its advantages in terms of transparency and communication with the public. The Bundesbank explained its choice of CBM in the following words: "[CBM] brings out the central bank's responsibility for monetary expansion especially clearly. The money creation of the banking system as a whole and the money creation of the central bank are closely linked through currency in circulation and the banks' obligation to maintain a certain portion of their deposits with the central bank. Central bank money, which comprises these two

components, can therefore readily serve as an indicator of both. A rise by a certain rate in central bank money shows not only the size of the money creation of the banking system but also the extent to which the central bank has provided funds for the banks' money creation" (quoted in Posen 1997).

4. The 2 percent figure was arrived at in part to compensate for the tendency of the consumer price index to overstate inflation by underestimating increases in the quality of goods, and also to avoid the zero lower-bound problem, which will be examined in chapter 9.

5. "From 1975 until 1987 the Bundesbank announced targets for the growth of the central bank money stock (CBM). CBM is defined as currency in circulation plus sight deposits, time deposits with maturity under four years, and savings deposits and savings bonds with maturity of less than four years, the latter three components weighted by their respective required reserve ratios as of January 1974. Since 1988, the Bundesbank has used growth in M3 as its announced target. Apart from not including savings deposits with longer maturities and savings bonds, the major difference between M3 and CBM is that the latter is a weighted sum aggregate while the former is a simple sum. The only source for large divergences between the growth of the two aggregates is significant fluctuations in the holdings of currency as compared to deposits. This potential divergence became critical in 1988 in the face of shifting financial incentives (leading to the switch in target aggregates), and again in 1990–91 after German monetary unification (Posen 1997).

Chapter Six

1. The snap election was brought about by the loss of the National Party's parliamentary majority occasioned by the declaration by a member of parliament, Marilyn Waring, that she intended to cross the aisle to vote with the opposition Labour Party. Subsequently, Waring was appointed to the Board of the Reserve Bank of New Zealand, where she served from 2005 until 2009.

Chapter Seven

1. See, e.g., Lucas 1976, 19–46.

2. "A further limitation of the current generation of DSGE models lies in the fact that, so far, they have not been entirely successful in modeling important relationships between the real sector and events in the financial sector. This shortcoming was obvious even before the financial market turbulence that commenced with the collapse of Lehman Brothers in September 2008. Although this applies equally to traditional macroeconomic models, it does make clear that a central bank cannot afford to eschew a broad-ranging approach to analysis" (Deutsche Bundesbank 2008, 33).

3. As we will see in the next chapter, an identical insight informs Graham Smart's analysis of the operation of the Bank of Canada's forecasting and policy model (Smart 2006, 85–136). Donald MacKenzie provides a similar insight on the option pricing models he studied: "The models ... are verbal and mathematical representations of markets or economic processes. These representations are deliberately simplified so that economic reasoning about those markets and economic processes can take precise mathematical form.... The models are the outcome of analytical thinking, of the manipulation of equations, and sometimes of geometric reasoning. They are underpinned by sophisticated economic thinking and sometimes advanced mathematics, but computationally they are not overwhelmingly complex" (MacKenzie 2006, 6).

4. Here is how two of the bank's officials described the role of the monetary pillar: "In sum, the monetary pillar ensures that longer-term risks to price stability emanating from the longer-run link between money growth and inflation are duly taken into account in the conduct of monetary policy. In this vein, the monetary pillar represents a commitment by the ECB not to disregard any information that can support its pursuit of the price stability objective in the medium term and the establishment of a nominal anchor for the euro area economy. Moreover, the monetary pillar represents a pragmatic solution to the challenges faced by all central banks in looking beyond standard forecasting horizons, notably when confronted by inflated asset prices and evolving financial imbalances. The empirically evident link between monetary developments and evolving imbalances in asset and credit markets implies that the two-pillar strategy, with its important role given to monetary analysis, may enable the detection of these imbalances at an early stage and a response to the implied risks to financial, economic and price stability in a timely, forward-looking, manner. Finally, in an environment of financial turmoil, the detailed analysis of quantitative developments in money and credit contributes to appropriately assessing the financing conditions of the economy and adjustments taking place in the banking sector.... [T]he ECB's monetary analysis relies on a suite of econometric tools for model-based assessment and detailed institutional analysis. The former includes, inter alia, empirical money and credit demand models, statistical filters, forecasting models, as well as small and medium-scale structural models. The latter entails, inter alia, an encompassing examination of the bank balance sheet data, including the components, counterparts and sectoral contributions to monetary aggregates. The multifaceted nature of monetary analysis implies that it can probably never be fully summarised in one single analytical framework, so that it will continue to rely on a suite of approaches. At the same time, the need to continuously enhance the monetary analysis in order to keep track of structural change in the economy will in all likelihood continue to be a challenge as well as a constant encouragement for scientific advancements in the future. Given that, as we argued before, many of the big policy mistakes of the past were due to a disregard for, or misinterpretation of, monetary developments, this

would appear to be an effort worth making for central banks" (Papademos and Stark 2010: 59–60).

5. Milton Friedman would of course agree that monetarism is about values, albeit a somewhat different constellations of values.

6. See Morris, Ongena, and Schuknech 2006. Their analysis appears to have informed Trichet's commentary.

Chapter Eight

1. See Mary Morgan's excellent account of the history of what she quite rightly refers to as the "Newlyn–Phillips Machine," acknowledging the role of Walter T. Newlyn in its creation (Morgan 2012, 172–216). Her account goes beyond a mere history, examining the deeper cultural processes mastered by the Newlyn–Phillips machine: "Turning . . . [an economic] metaphor, which begins as a figure of speech and idle likeness, into an analogical model involves both cognitive and imaginative work" (175).

2. Donald L. Kohn, a former vice chairman of the Federal Reserve System, commented on the centrality of Phillips's insights for navigating the then current (mid-2008) inflationary tempest: "A model in the Phillips curve tradition remains at the core of how most academic researchers and policymakers—including this one—think about fluctuations in inflation; indeed, alternative frameworks seem to lack solid economic foundations and empirical support. But the modern Phillips curve differs substantially from versions in use several decades ago; policymakers and academics alike are now attuned to the importance of expectations, the possibility of structural change, and the uncertainty that surrounds our understanding of the dynamics of wage and price adjustment. Moreover, the link between inflation and resource utilization often emphasized in a Phillips curve framework accounts for only a modest part of inflation fluctuations" (Kohn 2008).

3. My characterization of the fieldwork pursued by central bankers has aroused some skepticism. My colleague George Marcus was reading some of my notes and recognized Alan Bollard as someone he knew of from his time at the University of Auckland. He noted that Bollard had written an MA thesis on the monetization of the Tongan economy, which Marcus had found valuable for his own ethnographic research.

Chapter Nine

1. IS-LM stands for Investment Saving/Liquidity Preference Money Supply; see Krugman, n.d., "There is Something about Macro."

2. Svensson provided a simplified calculation of the real market rate: "Real

market rate = Nominal market rate – expected inflation = Repo rate + spread – expected inflation" (Svensson 2009, 12).

3. Svensson describes how this monetary logic might work: "It is easy for the central bank to implement part (2) and keep the exchange rate at a given level when the currency is strong and would appreciate if it were allowed to float. Initial doubts among the market participants and the risk of this method failing means that it would appear to be a good deal to buy domestic currency cheaply and then sell it at a higher price when the method fails. This would lead to a high demand for the domestic currency. The central bank, however, could sell as much domestic currency as it likes and would only see its foreign exchange reserves increase correspondingly. A large foreign exchange reserve and monetary base might be considered inflationary, but higher inflation and inflation expectations are exactly what the central bank wants in this situation.

"The difficult thing, in contrast, is to maintain a fixed exchange rate when the currency is weak and would depreciate if it was allowed to float, as was the case of the speculative attacks the Swedish krona was subjected to during the fixed exchange rate regime in the early 1990s. In such a situation, the central bank would have to buy the domestic currency and pay with foreign exchange reserves, which are finite and would eventually run out. When the market realises that there is a difference between maintaining a fixed exchange rate when the currency is strong and when it is weak, the high demand for the domestic currency will cease and the foreign exchange reserves will return to a more normal level (Svensson 2009, 7)."

4. This is the analytical basis of his second policy proposition: "When the interest rate is zero the exchange rate becomes an interesting indicator of expectations of the future price level. According to the interest rate parity condition, the current exchange rate is determined by the expected future exchange rate, current and expected future interest rate differentials between domestic and foreign interest rates and expected future currency risk premia. The future exchange rate depends on future price level, the future real exchange rate and future foreign price level. For exchange rates and price levels expressed in logarithms we can specify the following relation:

Current exchange rate = Expected future (exchange rate – interest rate differential + foreign exchange risk premium)

= Expected future (price level + real exchange rate – foreign price level – interest rate differential + foreign exchange risk premium)

With an expected future domestic interest rate that is zero or low, future interest rate differentials and foreign exchange risk premia for a small open economy are largely exogenous and given. At a reasonably long horizon, the expected future

real exchange rate is given by a neutral real equilibrium rate and is largely exogenous for a small economy. The expected future foreign price level is also exogenous for a small open economy. Consequently, under these conditions, the expected future price level is practically the only endogenous variable that affects
the current exchange rate. With this reasoning, the current exchange rate, all other
things being equal, becomes a direct indicator of the expected future price level.
By observing the exchange rate, the central bank can thus observe expectations of
the future price level. Higher inflation expectations and thereby a higher expected
future price level lead then to a depreciation of the currency today, all else being
equal. A measure that raises expectations of future inflation and the future price
level should thus show up in a depreciated currency. A strengthening of the currency may therefore be ominous and interpreted as a sign that inflation expectations are falling (Svensson 2009, 6)."

5. Svensson addressed the issue of competitive devaluation as follows: "Does
this method represent a competitive devaluation? The answer is that this is no
more of a competitive devaluation than any other form of monetary policy expansion. Note that if the zero lower bound for the interest rate did not exist, the
central bank could reduce the real interest rate by reducing the nominal rate. This
nominal rate reduction would lead to a depreciation of the currency. The currency
depreciation . . . achieves the same currency depreciation directly instead of indi-
rectly via a reduction of the nominal interest rate. The method is thus no more of
a competitive devaluation than a reduction of the nominal interest rate would be,
if such a reduction were possible. It is quite simply a method that entails a certain
degree of monetary policy expansion, but by using means other than the policy
rate" (Svensson 2009, 8).

Chapter Ten

1. Cutting the repo rate to 0.5 percent means that the interest rate corridor,
that is, the Riksbank's deposit and lending facilities, should be modified, as the current corridor construction would in this case entail a negative deposit rate. Material was presented proposing a slightly narrower corridor that entailed setting the
Riksbank's lending rate at 1.0 per cent and the deposit rate at 0.0 percent, with a
repo rate of 0.5 percent (Sveriges Riksbank 2009b).

Chapter Eleven

1. The nominal gross value added (GVA) contributed to the UK economy
by each region is as follows: Central Southern England (10.9%); East Midlands
(6.4%); Greater London (18.8%); North East (3.4%); North West (10.2%); North-

ern Ireland (2.3%); Scotland (8.2%); South East & East Anglia (12.3%); South West, Wales (3.9%); West Midlands & Oxfordshire (9.4%); and Yorkshire & the Humber (7.3%) (Ellis and Pike 2005, 426).

2. See chapter 3, note 4, for the longer version of the quote by Summers.

Chapter Twelve

1. Professor Miles's presentation was one of the finest accounts I had heard of the issues at stake in the crisis. Delivered to a group of high school students and their teachers, the talk had an impressive degree of analytical precision and communicative integrity.

Chapter Thirteen

1. The panel of experts briefing the ECON were themselves engaging in crisis management and institutional reform; they were fully integrated in the networks of technocrats who were drafting, revising, implementing and critically scrutinizing the various measures that were being promoted to address the crisis.

2. The intervention depended on an arcane debate on the Target 2 accounts of the bank (Sinn 2012).

3. Draghi, in his London comments, reviewed the breakdown of the transmission mechanism that had reversed monetary integration as follows: "There are some short-term challenges, to say the least. The short-term challenges in our view relate mostly to the financial fragmentation that has taken place in the euro area. Investors retreated within their national boundaries. The interbank market is not functioning. It is only functioning very little within each country by the way, but it is certainly not functioning across countries.

"And I think the key strategy point here is that if we want to get out of this crisis, we have to repair this financial fragmentation.

"There are at least two dimensions to this. The interbank market is not functioning, because for any bank in the world the current liquidity regulations make—to lend to other banks or borrow from other banks—a money losing proposition. So the first reason is that regulation has to be recalibrated completely.

"The second point is in a sense a collective action problem: because national supervisors, looking at the crisis, have asked their banks, the banks under their supervision, to withdraw their activities within national boundaries. And they ring fenced liquidity positions so liquidity can't flow, even across the same holding group because the financial sector supervisors are saying 'no.'

"So even though each one of them may be right, collectively they have been wrong. And this situation will have to be overcome of course.

"And then there is a risk aversion factor. Risk aversion has to do with counter-party risk. Now to the extent that I think my counterparty is going to default, I am not going to lend to this counterparty. But it can be because it is short of funding. And I think we took care of that with the two big LTROs where we injected half a trillion of net liquidity into the euro area banks. We took care of that" (Draghi 2012b).

4. In a subsequent speech entitled "Revisiting the European Social Contract," which was delivered by Benoît Cœuré, one of Draghi's close allies on the executive board of the ECB, these issues were further elaborated: "In the crisis, the ECB's continued commitment to price stability and the integrity of the euro has been one of the few elements of certainty in a highly volatile and uncertain environment. This commitment to monetary stability is not only grounded in its economic merits but is also a cornerstone of the social contract. It protects poorer households from the dire effects of inflation on purchasing power. It ensures that no redistribution of wealth takes place that is unsanctioned by democratic processes, which is exactly what inflation does. And it buttresses political stability by avoiding the social unrest that unchecked inflation can cause" (Cœuré 2013). Cœuré's went on to articulate, again in the language of European integration, the new role of the ECB as a key institutional actor in the project of creating and underwriting the multiple dimensions of European solidarity.

5. The project of solidarity and technocratic planning that Paul Rabinow (1989) dates to the early nineteenth century in France commences with infrastructural projects, public health programs, and the extension of insurance benefits to the public.

References

Abolafia, Mitchel Y. 1998. "Markets as Cultures." In *The Laws of the Markets*, edited by Michel Callon, 69–85. Oxford: Blackwell.

———. 2004. "Framing Moves: Interpretive Politics at the Federal Reserve." *Journal of Public Administration Research and Theory* 14 (3): 349–70.

———. 2005. "Making Sense of Recession." In *The Economic Sociology of Capitalism*, edited by Victor Nee and Richard Swedberg, 204–26. Princeton, NJ: Princeton University Press.

Ahamed, Liaquat. 2009. *Lords of Finance: The Bankers Who Broke the World*. New York: Penguin.

Akerlof, George A., William Dickens, and George Perry. 1996. "The Macroeconomics of Low Inflation." *Brookings Papers on Economic Activity* 1996 (1): 1–59.

Akerlof, George A., and Robert Shiller. 2009. *Animal Spirits: How Human Psychology Drives the Economy, and Why It Matters for Global Capitalism*. Princeton, NJ: Princeton University Press.

Althusser, Louis. 1971. "Ideology and Ideological State Apparatuses." In *Lenin and Philosophy and Other Essays*, translated by Ben Brewster, pt. 2, 121–76. New York: Monthly Review Press.

Ashley, James, Ronnie Driver, Simmon Hayes, and Chistopher Jeffery. 2005. "Dealing with Data Uncertainty." *Bank of England Quarterly Bulletin*, Spring: 23–29.

Åslund, Anders. 2012. "Why a Breakup of the Euro Area Must Be Avoided: Lessons from Previous Breakups." Peterson Institute for International Economics Policy Brief 12–20, August.

Austin, John L. 1961. *Philosophical Papers*, edited by J. O. Urmson and G. J. Warnock. Oxford: Oxford University Press.

Bagehot, Walter. 2006. *Lombard Street: A Description of the Monetary Market*. Charleston, SC: Biblobazaar.

Baldwin, Richard, and Charles Wyplosz. 2004. *The Economics of European Integration*. New York: McGraw Hill.

Ball, Laurence, and Niamh Sheridan. 2005. "Does Inflation Targeting Matter?" In *The Inflation-Targeting Debate*, edited by Ben S. Bernanke and Michael Woodford, 249–82. Chicago: University of Chicago Press.

Bank of England. 1999. "The Transmission Mechanism of Monetary Policy." Report prepared by Bank of England staff under the guidance of the Monetary Policy Committee in response to suggestions by the Treasury Committee of the House of Commons and the House of Lords Select Committee on the Monetary Policy Committee of the Bank of England. May.

———. 2002. "The MPC's Fan Charts." *Inflation Report, May 2002*. http://www.bankofengland.co.uk/publications/Documents/inflationreport/ir02mayfanbox.pdf.

———. 2007. "Explaining the New GDP Fan Chart." *Inflation Report, November 2007*. http://www.bankofengland.co.uk/publications/Documents/inflationreport/ir07novfanbox.pdf.

———. 2010a. "Agents' Summary of Business Conditions—July 2010." http://www.bankofengland.co.uk/publications/Documents/agentssummary/agsum10jul.pdf.

———. 2010b. *Inflation Report, May 2010*. http://www.bankofengland.co.uk/publications/Pages/inflationreport/ir1002.aspx.

———. 2010c. "Minutes of the Monetary Policy Committee Meeting, 7 and 8 July 2010." (published 21 July 2010).

———. 2011a. *Inflation Report, May 2011*. http://www.bankofengland.co.uk/publications/Pages/inflationreport/ir1102.aspx.

———. 2011b. "Minutes of the Monetary Policy Committee Meeting, 6 and 7 July 2011" (published 20 July 2011). http://www.bankofengland.co.uk/publications/minutes/Documents/mpc/pdf/2011/mpc1107.pdf.

———. n.d. "Bank of England/GfK NOP Inflation Attitudes Survey." http://www.bankofengland.co.uk/publications/Pages/other/nop.aspx.

———. n.d. "Core Purposes." http://www.bankofengland.co.uk/about/corepurposes/index.htm.

———. n.d. "Quantitative Easing Explained." http://www.bankofengland.co.uk/monetarypolicy/Pages/qe/assetpurchases2.aspx.

Barnes, Sebastian, and Colin Ellis. 2005. "Indicators of Short-Term Movements in Business Investment." *Bank of England Quarterly Bulletin*, Spring: 30–38.

Bean, Charles R. 2009. "The Great Moderation, the Great Panic, and the Great Contraction." Schumpeter Lecture, Annual Congress of the European Economic Association, Barcelona, 25 August. http://www.bankofengland.co.uk/publications/Documents/speeches/2009/speech399.pdf.

Belke, Ansgar, and Jens Klose. 2012. "ECB and FED Crisis Policies at the Zero-Lower Bound—An Empirical Assessment Based on Modified Reaction Functions." Paper presented at the European Parliament's Committee on Economic and Monetary Affairs Monetary Dialogue with the ECB-2012, July 9.

Berger, Peter L., and Thomas Luckmann. 1967. *The Social Construction of Reality: A Treatise in the Sociology of Knowledge.* New York: Anchor.

Bernanke, Ben S. 1983. "Nonmonetary Effects of the Financial Crisis in the Propagation of the Great Depression." *American Economic Review* 73 (3): 257–76.

———. 2002a. "Deflation: Making Sure 'It' Doesn't Happen Here." Speech presented at the National Economists Club, Washington, DC, November 21.

———. 2002b. "On Milton Friedman's Ninetieth Birthday." Speech presented at the Conference to Honor Milton Friedman, University of Chicago, November 8.

———. 2004. "Central Bank Talk and Monetary Policy." Speech presented at the Japan Society, New York, October 4.

———. 2007. "Federal Reserve Communications." Speech presented to the Cato Institute 25th Annual Monetary Conference, Washington, DC, November 17.

———. 2008. "Outstanding Issues in the Analysis of Inflation." Speech presented at the Federal Reserve Bank of Boston's 53rd Annual Economic Conference, Chatham, MA, June 9. www.federalreserve.gov/newsevents/speech/bernanke20080609a.htm.

———. 2009a. "The Federal Reserve's Balance Sheet." Speech presented at the Federal Reserve Bank of Richmond 2009 Credit Market Symposium, Charlotte, NC, April 3.

———. 2009b. "The Crisis and the Policy Response." Speech presented at the Stamp Lecture, London School of Economics, January 13. http://www.federalreserve.gov/newsevents/speech/bernanke20090113a.htm.

———. 2010a. "Monetary Policy and the Housing Bubble." Speech presented at the Annual Meeting of the American Economic Association, Atlanta, GA, January 3.

———. 2012. "Monetary Policy since the Onset of the Crisis." Speech presented at the Federal Reserve Bank of Kansas City Economic Symposium, Jackson Hole, WY, August 31–September 1.

Bernanke, Ben, Thomas Luabach, Fredric S. Mishkin, and Adam S. Posen. 1999. *Inflation Targeting: Lessons from the International Experience.* Princeton, NJ: Princeton University Press.

Bernanke, Ben, and Fredric Mishkin. 1997. "Inflation Targeting: A New Framework for Monetary Policy." *Journal of Economic Perspectives* 11: 97–116.

Bernanke, Ben, and Michael Woodford. 2005. Introduction to *The Inflation-Targeting Debate,* edited by Ben Bernanke and Michael Woodford, 1–10. Chicago: University of Chicago Press.

Besley, Timothy. 2009. "BOE's Besley Says Control of Public Finances Is 'What Counts'" (interview with Tom Keene). "On the Economy," Bloomberg Radio, May 26.

Beyer, Andreas, Vitor Gaspar, Christina Gerberding, Otmar Issing. Forthcoming. "Opting Out of the Great Inflation: German Monetary Policy after the Break

Down of Bretton Woods." In *The Great Inflation*, edited by Michael Bordo and Athanasios Orphanides. Chicago: University of Chicago Press.

Black, Fischer. 1986. "Noise." *Journal of Finance* 41: 529–43.

Blanchard, Olivier. 2008. "The State of Macro." NBER Working Paper No. 14259. National Bureau of Economic Research, Cambridge, MA.

Blanchard, Olivier, Giovanni Dell'Ariccia, and Paolo Mauro. 2010. "Rethinking Macroeconomic Policy." IMF Staff Position Note. Washington, DC: International Monetary Fund.

Blanchard, Olivier, and Jordi Galí. 2007. "Real Wage Rigidities and the New Keynesian Model." *Journal of Money, Credit, and Banking* 39 (1): 35–65.

Blanchflower, David G. 2007. "Recent Developments in the UK Economy: The Economics of Walking About." Bernard Corry Memorial Lecture, given at Queen Mary, University of London, May 30.

Blanchflower, David G., Jumana Saleheen, and Chris Shadforth. 2007. "The Impact of the Recent Migration from Eastern Europe on the UK Economy." Discussion Paper No. 17, Monetary Policy Committee Unit, Bank of England.

Blinder, Alan S. 1998. *Central Banking in Theory and Practice*. Cambridge, MA: MIT Press.

———. 2004. *The Quiet Revolution*. New Haven, CT: Yale University Press.

———. 2009. "Talking about Monetary Policy: The Virtues (and Vices?) of Central Bank Communication." BIS Working Paper No. 274. Basel, Switzerland: Bank for International Settlements.

———. 2012. "Central Bank Independence and Credibility During and After a Crisis." Paper presented at the Jackson Hole Symposium, September 1. http://www.kansascityfed.org/publicat/sympos/2012/ab.pdf.

Blinder, Alan S., Charles Goodhart, Philipp Hidebrand, David Lipton, and Charles Wyplosz. 2001. *How Do Central Banks Talk?* Geneva Report on the World Economy, 3. Geneva: International Center for Monetary and Banking Studies.

Blinder, Alan S., Jakob de Haan, Michael Ehrmann, Marcel Fratzscher, and David-Jan Jansen. 2008. "What We Know and What We Would Like to Know about Central Bank Communication." VoxEU.org, May 15. http://www.voxeu.org/index.php?q=node/1143.

Blinder, Alan S., and Ricardo Reis. 2005. "The Greenspan Standard." Paper presented at the Federal Reserve Bank of Kansas City Symposium, Jackson Hole, WY, August 25–27.

Bollard, Alan. 2010. *Crisis: One Central Bank Governor and the Global Financial Collapse*. Auckland, NZ: Auckland University Press.

Bollard, Alan, and Özer Karagedikli. 2006. "Inflation Targeting: The New Zealand Experience and Some Lessons." Paper presented at the Inflation Targeting Performance and Challenges Conference of the Central Bank of the Republic of Turkey, Istanbul, January 19–20.

Bordo, Michael D., and Athanasios Orphanides, eds. Forthcoming. *The Great Inflation*. Chicago: University of Chicago Press.

Borio, Claudio. 2011. "Central Banking Post-Crisis: What Compass for Unchartered Waters?" Keynote address presented at the SUERF–National Bank of Poland Conference "Monetary Policy after the Crisis," Warsaw, March 4.

Borup, Mads, Nik Brown, Kornelia Konrad, and Lente H. Van. 2006. "The Sociology of Expectations in Science and Technology." *Technology Analysis & Strategic Management* 18 (3): 285–98.

Boyer, Dominic. 2005. *Spirit and System: Media, Intellectuals, and the Dialectic in Modern German Culture*. Chicago: University of Chicago Press.

———. 2012. "From Media Anthropology to Anthropology of Mediation." In *The Sage Handbook of Social Anthropology*, edited by Richard Fardon, Olivia Harris, Trevor H. J. Marchand, Mark Nuttall, Cris Shore, Veronica Strang, and Richard A. Wilson, 383–93. London: Sage.

Brash, Donald T. 1996a. "Monetary Policy and the Free-Market Economy." Speech presented at the Auckland Manufacturers Association, Auckland, New Zealand, February 2.

———. 1996b. "New Zealand's Remarkable Reforms." Speech presented at the Fifth Annual Hayek Memorial Lecture, Institute of Economic Affairs, London, June 4.

———. 1997. "An Address to the Canterbury Employers Chamber of Commerce," Christchurch, NZ, January 26.

———. Forthcoming. "Practical Experiences in Reducing Inflation: The Case of New Zealand." In *The Great Inflation*, edited by Michael Bordo and Athanasios Orphanides. Chicago: University of Chicago Press.

Brenneis, Donald. 1999. "New Lexicon, Old Language: Negotiating the 'Global' at the National Science Foundation." In *Critical Anthropology Now: Unexpected Contexts, Shifting Constituencies, Changing Agendas*, edited by George E. Marcus, 123–46. Santa Fe, NM: School of American Research Press.

Brown, Nik, Brian Rappert, and Andrew Webster. 2000. *Contested Futures: A Sociology of Prospective Technoscience*. Surrey, UK: Ashgate Press.

Brunner, Karl. 1971. "The Uses of Money: Money in the Theory of an Exchange Economy." *American Economic Review* 61 (5): 784–805.

———. 1981. "The Art of Central Banking." Working Paper No. GPB 81–6. University of Rochester Center for Research in Government Policy and Business.

Brunner, Karl, and Allan H. Meltzer. 1976. "An Aggregate Theory for a Closed Economy." In *Monetarism*, edited by Jerome Stern. New York: American Elsevier.

Buiter, Willem. 2011. "The Terrible Consequences of a Eurozone Collapse." *Ft.com*, December 7. http://www.ft.com/intl/cms/s/0/6cf8ce18-2042-11e1-9878-00144 feabdco.html#axzz2KzS8FgeZ.

Burke, Kenneth. 1974. *A Grammar of Motive*. Berkeley: University of California Press.

Callon, Michel. 1986. "Some Elements of a Sociology of Translation: Domestication of the Scallops and the Fishermen of St. Brieuc Bay." In *Power, Action, and*

Belief: A New Sociology of Knowledge, edited by John Law. London: Routledge and Kegan Paul.

———. 1998. "An Essay on Framing and Overflowing: Economic Externalities Revisited by Sociology." In *The Laws of the Markets*, edited by Michel Callon, 244–69. Oxford: Blackwell.

———. 2007. "Performative Economics." In *Do Economists Make Markets?*, edited by Donald MacKenzie, Fabian Muniesa, and Lucia Siu, 311–57. Princeton, NJ: Princeton University Press.

Callon, Michel, and Koray Caliskan. 2005. "New and Old Directions in the Anthropology of Markets." Paper presented at the Wenner-Gren Foundation for Anthropological Research, New York, April.

Callon, Michel, and John Law. 2005. "On Qualculation, Agency, and Otherness." *Environment and Planning D: Society and Space* 23 (5): 717–33.

Capie, Forrest. 2010. *The Bank of England: 1950s to 1979*. Cambridge: Cambridge University Press.

Castle, Jennifer, and Colin Ellis. 2002. "Building a Real-Time Database for GDP(E)." *Bank of England Quarterly Bulletin*, Spring: 42–49.

Cecchetti, Stephen. 2008. "Our Need to Sustain the 'Great Moderation.'" *FT.com*, June 22. http://www.ft.com//cms/s/0/71772496-4065-11dd-bd48-0000779fd2ac .html.

Chehal, Puneet, and Bharat Trehan. 2009. "Talking about Tomorrow's Monetary Policy Today." *FRBSF Economic Letter* 2009–35 (November 9). http://www .frbsf.org/publications/economics/letter/2009/el2009-35.html.

Clarida, Richard, Jordi Galí, and Mark Gertler. 1999. "The Science of Monetary Policy: A New-Keynesian Perspective." *Journal of Economic Literature* 37 (4): 1661–1707.

Clifford, James, and George Marcus, eds. 1986. *Writing Culture: The Poetics and Politics of Representation*. Berkeley: University of California Press.

Cœuré, Benoît. 2013. "Revisiting the European Social Contract." Speech presented at the European Conference at Harvard, "Europe 2.0: Taking the Next Step," Cambridge, MA, March 2.

Collier, Stephen J. 2011. *Post-Soviet Social: Neoliberalism, Social Modernity, Biopolitics*. Princeton, NJ: Princeton University Press.

Comaroff, Jean, and John Comaroff. 2003. "Transparent Fictions, or the Conspiracies of a Liberal Imagination: An Afterword." In *Transparency and Conspiracy: Ethnographies of Suspicion in the New World Order*, edited by Harry G. West and Todd Sanders. Durham, NC: Duke University Press.

Connolly, Bernard. 1995. *The Rotten Heart of Europe: The Dirty War for Europe's Money*. London: Faber and Faber.

Copernicus, Nicolaus. 1995. *Minor Works*. Translated by Edward Rosen. Baltimore: Johns Hopkins University Press.

Dale, Spencer, Athanasios Orphanides, and Pär Österholm. 2008. "Imperfect Central Bank Communication—Information versus Distraction." International Monetary Fund Working Paper No. WP/08/60. Washington, DC: International Monetary Fund.

Davies, Gavyn. 2012a. "Draghi Breaks the Ultimate Euro Taboo." *FT.com*, August 5. http://blogs.ft.com/gavyndavies/2012/08/05/draghi-breaks-the-ultimate -euro-taboo/.

———. 2012b. "Major Change in Bernanke's Policy Reaction Function." *FT.com*, December 16. http://blogs.ft.com/gavyndavies/2012/12/16/a-major-change-in -bernankes-policy-reaction-function/.

Deutsche Bundesbank. 2000. *Macro-Econometric Multi-Country Model: MEMMOD*. Frankfurt am Main: Deutsche Bundesbank.

———. 2008. "Development and Application of DSGE Models for the German Economy." Deutsche Bundesbank Monthly Report. July.

Dewey, John. (1927) 1991. *The Public and Its Problems*. Athens, OH: Swallow Press/Ohio University Press.

Douglas, Roger, and Louise Callan. 1987. *Toward Prosperity: People and Politics in the 1980s in NZ: A Personal View*. Auckland, NZ: D. Bateman.

Draghi, Mario. 2012a. "Introductory Statement by Mario Draghi, President of the ECB, Brussels, 9 July 2012." Hearing at the Committee on Economic and Monetary Affairs of the European Parliament. http://www.ecb.int/press/key /date/2012/html/sp120709.en.html.

———. 2012b. "Speech by Mario Draghi, President of the European Central Bank at the Global Investment Conference in London, 26 July 2012." http://www.ecb .int/press/key/date/2012/html/sp120726.en.html.

Duke, Elizabeth. 2010. "Come with Me to the FOMC." Speech presented to the Money Marketeers of New York University, October 19.

Durkheim, Émile. (1897) 1997. *On Suicide: A Study in Sociology*. New York: The Free Press.

ECB (European Central Bank). 2004. "Introductory Statement, by Lucas Papademos, Vice-President of the European Central Bank and Chairman of the Jury for the International Urban Planning and Architectural Design Competition for the New ECB Premises, at the Deutsches Architektur Museum, Frankfurt am Main, 20 February 2004." http://www.ecb.int/press/key/date/2004/html /sp040220.en.html.

———. 2006. "Introductory Statement with Q&A, by Jean-Claude Trichet, President of the ECB, Lucas Papademos, Vice President of the ECB, and Jaime Caruana, Governor of the Banco de España, Madrid, 6 June 2006." http://www .ecb.int/press/pressconf/2006/html/is060608.en.html.

———. 2009. "Coop Himmelb(l)au's Design For A Vertical City In Frankfurt, Germany." Reprinted in *archiCentral: architecture//news//daily*, May 27, http://www .archicentral.com/coop-himmelblaus-design-for-a-vertical-city-in-frankfurt -germany-18500/.

———. 2012. "Press Release, 6 September 2012—Technical Features of Out-right Monetary Transactions." http://www.ecb.int/press/pr/date/2012/html/pr120906_1.en.html.

———. 2013 "Inflation in the Euro Area." http://www.ecb.int/mopo/html/index.en.html.

———. n.d. "New Premises." http://www.ecb.int/ecb/premises/html/index.en.html.

———. n.d. "Transparency." http://www.ecb.int/ecb/orga/transparency/html/index.en.html.

Eckersley, Philip, and Pamela Webber. 2003. "The Bank's Regional Agencies." *Bank of England Quarterly Bulletin*, Spring: 92–96.

Eggertsson, Gauti B. 2008. "Liquidity Trap." http://www.newyorkfed.org/research/economists/eggertsson/palgrave.pdf.

Eggertsson, Gauti B., and Michael Woodford. 2003. "The Zero Bound on Interest Rates and Optimal Monetary Policy." *Brookings Papers on Economic Activity* 2003 (1): 139–211.

Eichengreen, Barry. 1992. *Golden Fetters: The Gold Standard and the Great Depression, 1919–1939*. Oxford: Oxford University Press.

Ellis, Colin, and Tim Pike. 2005. "Introducing the Agents' Scores." *Bank of England Quarterly Bulletin*, Winter: 424–30.

Elyachar, Julia. 2005. *Markets of Dispossession: NGOs, Economic Development, and the State in Cairo*. Durham, NC: Duke University Press.

———. 2013. "Memoirs of Debt: A Research Assistant at the Fed in 1982." Unpublished manuscript, in author's possession.

Englund, Peter. 1999. "The Swedish Banking Crisis: Roots and Consequences." *Oxford Review of Economic Policy* 15: 80–97.

Escobar, Brian. 2008. "On Complexity and Emerging Modes of Engagement with Knowledge and Its Objects in Complex Systems Engineering, Science, and Their Audiences." B.A. Honors Thesis, Department of Anthropology, State University of New York at Binghamton.

Evans, Robert. 1999. *Macroeconomic Forecasting: A Sociological Appraisal*. London: Routledge.

Fagan, Gabriel, and Julian Morgan. 2005. *Econometric Models of the Euro-area Central Banks*. Cheltenham, UK: Edward Elgar.

Feldstein, Martin. 1997. "The Political Economy of the European Economic and Monetary Union: Political Sources of Economic Liability." NBER Working Paper No. 6150. Cambridge, MA: National Bureau of Economic Research.

Fischer, Michael M. J. 2007. "Culture and Cultural Analysis as Experimental Systems." *Cultural Anthropology* 22 (1): 1–65.

Fischhoff, Baruch, and John Kadvany. 2011. *Risk: A Very Short Introduction*. Oxford: Oxford University Press.

Fisher, Melissa. 2012. *Wall Street Women*. Durham NC: Duke University Press.

Fisher, Irving. 1933. "The Debt-Deflation Theory of Great Depressions." *Econometrica* 1: 337–57.

———. 1973. "I Discovered the Phillips Curve: 'A Statistical Relation between Un-employment and Price Changes.'" *Journal of Political Economy* 81 (2): 496–502.

Fligstein, Neil. 2001. *The Architecture of Markets: An Economic Sociology of Twenty-First-Century Capitalist Societies.* Princeton, NJ: Princeton University Press.

Fligstein, Neil, and Iona Mara-Drita. 1996. "How to Make a Market: Reflections on the Attempt to Create a Single Market in the European Union." *American Journal of Sociology* 102 (1): 1–33.

Fortun, Kim. 2003. "Ethnography in/of/as Open Systems." *Reviews in Anthropology* 32 (2): 171–90.

FRB (Federal Reserve Board of Governors). 1923. "Annual Report."

———. 2000a. "Press Release." December 19. http://www.federalreserve.gov /boarddocs/press/general/2000/20001219/.

———. 2000b. "Meeting of the Federal Open Market Committee" (transcript). December 19. http://www.federalreserve.gov/monetarypolicy/files/FOMC 20001219meeting.pdf.

———. 2001a. "Press Release." January 3. http://www.federalreserve.gov/boarddocs /press/general/2001/20010103/.

———. 2001b. "Federal Open Market Committee Conference Call" (transcript). January 3. http://www.federalreserve.gov/monetarypolicy/files/FOMC20010103 ConfCall.pdf.

———. 2001c. "Federal Reserve Districts: Second District—New York" (The Beige Book). October 24. http://www.federalreserve.gov/fomc/beigebook/2001 /20011024/2.htm.

———. 2011. "Directors of Federal Reserve Banks and Branches." http://www .federalreserve.gov/generalinfo/listdirectors/about.htm.

———. 2012a. "Press Release." January 25. http://www.federalreserve.gov/news events/press/monetary/20120125c.htm.

———. 2012b. "Press Release." December 12. http://www.federalreserve.gov/news events/press/monetary/20121212a.htm.

———. n.d. "Federal Open Market Committee." http://www.federalreserve.gov /monetarypolicy/fomc.htm.

———. n.d. *Role and Responsibilities of Federal Reserve Directors.* Washington, DC: Board of Governors of the Federal Reserve System. http://www.federal reserve.gov/aboutthefed/directors/pdf/roles_responsibilities_FINAL web013013.pdf.

Friedman, Benjamin. 1995. "The Rise and Fall of Money Growth Targets as Guide-lines for U.S. Monetary Policy." Mimeo, Bank of Japan Monetary Conference, October.

Friedman, Jonathan. 2008. "Commentary on Jane Guyer." *American Ethnologist* 34: 426–29.

Friedman, Milton. 1962. *Capitalism and Freedom.* Chicago: University of Chicago Press.

———. 1968. The Role of Monetary Policy. *American Economic Review* 58 (1): 1–17.

———. 1970. "The Counter-Revolution in Monetary Theory: First Wincott Memorial Lecture, delivered at the Senate House, University of London, 16 September 1970." London: Published for the Wincott Foundation by the Institute of Economic Affairs.

———. 1984. "Lessons from the 1979–1982 Monetary Policy Experiment." *American Economic Review* 74: 397–401.

Friedman, Milton, with Anna J. Schwartz. 1963. A Monetary History of the United States, 1867–1960. Princeton, NJ: Princeton University Press.

Friedman, Thomas L. 2012. "Two Worlds Cracking Up" (op-ed piece). *New York Times*, June 12. http://www.nytimes.com/2012/06/13/opinion/friedman-two-worlds-cracking-up.html.

Gal, Susan. 1991. "Bartok's Funeral: Representations of Europe in Hungarian Political Rhetoric." *American Ethnologist* 18 (3): 440–58.

———. 2007. Circulation in the "New" Economy: Clasps and Copies. Paper presented at the 106th Annual Meeting of the American Anthropological Association, Washington, DC, November 29–December 2.

Galí, Jordi, Stefan Gerlach, Julio Rotemberg, Harald Uhlig, and Michael Woodford. 2004. *The Monetary Policy Strategy of the ECB Reconsidered: Monitoring the European Central Bank 5*. London: Centre for Economic Policy Research.

Galí, Jordi, and Mark Gertler. 1999. "Inflation Dynamics: A Structural Econometric Analysis." *Journal of Monetary Economics* 44 (2): 195–222.

Garsten, Christina, and Monica Lindh De Montoya. 2008. "Introduction: Examining the Politics of Transparency." In *Transparency in a New Global Order: Unveiling Organizational Visions*, edited by Christina Garsten and Monica Lindh De Montoya, 1–25. Cheltenham, UK: Edward Elgar.

Geertz, Clifford. 1973. "Thick Description: Toward an Interpretive Theory of Culture." In *The Interpretation of Cultures: Selected Essays*, 2–30. New York: Basic Books.

Giles, Chris. 2012. "The Court of King Mervyn." *FT Magazine*, May 5. http://www.ft.com/intl/cms/s/2/f853d068-94b7-11e1-bb0d-00144feab49a.html#axzz2Kola RtrE.

Goodhart, Charles. 1975. "Monetary Relationships: A View from Threadneedle Street." Papers in Monetary Economics. Reserve Bank of Australia.

———. 1998. "The Two Concepts of Money: Implications for the Analysis of Optimal Currency Areas." *European Journal of Political Economy* 14 (3): 407–32.

———. 2010. "The Changing Roles of Central Banks." Bank for International Settlements Working Paper No. 326. Basel, Switzerland: Bank for International Settlements.

Graeber, David. 2001. *Toward an Anthropological Theory of Value: The False Coin of Our Dreams*. New York: Palgrave.

Granovetter, Mark. 1985. "Economic Action and Social Structure: The Problem of Embeddedness." *American Journal of Sociology* 91 (3): 481–510.

Greider, William. 1987. *Secrets of the Temple: How the Federal Reserve Runs the Country*. New York: Touchstone.

Grimes, Arthur. 2001. "Review of New Zealand Monetary Policy." *Agenda* 8 (4): 303–20.

Gros, Daniel, Cinzia Alcidi, and Alessandro Giovanni. 2012. "Central Banks in Times of Crisis: The FED versus the ECB." Paper presented at the European Parliament's Committee on Economic and Monetary Affairs Monetary Dialogue with the ECB-2012, July 9.

Grossman, Emiliano, Emilio Luque, and Fabian Musiena. 2008. "Economies through Transparency." In *Transparency in a New Global Order: Unveiling Organizational Visions*, edited by Christina Garsten and Monica Lindh De Montoya, 97–121. Cheltenham, UK: Edward Elgar.

Gusterson, Hugh. 1997. "Studying Up Revisited." *PoLAR: Political and Legal Anthropology Review* 20 (1): 114–19.

Guthrie, Graeme, and Julian Wright. 2000. "Open Mouth Operations." *Journal of Monetary Economics* 46 (2): 489–516.

Guyer, Jane. 2004. *Marginal Gains: Monetary Transactions in Atlantic Africa*. Chicago: University of Chicago Press.

———. 2007. "Prophecy and the Near Future: Thoughts on Macroeconomic, Evangelical, and Punctuated Time." *American Ethnologist* 34 (3): 409–21.

Haas, Ernst B. 1958. *The Uniting of Europe: Political, Social, and Economic Forces, 1950–1957*. Stanford, CA: Stanford University Press.

Habermas, Jürgen. 1984–87. *The Theory of Communicative Action*. Translated by Thomas McCarthy. 2 vols. Boston: Beacon Press.

———. 1991. *The Structural Transformation of the Public Sphere: An Inquiry into a Category of Bourgeois Society*. Translated by Thomas Burger. Cambridge, MA: MIT Press.

Hacking, Ian. 1983. *Representing and Inventing: Introductory Topic in the Philosophy of Natural Science*. Cambridge: Cambridge University Press.

Hamburg, Britta, and Karl-Heinz Töder. 2005. "The Macroeconometric Multi-Country Model of the Deutsche Bundesbank." In *Econometric Models of the Euro-Area Central Banks*, edited by Gabriel Fagan and Julian Morgan, 119–36. Cheltenham, UK: Edward Elgar.

Hann, Chris, and Keith Hart, eds. 2009. *Market and Society: The Great Transformation Today*. Cambridge: Cambridge University Press.

———. 2011. *Economic Anthropology: History, Ethnography, Critique*. Cambridge: Polity Press.

Haraway, Donna. 1988. "Situated Knowledges: The Science Question in Feminism and the Privilege of Partial Perspectives." *Feminist Studies* 14 (3): 575–99.

Harding, Robin. 2012. "Central Bankers Give Voice to a Revolution." *FT.com*,

December 14. http://www.ft.com/intl/cms/s/o/cbfae4f4-45e0-11e2-b7ba-00144 feabdco.html#axzz2KzS8FgeZ.

Harrison, Richard, Kalin Nikolov, Meghan Quinn, Gareth Ramsay, Alasdair Scott, and Ryland Thomas. 2005. *The Bank of England Quarterly Model*. London: Bank of England.

Hart, Keith. 2000. *The Memory Bank: Money in an Unequal World*. London: Profile Books.

Hart, Keith, Jean-Louis Laville, and Antonio David Cattani. 2010. *The Human Economy*. London: Polity Press.

Hawtrey, Ralph G. 1970. *The Art of Central Banking*. 2nd ed. London: Frank Cass and Co.

Hayek, Fredrick. 1948a. "Economics and Knowledge." In *Individualism and Economic Order*, 35–56. Chicago: University of Chicago Press.

———. 1948b. "The Uses of Knowledge in Society." In *Individualism and Economic Order*, 77–91. Chicago: University of Chicago Press.

Heikensten, Lars, and Anders Vredin. 2002. "The Art of Targeting Inflation." *Swidish Riksbank Economic Review*, Fourth Quarter: 3–34.

Helmreich, Stephan. 2001. "After Culture: Reflections on the Apparition of Anthropology in Artificial Life, a Science of Simulation." *Cultural Anthropology* 16 (4): 612–27.

Herzfeld, Michael. 1992. *The Social Production of Indifference: Exploring the Symbolic Roots of European Bureaucracy*. Chicago: University of Chicago Press.

———. 2004. *Cultural Intimacy: Social Poetics in the Nation-State*. London: Routledge.

———. 2009. *Evicted from Eternity: The Restructuring of Modern Rome*. Chicago: University of Chicago Press.

Hicks, John. 1937. "Mr. Keynes and the 'Classics': A Suggested Interpretation." *Econometrica* 5 (2): 147–59.

———. 1980–81. "IS-LM: An Explanation." *Journal of Post Keynesian Economics* 3 (2): 139–55.

Hilgartner, Stephen, Nicole Nelson, and Anna Geltzer. 2008. "Introduction: The Anticipatory State: Making Policy-Relevant Knowledge about the Future." *Science and Public Policy* 35 (8): 546–550.

Ho, Karen. 2009. *Liquidated: An Ethnography of Wall Street*. Durham, NC: Duke University Press.

Holmes, Douglas R. 1989. *Cultural Disenchantments: Worker Peasantries in Northeast Italy*. Princeton, NJ: Princeton University Press.

———. 2000. *Integral Europe: Fast-Capitalism, Multiculturalism, Neofascism*. Princeton, NJ: Princeton University Press.

———. 2009. "Economy of Words." *Cultural Anthropology* 24 (3): 381–419.

Holmes, Douglas R., and George E. Marcus. 2005. "Cultures of Expertise and the Management of Globalization: Toward the Re-Functioning of Ethnography."

In *Global Assemblages*, edited by Aihwa Ong and Stephen J. Collier, 235–52. Oxford: Blackwell.

———. 2006. "Fast-Capitalism: Paraethnography and the Rise of the Symbolic Analyst." In *Frontiers of Capital: Ethnographic Perspectives on the New Economy*, edited by Melissa Fisher and Greg Downey, 33–37. Durham, NC: Duke University Press.

———. 2008. "Collaboration Today and the Re-Imagination of the Classic Scene of Fieldwork Encounter." *Collaborative Anthropologies*, no. 1: 136–70.

———. 2012. "Collaborative Imperatives: A Manifesto, of Sorts, for the Re-Imagination of the Classic Scene of Fieldwork Encounter." In *Collaborators Collaborating: Counterparts in Anthropological Knowledge and International Research Relations*, edited by Monica Konrad, 126–43. Oxford: Berghahn Books.

Hume, David. 1987. "Of Interest." In *Essays, Moral, Political, and Literary*, edited by Eugene Miller. Rev. ed. Indianapolis: LibertyClassics. Based on the 1777 edition originally published as vol. 1 of *Essays and Treatises on Several Subjects*.

IMF (International Monetary Fund). 2012. "2012 Article IV Consultation with Spain: Concluding Statement of IMF Mission." June 14. http://www.imf.org/external/np/ms/2012/061512.htm.

Independent Commission on Banking. 2011. "Final Report: Recommendations." London: Produced by the Domarn Group for the Independent Commission on Banking. http://www.hm-treasury.gov.uk/d/ICB-Final-Report.pdf.

Issing, Otmar. 1997. "Monetary Targeting in Germany: The Stability of Monetary Policy and the Monetary System." *Journal of Monetary Economics* 39 (1): 67–79.

———. 2005. "The Monetary Pillar of the ECB." Speech presented at "The ECB and Its Watchers VII" Conference, Frankfurt am Main, June 3. http://www.ecb.int/press/key/date/2005/html/sp050603.en.html.

———. 2011. "Slithering to the Wrong Kind of Union." *FT.com*, August 8. http://www.ft.com/intl/cms/s/0/c4159b34-c1a8-11e0-acb3-00144feabdc0.html#axzz1UUUNwEPr.

Jansson, Per, and Anders Vredin. 2004. "Preparing the Monetary Policy Decision in an Inflation-Targeting Central Bank: The Case of the Sveriges Riksbank." In *Practical Experience with Inflation Targeting: International Conference Held at the Czech National Bank, May 13–14, 2004*, 73–94. Prague: Czech National Bank.

Jeanne, Olivier, and Lars E. O. Svensson. 2007. "Credible Commitment to Optimal Escape from a Liquidity Trap: The Role of the Balance Sheet of an Independent Central Bank." *American Economic Review* 97 (1): 474–90.

Joyce, Michael, Matthew Tong, and Robert Woods. 2011. "The United Kingdom's Quantitative Easing Policy: Design, Operation, and Impact." *Bank of England Quarterly Bulletin*, Fall: 200–212.

Jung, Taehun, Yuki Teranishi, and Tsutomu Watanabe. 2005. "Optimal Monetary Policy at the Zero-Interest-Rate Bound." *Journal of Money, Credit, and Banking* 37 (5): 813–36.

Kalb, Don. 1998. *Expanding Class: Power and Everyday Politics in Industrial Communities, The Netherlands, 1850–1950*. Durham, NC: Duke University Press.

Kelty, Christopher. 2005. "Geeks, Social Imaginaries, and Recursive Publics." *Cultural Anthropology* 20 (2): 185–214.

Keynes, John Maynard. (1923) 1971. *The Collected Writings of John Maynard Keynes*. Vol. 4, *A Tract on Monetary Reform*. Edited by Donald Moggridge. London: Macmillan for the Royal Economic Society.

———. (1936) 2007. *The General Theory of Employment, Interest, and Money*. Basingstoke, UK: Palgrave Macmillan.

———. 1983. *The Collected Writing of John Maynard Keynes*. Vol. 11, *Economic Articles and Correspondence, Academic*. Edited by Elizabeth S. Johnson and Donald Edward Moggridge. London: Macmillan for the Royal Economic Society.

King, Mervyn. 2002. "No Money, No Inflation—The Role of Money in the Economy." *Bank of England Quarterly Bulletin*, Summer: 162–77.

———. 2004. "The Institutions of Monetary Policy." *American Economic Review* 94 (2): 1–13.

———. 2005a. "What Has Inflation Targeting Achieved?" In *The Inflation Targeting Debate*, edited by Ben Bernanke and Michael Woodford, 11–16. Chicago: University of Chicago Press.

———. 2005b. "Monetary Policy: Practice Ahead of Theory." Mais Lecture, delivered at Cass Business School, London, May 17.

———. 2005c. "Remarks to the Central Bank Governors' Panel." Paper presented at the Federal Reserve Bank of Kansas City Symposium, Jackson Hole, Wyoming, August 25–27.

King, Michael. 2005. "Epistemic Communities and Diffusion of Ideas: Central Bank Reform in the United Kingdom." *West European Politics* 28 (1): 94–123.

Knorr-Cetina, Karin. 1999. *Epistemic Cultures: How the Sciences Make Knowledge*. Cambridge, MA: Harvard University Press.

———. 2007. "Culture in Global Knowledge Societies: Knowledge Cultures and Epistemic Cultures." *Interdisciplinary Reviews of Science* 32 (4): 361–75.

Knorr-Cetina, Karin, and Urs Bruegger. 2002. "Global Microstructures: The Virtual Societies of Financial Markets." *American Journal of Sociology* 107 (4): 905–50.

Knorr-Cetina, Karin, and Alex Preda. 2005. Introduction to *The Sociology of Financial Markets*, edited by Karin Knorr-Cetina and Alex Preda, 1–14. Oxford: Oxford University Press.

Kohn, Donald L. 2008. "Lessons for Central Bankers from a Phillips Curve Framework." Paper presented at the 52nd Annual Economic Conference sponsored by the Federal Reserve Bank of Boston, Chatham, Massachusetts, June 11.

———. 2009. "Monetary Policy and Asset Prices Revisited." Speech presented at the Cato Institute's 26th Annual Monetary Policy Conference, Washington DC, November.

Krugman, Paul. 1998. "It's Baaack: Japan's Slump and the Return of the Liquidity Trap." *Brookings Papers on Economic Activity* 1998 (2): 137–205.

———. 1999. "Thinking about the Liquidity Trap." http://web.mit.edu/krugman /www/trioshrt.html.

———. 2000. "How Complicated Does the Model Have to Be?" *Oxford Review of Economic Policy* 16 (4): 33–42.

———. 2007. Introduction to *The General Theory of Employment, Interest, and Money*, by John Maynard Keynes, xxv–xxxviii. Basingstoke, UK: Palgrave Mac-Millan.

———. 2011. "IS-LMentary." Conscience of a Liberal blog. *New York Times*, October 9. http://krugman.blogs.nytimes.com/2011/10/09/is-lmentary/.

———. 2012. "Eurozone Problems." *New York Times*, January 30.

———. n.d. "There is Something about Macro." http://web.mit.edu/krugman/ www/islm.html.

Lakoff, George, and Mark Johnson. 1980. *Metaphors We Live By*. Chicago: University of Chicago Press.

Lambert, Richard. 2005. "Inside the MPC." *Bank of England Quarterly Bulletin*, Spring: 56–65.

Latour, Bruno. 1987. *Science in Action: How to Follow Scientists and Engineers through Society*. Cambridge, MA: Harvard University Press.

———. 1988. *The Pasteurization of France*. Translated by Alan Sheridan and John Law. Cambridge, MA: Harvard University Press.

———. 1999. *Pandora's Hope: Essays on the Reality of Science Studies*. Cambridge, MA: Harvard University Press.

———. 2005. *Reassembling the Social: An Introduction to Actor-Network Theory*. Oxford: Oxford University Press.

Laubach, Thomas, and Adam S. Posen. 1997a. "Disciplined Discretion: The German and Swiss Monetary Frameworks in Operation." Federal Reserve Bank of New York Research Paper No. 9707. March.

———. 1997b. "Some Comparative Evidence on the Effectiveness of Inflation Targeting." Federal Reserve Bank of New York Research Paper No. 9714. May.

Law, John, and John Hassard. 1999. *Actor Network Theory and After*. Oxford: Blackwell/Sociological Review.

Lee, Benjamin, and Edward LiPuma. 2002. "Cultures of Circulation: The Imaginations of Modernity." *Public Culture* 14 (1): 191–213.

Leeper, Eric, Christopher Sims, and Tao Zha. 1996. "What Does Monetary Policy Do?" *Brookings Institutions Papers on Economic Activity*, no. 2: 1–63.

Leijonhufvud, Alex. 1968. *On Keynesian Economics and the Economics of Keynes*. New York: Oxford University Press.

———. 2008. "Keynes and the Crisis." *CEPR Policy Insight*, no. 23: 1–7.

Lépinay, Vincent-Antonin. 2007. "Decoding Finance: Articulation and Liquidity around a Trading Room." In *Do Economists Make Markets?*, edited by Donald MacKenzie, Fabian Muniesa, and Lucia Siu, 87–127. Princeton, NJ: Princeton University Press.

———. 2011. *Codes of Finance: Engineering Derivatives in a Global Bank.* Princeton, NJ: Princeton University Press.

Lippmann, Walter. (1927) 2002. *The Phantom Public.* New Brunswick, NJ: Transaction Publishers.

Lucas, Robert, Jr. 1976. "Econometric Policy Evaluation: A Critique." In *The Phillips Curve and Labor Markets*, edited by Karl Brunner and Alan Meltzer, 19–46. Carnegie-Rochester Conference Series on Public Policy, vol. 1. New York: American Elsevier.

———. 1986. "Adaptive Behavior and Economic Theory." *Journal of Business* 59 (4): 401–26.

———. 1997. "Monetary Neutrality: Prize Lecture, December 7, 1995." In *Nobel Lectures, Economic Sciences, 1991–1995*, edited by Torsten Persson, 246–65. London: World Scientific Publishing Co.

MacKenzie, Donald. 2001. "Physics and Finance: S-Terms and Modern Finance as a Topic for Science Studies." *Science, Technology, and Human Values* 26 (2): 115–44.

———. 2003. "An Equation and Its Worlds: Bricolage, Exemplars, Disunity, and Performativity in Financial Economics." *Social Studies of Science* 33 (6): 831–68.

———. 2006. *An Engine, Not a Camera: How Financial Models Shape Markets.* Cambridge, MA: MIT Press.

MacKenzie, Donald, Fabian Muniesa, and Lucia Siu. 2007. Introduction to *Do Economists Make Markets? On the Performativity of Economics*, 1–19. Princeton, NJ: Princeton University Press.

Malin, Adolfson, Michael K. Derssson, Jesper Lindé, Mattias Villani, and Anders Vredin. 2007. "Modern Forecasting, Models in Action: Improving Macroeconomic Analyses at Central Banks." *International Journal of Central Banking* 3 (4): 111–44.

Mankiw, Gregory. 2006. "The Macroeconomist as Scientist and Engineer." NBER Working Paper No. 12349. Cambridge, MA: National Bureau of Economic Research.

Mankiw, Gregory, and Ricardo Reis. 2002. "Sticky Information versus Sticky Prices: A Proposal to Replace the New Keynesian Phillips Curve." *Quarterly Journal of Economics* 117 (4): 1295–1328.

Marcus, George E. 2007. "Ethnography Two Decades after Writing Culture: From the Experimental to the Baroque." *Anthropological Quarterly* 80 (4): 1127–45.

———. 2008. "The End(s) of Ethnography: Social/Cultural Anthropology's Signature Form of Producing Knowledge in Transition." *Cultural Anthropology* 23 (1): 1–14.

———. 2012. "The Legacies of Writing Culture and the Near Future of the Ethnographic Form: A Sketch." *Cultural Anthropology* 27: 427–445.

Masco, Joseph. 2009. "'Survival Is Your Business': Engineering Ruins and Affect in Nuclear America." *Cultural Anthropology* 23 (2): 361–98.

———. 2010. "'Sensitive but Unclassified': Secrecy and the Counterterrorist State." *Public Culture* 22 (3): 433–63.

Maurer, Bill. 1995. "Complex Subjects: Offshore Finance, Complexity Theory, and the Dispersion of the Modern." *Socialist Review* 25 (3–4): 113–45.

———. 2002a. "Repressed Futures: Financial Derivatives' Theological Unconscious." *Economy and Society* 31 (1): 15–36.

———. 2002b. "Redecorating the International Economy: Keynes, Grant, and the Queering of Bretton Woods." In *Queer Globalizations: Citizenship and the Afterlife of Colonialism*, edited by A. Cruz-Malave and M. Manalansan, 100–33. New York: New York University Press.

———. 2005a. "Introduction to Ethnographic Emergences." *American Anthropologist* 107 (1): 1–4.

———. 2005b. *Mutual Life, Limited: Islamic Banking, Alternative Currencies.* Princeton, NJ: Princeton University Press.

———. 2005c. "Due Diligence and 'Reasonable Man,' Offshore." *Cultural Anthropology* 20 (4): 474–505.

Mauss, Marcel. (1922) 1990. *The Gift: Forms and Functions of Exchange in Archaic Societies.* London: Routledge.

McCallum, Bennett T. 2000. "Theoretical Analysis Regarding a Zero Lower Bound on Interest Rates." *Journal of Money, Credit, and Banking* 32 (4): 870–904.

———. 2008. "Monetarism." In *The Concise Encyclopedia of Economics.* Library of Economics and Liberty. http://econlib.org/library/Enc/Monetarism.html.

McCloskey, Deidre. 1985. *The Rhetoric of Economics.* Madison: University of Wisconsin Press.

———. 1990. *If You're So Smart: The Narrative of Economic Expertise.* Chicago: University of Chicago Press.

———. 1994. *Knowledge and Persuasion in Economics.* Cambridge: Cambridge University Press.

McNamara, Kathleen. 1998. *The Currency of Ideas: Monetary Politics in the European Union.* Ithaca, NY: Cornell University Press.

Menand, Louis. 2002. *The Metaphysical Club: A Story of Ideas in America,* New York: Farrar, Straus and Giroux.

Merton, Robert K. 1948. "The Self-Fulfilling Prophecy." *Antioch Review* 8 (2): 193–210.

Mitchell, Timothy. 2002. *Rule of Experts: Egypt, Techno-Politics, Modernity.* Berkeley: University of California Press.

Mishkin, Fredric. 2004. *The Economics of Money, Banking, and Financial Markets.* 7th ed. Boston: Addison Wesley.

Mitrany, David. 1965. "The Prospect of European Integration: Federal or Functional." *Journal of Common Market Studies* 4 (6): 119–49.

Miyazaki, Hirokazu. 2003. "The Temporalities of the Market." *American Anthropologist* 105 (2): 255–65.

———. 2004. *The Method of Hope: Anthropology, Philosophy, and Fijian Knowledge*. Stanford, CA: Stanford University Press.

———. 2006a. "Economy of Dreams: Hope in Global Capitalism and Its Critiques." *Cultural Anthropology* 21 (2): 147–72.

———. 2006b. "Documenting the Present." In *Documents: Artifacts of Modern Knowledge*, edited by Annelise Riles. Ann Arbor: University of Michigan Press.

———. 2013. *Arbitraging Japan: Dreams of Capitalism at the End of Finance*. Berkeley, CA: University of California Press.

Miyazaki, Hirokazu, and Annelise Riles. 2005. "Failure as an Endpoint." In *Global Assemblages*, edited Aihwa Ong and Stephen Collier, 320–31. Oxford: Blackwell.

Monnet, Jean. 1976. *Memoires*. Paris: Arthème Fayard.

Moravcsik, Andrew. 1998. *The Choice for Europe: Social Purpose and State Power from Messina to Maastricht*. Ithaca, NY: Cornell University Press.

Morgan, Mary S. 2012. *The World in the Model: How Economists Work and Think*. Cambridge: Cambridge University Press.

Morris, Richard, Hedwig Ongena, and Ludger Schuknech. 2006. "The Reform and Implementation of the Stability and Growth Pact." ECB Occasional Paper No. 47. Frankfurt am Main: European Central Bank.

Muehlebach, Andrea. 2012. *Moral Neoliberalism: Welfare and Citizenship in Italy*. Chicago: University of Chicago Press.

Müller, Jan-Werner. 2007. *Constitutional Patriotism*. Princeton, NJ: Princeton University Press.

Mundell, Robert A. 1961. "A Theory of Optimum Currency Areas." American Economic Review 51 (4): 657–65.

Muniesa, Fabian, and Michel Callon. 2007. "Economic Experiments and the Construction of Markets." In *Do Economists Make Markets?*, edited by Donald MacKenzie, Fabian Muniesa, and Lucia Siu, 163–89. Princeton, NJ: Princeton University Press.

Munn, Nancy. 1992. "The Cultural Anthropology of Time: A Critical Essay." *Annual Review of Anthropology*, no. 21: 93–123.

Muth, John. 1961. "Rational Expectations and the Theory of Price Movements." *Econometrica* 29 (3): 315–35.

Narotzky, Susana, and Gavin Smith. 2006. *Immediate Struggles: People, Power, and Place in Rural Spain*. Berkeley: University of California Press.

Nelson, Stephen, and Peter Katzenstein. 2010. "Uncertainty and Risk in the Crisis of 2008." Paper presented at the Politics in Hard Times Workshop Honoring Peter Gourevitch, University of California at San Diego, April 23–24.

Nergiz, Dincer, and Barry Eichengreen. 2009. "Central Bank Transparency: Causes, Consequences, and Update." NBER Working Paper No. 14791. Cambridge MA: National Bureau of Economic Research.

Orphanides, Athanasios. 2002. "Monetary-Policy Rules and the Great Inflation." *American Economic Review* 92 (2): 115–20.

Orphanides, Athanasios, and John C. Williams. 2007. "Robust Monetary Policy with Imperfect Knowledge." *Journal of Monetary Economics* 54 (5): 1406–35.

Pagan, Adrain. 2003. "Report on Modelling and Forecast at the Bank of England." *Bank of England Quarterly Bulletin*, Spring: 1–29.

Papademos, Lucas, and Jürgen Stark, eds. 2010. *Enhancing Monetary Analysis*. Frankfurt am Main: European Central Bank.

Parker, George, and Peter Thal Larsen. 2005. "EU States Accused of 'Hiding' Deficits." *FT.com*, October 5. http://www.ft.com/intl/cms/s/0/cd1192f0-35cd-11da-903d-00000e2511c8.html#axzz2KzS8FgeZ.

Petryna, Adriana. 2002. *Life Exposed: Biological Citizens after Chernobyl*. Princeton, NJ: Princeton University Press.

Phelps, Edmund. 1968. "Money-Wage Dynamics and Labor-Market Equilibrium." *Journal of Political Economy* 76 (1): 678–711.

Phelps, Edmund, and John Taylor. 1997. "Stabilizing Powers of Monetary Policy under Rational Expectations." *Journal of Political Economy* 85 (1): 163–90.

Phillips, A. William. 1954. "Stabilization Policy in a Closed Economy." *Economic Journal* 64 (254): 290–323.

———. 1958. "The Relationship between Unemployment and the Rate of Change of Money Wages in the United Kingdom, 1861–1957." *Economica* 25 (100): 283–99.

Polanyi, Karl. 1968. "The Semantics of Money Uses." In *Primitive, Archaic, and Modern Economics: Essays of Karl Polanyi*, edited by George Dalton, 175–203 New York: Doubleday.

———. 2001. *The Great Transformation: The Political and Economic Origins of Our Time*. Boston: Beacon Press.

———. 2011. "The Economy as Instituted Process." In *The Sociology of Economic Life*, edited by Mark Granovetter and Richard Swedberg, 22–51. Boulder, CO: Westview Press.

Poovey, Mary. 1998. *A History of the Modern Fact: Problems of Knowledge in the Sciences of Wealth and Society*. Chicago: University of Chicago Press.

Porter, Theodore. 1995. *Trust in Numbers: The Pursuit of Objectivity in Science and Public Life*. Princeton, NJ: Princeton University Press.

Posen, Adam S. 1997. "Lessons from the Bundesbank on the Occasion of Its 40th (and Second to Last?) Birthday." IIE Working Paper No. 97-4. Washington, DC: Peterson Institute for International Economics. http://www.iie.com/publications/wp/wp.cfm?ResearchID=153.

———. 2009. "Finding the Right Tool for Dealing with Asset Price Booms." Speech presented at the MPR Monetary Policy and the Economy Conference, London, December 1.

———. 2010a. "The Realities and Relevance of Japan's Great Recession: Neither *Ran* nor *Rashomon.*" STICERD Public Lecture, London School of Economics, May 24.

———. 2010b. "The British Recovery in International Comparison." Speech presented at "Sustaining the Recovery," the Society of Business Economists Annual Conference, London, June 30.

Rabinow, Paul. 1986. Representations are Social Fact." In *Writing Culture: The Poetics and Politics of Representation*, edited by James Clifford and George Marcus. Berkeley: University of California Press.

———. 1989. *French Modern: Norms and Forms of the Social Environment.* Chicago: University of Chicago Press.

———. 2008. *Marking Time: On the Anthropology of the Contemporary.* Princeton, NJ: Princeton University Press.

Rabinow, Paul, George E. Marcus, James D. Faubion, and Tobias Rees. 2008. *Designs for an Anthropology of the Contemporary.* Durham, NC: Duke University Press.

Razsa, Maple, and Andrej Kurnik. 2012. "The Occupy Movement in Žižek's Hometown: Direct Democracy and a Politics of Becoming." *American Ethnologist* 39 (2): 238–58.

RBNZ (Reserve Bank of New Zealand). 1990. "Policy Targets Agreement (March 1990)." http://www.rbnz.govt.nz/monpol/pta/0073109.html.

———. 2004. *The Reserve Bank's Forecasting and Policy System.* Prepared by Dominick Stephens. Economics Department, Wellington: Reserve Bank of New Zealand.

———. 2007a. *Finance and Expenditure Select Committee Inquiry into the Future Monetary Policy Framework: Submission by the Reserve Bank of New Zealand.* Wellington: Reserve Bank of New Zealand.

———. 2007b. "Monetary Policy Statement, September 2007—Policy Assessment" (press release). http://www.rbnz.govt.nz/monpol/statements/3117428 .html.

———. 2008a. "Monetary Policy Statement, June 2008—Policy Assessment" (press release). http://www.rbnz.govt.nz/monpol/statements/3335309.html.

———. 2008b. "Monetary Policy Statement, June 2008." http://www.rbnz.govt.nz /monpol/statements/jun08.pdf.

———. 2008c. "Monetary Policy Statement, December 2008." http://www.rbnz .govt.nz/monpol/statements/dec08.pdf.

———. 2009a. "OCR Reduced to 3.5 Percent" (press release). 29 January. http:// www.rbnz.govt.nz/news/2009/3544313.html.

———. 2009b. "What Is the Policy Targets Agreement?" September. http://www .rbnz.govt.nz/monpol/pta/3027620.html.

———. n.d. "A. W. H. (Bill) Phillips, (MBE) and the MONIAC" (museum fact-sheet). http://www.rbnz.govt.nz/research_and_publications/fact_sheets_and_guides/3121411.pdf.

Rheinberger, Hans-Jorg. 1997. *Toward a History of Epistemic Things: Synthesizing Proteins in the Test Tube.* Stanford, CA: Stanford University Press.

———. 1998. "Experimental Systems, Graphematic Spaces." In *Inscribing Science: Scientific Texts and the Materiality of Communication*, edited by Timothy Lenoir. Stanford, CA: Stanford University Press.

Rhinehart, Carmen, and Kenneth Rogoff. 2009. *This Time Is Different: Eight Centuries of Financial Folly.* Princeton, NJ: Princeton University Press.

Riles, Annelise. 2000. *The Network Inside Out.* Ann Arbor: University of Michigan Press.

———. 2001. "Real-Time: Governing the Market after the Failure of Knowledge." Paper presented at the University of California at Berkeley Department of Anthropology, January 18.

———. 2004. "Real Time: Unwinding Technocratic and Anthropological Knowledge." *American Ethnologist* 31 (3): 392–405.

———. 2006. Introduction to *Documents: Artifacts of Modern Knowledge*, edited by Annelise Riles, 1–38. Ann Arbor: University of Michigan Press.

———. 2010. "Collateral Expertise: Legal Knowledge in the Global Financial Markets." *Current Anthropology* 51 (6): 795–818.

———. 2011. *Collateral Knowledge: Legal Reasoning in the Global Financial Markets.* Chicago: University of Chicago Press.

Roitman, Janet. 2004. *Fiscal Disobedience: An Anthropology of Economic Regulation in Central Africa.* Princeton, NJ: Princeton University Press.

———. 2013. *Anti-Crisis.* Durham, NC: Duke University Press.

Rosengren, Eric S. 2008. "Opening Remarks: Empirical Questions in Modeling Inflation and Understanding the Implications for Policy." Paper presented at the 52nd Annual Economic Conference sponsored by the Federal Reserve Bank of Boston, Chatham, Massachusetts, June 11.

Rotemberg, Julio, and Michael Woodford. 1997. "An Optimization-Based Econometric Framework for the Evaluation of Monetary Policy." *NBER Macroeconomics Annual 1997*, no. 12: 297–346.

Roubini, Nouriel. 2006. "Why Central Banks Should Burst Bubbles." *International Finance* 9 (1): 87–107.

———. 2011. "The Eurozone Heads for Break-Up." *Ft.com*, June 11. http://blogs.ft.com/the-a-list/2011/06/13/the-eurozone-heads-for-break-up/#axzz2PYAoNmnS.

Rudnyckyj, Daromir. 2010. *Spiritual Economies: Islam, Globalization, and the Afterlife of Development.* Ithaca, NY: Cornell University Press.

Rudnyckyj, Daromir, and Analiese Richard. 2009. "Economies of Affect." *Journal of the Royal Anthropological Institute* 15 (1): 57–77.

Salemi, Michael. 2008. "Hyperinflation." In *The Concise Encyclopedia of Economics.* Library of Economics and Liberty. http://econlib.org/library/Enc/Hyperinflation .html.

Samuelson, Paul. 2001. "Progress and Pitfall in the State of Modern Finance Theory." Speech presented at Renaissance Technologies, East Setauket, NY.

———. 2008. "Thoughts about the Phillips Curve." Paper presented at the 52nd Annual Economic Conference sponsored by the Federal Reserve Bank of Boston, Chatham, Massachusetts, June 3.

Samuelson, Paul, and Robert Solow. 1960. "Analytical Aspects of Anti-Inflation Policy." *American Economic Review* 50 (2): 177–94.

Schäuble, Wolfgang. 2011. "Why Austerity Is Only Cure for the Eurozone." *FT.com,* September 5. http://www.ft.com/intl/cms/s/0/97b826e2-d7ab-11e0-a06b-00144 feabdco.html#axzz1X5xWHHol.

Scheller, Hanspeter. 2004. *The European Central Bank: History, Role, and Function.* Frankfurt am Main: European Central Bank.

Scott, James. 1979. *The Moral Economy of the Peasant: Rebellion and Subsistence in Southeast Asia.* New Haven, CT: Yale University Press.

Searle, John. 1969. *Speech Acts: An Essay in the Philosophy of Language.* Cambridge: Cambridge University Press.

Sherwin, Murray. 1999. "Inflation Targeting: 10 Years On." Speech presented at the New Zealand Association of Economists Conference, Rotorua, NZ. Reprinted in *Reserve Bank of New Zealand Bulletin* 62 (2): 72–80.

Shore, Cris. 2000. *Building Europe: The Cultural Politics of European Integration.* London: Routledge.

Shore Cris, and Susan Wright. 2000. "Coercive Accountability: The Rise of Audit Culture in Higher Education." In *Audit Culture: Anthropological Studies in Accountability, Ethics, and the Academy,* edited by Marilyn Strathern, 57–89. London: Routledge.

Sibert, Anne. 2012. "Non-Standard Policy Measures—A First Assessment." Paper presented at the European Parliament's Committee on Economic and Monetary Affairs Monetary Dialogue with the ECB-2012, July 9.

Silverstein, Michael, and Greg Urban. 1996. *Natural Histories of Discourse.* Chicago: University of Chicago Press.

Sims, Christopher. 2002. "The Role of Models and Probabilities in the Monetary Policy Process." *Brookings Papers on Economic Activity* 2002 (2): 1–62.

———. 2008. "Inflation Expectations, Uncertainty, the Phillips Curve, and Monetary Policy." Paper presented at the 52nd Annual Economic Conference sponsored by the Federal Reserve Bank of Boston, Chatham, Massachusetts, June 11.

Singleton, John, with Arthur Grimes, Gary Hawke, and Frank Holmes. 2006. *Innovation and Independence: The Reserve Bank of New Zealand.* Auckland, NZ: Auckland University Press.

Sinn, Hans-Werner. 2011. "The ECB's Stealth Bailout." VoxEU.org, June 1. http://www.voxeu.org/article/ecb-s-stealth-bailout.

———. 2012. "Fed versus ECB: How TARGET Debts Can Be Repaid." VoxEU.org, March 10. http://www.voxeu.org/article/fed-versus-ecb-how-target-debts-can-be-repaid.

Sinn, Hans-Werner, and Timo Wollmershäuser. 2012. "Target Loans, Current Account Balances, and Capital Flows: The ECB's Rescue Facility." *International Tax and Public Finance* 19 (4): 468–508.

Skidelsky, Robert. 1983. *John Maynard Keynes.* Vol. 1, *Hopes Betrayed, 1883–1920.* New York: Penguin.

———. 1992. *John Maynard Keynes.* Vol. 2, *The Economist as Savior, 1920–1937.* New York: Penguin.

———. 2000. *John Maynard Keynes.* Vol. 3, *Fighting for Britain, 1937–1946.* New York: Penguin.

———. 1996. *Keynes.* Past Masters Series. Oxford: Oxford University Press.

———. 2009. *Keynes: The Return of the Master.* New York: Public Affairs.

———. 2010. "House of Lords Debate: Comprehensive Spending Review" (Hansard Column 1501–1503). November 1. http://www.skidelskyr.com/site/article/house-of-lords-debate-comprehensive-spending-review/.

Smart, Graham. 1999. "Storytelling in a Central Bank: The Role of Narrative in the Creation and Use of Economic Knowledge." *Journal of Business and Technical Communication* 13 (3): 249–73.

———. 2006. *Writing the Economy: Activity, Genre, and Technology in the World of Banking.* London: Equinox.

Smets, Frank, and Raf Wouters. 2004. "Forecasting with a Bayesian DSGE Model: An Application to the Euro Area." *Journal of Common Market Studies* 42 (4): 841–67.

Smith, Gavin. 1999. *Confronting the Present: Towards a Politically Engaged Anthropology.* Oxford: Berg.

Solow, Robert. 2010. Statement at Congressional Hearing on *Building a Science of Economics for the Real World,* made before the House Subcommittee on Investigations and Oversight of the Committee on Science and Technology. 111th Cong., 2nd sess., July 10.

Solow, Robert, and John B. Taylor. 2001. *Inflation, Unemployment, and Monetary Policy.* Cambridge, MA: MIT Press.

Soros, George. 1994. "The Theory of Reflexivity." Paper presented at the MIT Department of Economics World Economy Laboratory Conference, Washington, DC, April 26.

———. 2008. *The New Paradigm for Financial Markets: The Credit Crisis of 2008 and What It Means.* Philadelphia: PublicAffairs.

Stiglitz, Joseph. 2009. *Selected Works of Joseph E. Stiglitz.* Vol. 1, *Information and Economic Analysis.* New York: Oxford University Press.

Stoler, Ann. 2008. *Along the Archival Grain: Epistemic Anxieties and Colonial Common Sense*. Princeton, NJ: Princeton University Press.

Strassler, Karen. 2009. "The Face of Money: Currency, Crisis, and Remediation in Post-Suharto Indonesia." *Cultural Anthropology* 24 (1): 68–103.

Strathern, Marilyn. 2000. *Audit Culture: Anthropological Studies in Accountability, Ethics, and the Academy*. London: Routledge.

Summers, Lawrence H. 1991. "The Scientific Illusion in Empirical Macroeconomics." *Scandinavian Journal of Economics* 93 (2): 129–48.

Sunder Rajan, Kaushik. 2006. *Biocapital: The Constitution of Postgenomic Life*. Durham, NC: Duke University Press.

———. 2012. *Lively Capital: Biotechnologies, Ethics, and Governance in Global Markets*. Durham, NC: Duke University Press.

Svensson, Lars E. 2001a. "Independent Review of the Operation of Monetary Policy in New Zealand" (report to the Ministry of Finance). *Reserve Bank of New Zealand Bulletin* 64 (1): 4–11.

———. 2001b. "The Zero Bound in an Open Economy: A Foolproof Way of Escaping from a Liquidity Trap." *Monetary and Economic Studies* 19 (S1): 277–312.

———. 2003. "Escaping from a Liquidity Trap and Deflation: The Foolproof Way and Others." *Journal of Economic Perspectives* 17 (4): 145–66.

———. 2006. "Monetary Policy and Japan's Liquidity Trap." CEPS Working Paper No. 126. http://www.princeton.edu/ceps/workingpapers/126svensson.pdf.

———. 2009. "Monetary Policy with a Zero Interest Rate." Speech presented at the SNS Center for Business and Policy Studies, Stockholm, Sweden, February 17. http://www.riksbank.se/Pagefolders/39304/090217e.pdf.

Sveriges Riksbank. 2009a. "Separate Appendix to the Riksbank's Communication Policy." April 2. http://www-riksbank-se.cdn.episerverhosting.com/Pagefolders/40148/nr34e_appendix_communication_policy09.pdf.

———. 2009b. "Minutes of the Executive Board's Monetary Policy Meeting on 20 April 2009." http://www.riksbank.se/en/Press-and-published/Minutes-of-the-Executive-Boards-monetary-policy-meetings/2009/Minutes-of-the-Executive-Boards-monetary-policy-meeting-on-20-April-2009/.

Swedberg, Richard. 1999. "Civil Courage (Zivilcourage): The Case of Knut Wicksell." *Theory and Society* 28 (4): 501–28.

Tett, Gillian. 2009. *Fool's Gold: The Inside Story of J. P. Morgan and How Wall Street Greed Corrupted Its Bold Dream and Created a Financial Catastrophe*. New York: Free Press.

Tily, Geoff. 2009. "John Maynard Keynes and the Development of National Accounts in Britain, 1895–1941." Review of Income and Wealth 55 (2): 331–59.

Tobin, James. 1972a. "Friedman's Theoretical Framework." *Journal of Political Economy* 80 (5): 852–63.

———. 1972b. "Inflation and Unemployment." *American Economic Review* 62 (1): 1–18.

———. 1999–2010. "Monetary Policy." In *The Concise Encyclopedia of Economics*. Library of Economics and Liberty. http.//www.econlib.org/library/Enc /MonetaryPolicy.html.

Trichet, Jean-Claude. 2005. "Monetary Policy and 'Credible Alertness'." Paper presented at the Monetary Policy Strategies: A Central Bank Panel, Federal Reserve Bank of Kansas City Symposium, Jackson Hole, WY, August 25–27.

Tucker, Paul. 2009. "Report to the Treasury Select Committee" (Bank of England February 2009 Inflation Report). March 18. http://www.parliament.the -stationery-office.co.uk/pa/cm200809/cmselect/cmtreasy/376-i/376we06 .htm.

Tufte, Edward R. 1983. *The Visual Display of Quantitative Information*. Cheshire, CT: Graphics Press.

———. 1990. *Envisioning Information*. Cheshire, CT: Graphics Press.

———. 1997. *Visual Explanations: Images and Quantities, Evidence and Narrative*. Cheshire, CT: Graphics Press.

Turner, Terence. 2008. "Marxian Value Theory: An Anthropological Perspective." *Anthropological Theory* 8 (1): 43–56.

Volckart, Oliver. 1973. "Early Beginnings of the Quantity Theory of Money and Their Context in Polish and Prussian Monetary Policies, c. 1520–1550." *Economic History Review*, n.s., 50 (3): 430–49.

Westbrook, David. 2004. *City of Gold: An Apology for Global Capitalism in a Time of Discontent*. London: Routledge.

———. 2008. *Navigators of the Contemporary: Why Ethnography Matters*. Chicago: University of Chicago Press.

———. 2009. *Out of Crisis: Rethinking Our Financial Markets*. Boulder, CO: Paradigm Publishers.

Wetterberg, Gunnar. 2009. *Money and Power: From Stockholms Banco 1656 to Sveriges Riksbank Today*. Translated by Patrick Hort. Stockholm: Sveriges Riksbank.

Williams, Raymond. 1981. *Politics and Letters: Interviews with "New Left Review."* London: Verso.

Wood, John H. 2005. *A History of Central Banking in Great Britain and the United States*. Cambridge: Cambridge University Press.

Woodford, Michael. 2001. "Imperfect Common Knowledge and the Effects of Monetary Policy." NBER Working Paper No. 876. Cambridge, MA: National Bureau of Economic Research.

———. 2003. *Interest and Prices: Foundations of a Theory of Monetary Policy*. Princeton, NJ: Princeton University Press.

———. 2005. "Central-Bank Communication and Policy Effectiveness." Paper presented at the Federal Reserve Bank of Kansas City Symposium, Jackson Hole, WY, August 25–27.

———. 2008a. "The Fed's Enhanced Communication Strategy: Stealth Inflation

Targeting?" Voxeu.org, January 8. http://www.voxeu.org/article/feds-enhanced
-communication-strategy-stealth-inflation-targeting.

———. 2008b. "Does a 'Two-Pillar Phillips Curve' Justify a Two-Pillar Monetary
Policy Strategy?" In *The Role of Money: Money and Monetary Policy in the
Twenty-First Century*, edited by Andreas Beyer and Lucrzia Reichlin, 56–82.
Frankfurt am Main: European Central Bank.

———. 2008c. "Convergence in Macroeconomics: Elements of the New Synthesis."
Paper presented at the session "Convergence in Macroeconomics?" at the Annual Meeting of the American Economics Association, New Orleans, January 4.

———. 2012. "Methods of Policy Accommodation at the Interest-Rate Lower
Bound." Paper presented "The Changing Policy Landscape," Federal Reserve
Bank of Kansas City Symposium, Jackson Hole, WY, August 31–September 1.

Wyplosz, Charles. 2012. "The Role of the ECB in Fiscal Adjustment Programmes."
Paper presented at the European Parliament's Committee on Economic and
Monetary Affairs Monetary Dialogue with the ECB-2012, July 9.

Yellen, Janet. 2013. "Communications in Monetary Policy." Speech presented at
the Society of American Business Editors and Writers 50th Anniversary Conference, Washington DC, April 4.

Zaloom, Caitlin. 2003. "Ambiguous Numbers: Trading Technologies and Interpretation in Financial Markets." *American Ethnologist* 30 (2): 258–72.

———. 2004. "The Productive Life of Risk." *Cultural Anthropology* 19 (3): 365–91.

———. 2006. *Out of the Pits: Traders and Technology from Chicago to London.*
Chicago: University of Chicago Press.

———. 2009. "How to Read the Future: The Yield Curve, Affect, and Financial
Prediction." *Public Culture* 21 (2): 243–66.

Zingales, Luigi. 2012. "Banking Union Is Last Gambit to Save Euro Dream."
Bloomberg.com, July 29. http://www.bloomberg.com/news/2012-07-29/banking
-union-is-last-gambit-to-save-euro-dream.html.

Index